In this book, John Peters investigates the impact of impressionism on Conrad and links this to his literary techniques as well as his philosophical and political views. Impressionism, Peters argues, enabled Conrad to encompass both surface and depth not only in visually perceived phenomena but also in his narratives and objects of consciousness, be they physical objects, human subjects, events, or ideas. Though traditionally thought of as a skeptical writer, Peters claims that through impressionism Conrad developed a coherent and mostly traditional view of ethical and political principles, a claim he supports through reference to a broad range of Conrad's texts. *Conrad and Impressionism* investigates the sources and implications of Conrad's impressionism in order to argue for a consistent link between his literary technique, philosophical presuppositions and sociopolitical views. The same core ideas concerning the nature of human experience run throughout his works.

JOHN G. PETERS is Assistant Professor of English at the University of Wisconsin-Superior. He won the Joseph Conrad Society of America's Young Scholar Award for 1999. This is his first book.

CONRAD AND IMPRESSIONISM

JOHN G. PETERS

CAMBRIDGE
UNIVERSITY PRESS

PUBLISHED BY THE PRESS SYNDICATE OF THE UNIVERSITY OF CAMBRIDGE
The Pitt Building, Trumpington Street, Cambridge, United Kingdom

CAMBRIDGE UNIVERSITY PRESS
The Edinburgh Building, Cambridge, CB2 2RU, UK
40 West 20th Street, New York, NY 10011–4211, USA
477 Williamstown Road, Port Melbourne, VIC 3207, Australia
Ruiz de Alarcón 13, 28014 Madrid, Spain
Dock House, The Waterfront, Cape Town 8001, South Africa

http://www.cambridge.org

First published 2001
Reprinted 2002

Printed in Great Britain by Biddles Limited, Guildford & King's Lynn.

Typeset in Baskerville 11/12.5pt [VN]

A catalogue record for this book is available from the British Library

ISBN 0 521 79173 1 hardback

For Deanna

"We had approached nearer to absolute Truth, which, like Beauty itself, floats elusive, obscure, half submerged, in the silent still waters of mystery."

Lord Jim

Contents

Preface

Before beginning my inquiry proper, it is necessary to lay some ground-work. On a purely stylistic level, concerning quoted material, I follow standard practice and attribute passages using italics for emphasis either to myself or to the cited author depending on whose emphasis it is. Also, unless otherwise noted, bracketed information and ellipsis within quoted material are mine.

A few other nonstylistic issues must also be addressed. When dealing with any writer's literary works, it is difficult (if not impossible) to separate the writer's own views from those of a work's narrating voice, and with Joseph Conrad this difficulty is particularly problematic be-cause of the presence of multiple narrators and such narrator characters as Marlow and the teacher of foreign languages. When an idea appears consistently throughout Conrad's works, though, I have felt comfortable attributing that idea to Conrad himself, especially when Conrad's own comments in his letters and essays further support that idea or when others who knew Conrad have attributed such an idea to him. Nat-urally, in considering any of these sources, one must remain skeptical. At different times, Conrad may have expressed different opinions on the same topic to different people; furthermore, commentators have some-times accused Conrad of doctoring events (as they do his friend Ford Madox Ford, whom I also cite on occasion). When general consistency exists among sources, however, I thought it safe to attribute a particular idea to Conrad.

In addition, as much as possible, I have tried to limit comments concerning human nature, the nature of western civilization, and the nature of the universe to those views that I believe to have been Conrad's own. I have simply tried to report what seems to appear in the various sources I have investigated. However, to avoid constantly intro-ducing sentences with "for Conrad" or "according to Conrad" or some other qualification, I have sometimes simply stated an idea without the qualification.

In this same vein, Christopher GoGwilt and others have argued convincingly that the west is not a single concept but rather a variety of concepts put forward at various times for various reasons.[1] However, Conrad particularly seems to question a certain popularized and mono-lithic view of western civilization that saw its methods and practices as originating from absolute truth. Concurrent with this view was the belief in the necessity of civilizing the rest of the world and thus bringing other peoples to a knowledge of the truth. The clearest manifestation of this attitude appears in "Heart of Darkness" when Marlow summarizes his aunt's view: "It appeared, however, I was also one of the Workers, with a capital – you know. Something like an emissary of light, something like a lower sort of apostle. There had been a lot of such rot let loose in print and talk just about that time, and the excellent woman, living right in the rush of all that humbug, got carried off her feet" (*Y* 59). Conrad rejects such a view. For this reason, when I refer to western civilization in this book, I am typically referring to this popularized view of the role and position of the west in the world at that time.

Regarding impressionist theory, Diego Martelli remarked of impres-sionist painters that they do not "fabricate their theories first and then adapt the paintings to them, but on the contrary ... the pictures were born of the unconscious visual phenomenon of men of art who, having studied, afterward produced the reasoning of the philosophers."[2] Simi-larly, since literary impressionists left behind no philosophical treatise and usually wrote little by way of helpful commentary concerning their works, I have generally had to reconstruct impressionist literary theory – in a sense archaeologically – from the impressionists' works themselves rather than from their comments about their works.

Finally, even though I discuss impressionist literary theory in general, because this book is primarily about Conrad's impressionism, most of my illustrations of impressionist techniques will, of course, come from Conrad's works. To a lesser extent, I also quote from the works of Ford Madox Ford, Stephen Crane, and Henry James since they are almost universally acknowledged as impressionists and would also be well known to most readers. In so doing, though, I am not implying that these authors were the only impressionist writers – merely that there is not enough space in this book to argue for the impressionism of other authors less categorically associated with this literary movement.

Acknowledgments

I would like to thank a number of people without whose help and support this book could not have reached its completion. First, I would like to thank those people at the Pennsylvania State University who were invaluable resources during the early stages of this project: Sanford Schwartz, my thesis director (and continuing supporter), Stanley Weintraub, Wendell Harris, Joseph Kockelmans, and the late Salim Kemal, my committee members, all of whom were instrumental in helping me to see what is necessary to produce good scholarship.

I am also grateful to the English faculty in general at Louisiana State University for their graciousness in offering help and advice during the initial revision and submission phase. Sharon Weltman, Elsie Michie, Panthea Reid, Rick Moreland, Bainard Cowan, Joseph Kronick, and Gerald Kennedy were especially helpful, and I am most appreciative of Jim Springer Borck's friendship and support.

Others who warrant my warmest gratitude include the entire English faculty at the University of Wisconsin-Superior for their encouragement, particularly Anthony Bukoski, Nicholas Sloboda, Joan Bischoff, and Barton Sutter; the department's administrative assistant, Carmen Britton, who never makes mistakes and never questions what happens to all that paper I request; Dr. Ray Ryan, my editor at Cambridge University Press, for his generous help and advice in preparing the manuscript; Rachel De Wachter and Hilary Hammond of Cambridge University Press for their help in the final stages of the editing process; Richard Hudelson, Nicholas Joukovsky, Robert Hume, Marie Secor, David Galef, Robert Lougy, Robert Edwards, Patrick Cheney, Carla Mulford, Maximillian Novak, and Anna Nardo, for their willingness to read prospective articles and otherwise support my scholarship; Gordon Thomas, Jean Anne Waterstradt, and Peter Jourdain for their friendship and general support for my scholarly endeavors; Robert Hass for his constant friendship and moral support; the Joseph Conrad Society of

America for the confidence they showed in my work by presenting me with their Young Scholar Award for 1999; and Richard Poulsen for his friendship as well as his unfailing support and unwavering confidence in my abilities ever since my undergraduate days. A version of part of chapter 4 appeared in *Studies in the Novel* 5.32 (winter 2000), copyright 2000 by the University of North Texas, reprinted by permission of the publisher.

Finally, I would like to thank my family in general for their support, particularly my mother, Virginia Long, my aunt and uncle, Ruth and George Snider, and my mother and father-in-law, Shirley and Alfred Davis, for their support and interest throughout this project. Furthermore, I would like to thank my grandfather, George Snider, for his moral support and my late grandmother, Ruth Snider, for her endless faith in me. I am also grateful to my two-year-old daughter, Kaitlynne, who I suspect cares nothing for Conrad but is nevertheless a great joy to be around. Most important, though, I would like to express my deepest appreciation to my wife, Deanna, who has been patient, supportive, and loving during the long, difficult, and often discouraging graduate-school and job-search experience that has gone hand in hand (as did we) with the writing of this book.

Abbreviations

Throughout this book, when quoting from *Almayer's Folly* and *The Secret Agent*, I will use the Cambridge editions of these works. For Conrad's other works, unless otherwise stated, I will use the standard 1928 Doubleday edition. The abbreviations I use are as follows:

AF	*Almayer's Folly*	Ro	*The Rover*
AG	*The Arrow of Gold*	S	*Suspense*
C	*Chance*	SA	*The Secret Agent*
I	*The Inheritors*	SL	*The Shadow Line*
LJ	*Lord Jim*	SS	*A Set of Six*
MS	*The Mirror of the Sea*	T	*Typhoon and Other Stories*
N	*Nostromo*	TH	*Tales of Hearsay*
NLL	*Notes on Life and Letters*	TLS	*'Twixt Land and Sea*
NN	*The Nigger of the "Narcissus"*	TU	*Tales of Unrest*
OI	*An Outcast of the Islands*	UWE	*Under Western Eyes*
PR	*A Personal Record*	V	*Victory*
R	*Romance*	WT	*Within the Tides*
Re	*The Rescue*	Y	*Youth and Two Other Stories*

Objects of consciousness in Conrad's impressionist world

"The unwearied self-forgetful attention to every phase of the living universe reflected in our consciousness may be our appointed task on this earth."

A Personal Record

I

In this book, I investigate the far-reaching effects of impressionism in the works of Joseph Conrad. In particular, I look at the sources and implications of his impressionism in order to argue for a consistent link between his literary technique, philosophical presuppositions, and sociopolitical views. The same core ideas concerning the nature of human existence and human experience run throughout his works. In the process of investigating these issues, I present a generally unified Conrad that contrasts with the fragmented Conrad popular in some circles. Furthermore, I posit a much-needed definition of literary impressionism based upon philosophical groundings rather than upon the visual arts. In this way, I hope to demonstrate literary impressionism's broad power and significant influence and by so doing argue for a much more important role for this movement in literary history than is generally accorded it.

Running in the background of this study will be an attempt to show that Conrad's narrative techniques and philosophical inquiries result in part from the intellectual environment in which he wrote. Nevertheless, it would be misleading to suggest that my reading of Conrad is either an attempt at cultural studies or intellectual history. Instead, the intellectual and cultural environment is a means of orienting Conrad's works and a backdrop for the philosophical investigations in which I will be engaging. Furthermore, although this book will be a philosophical investigation into epistemological processes and their sociopolitical implications in Conrad's works, I do not systematically apply the ideas of any specific philosophical school of thought nor the philosophical ideas of any specific thinker (although the views of certain philosophers or schools of philosophy may occasionally inform my argument). Instead, I try to uncover the underlying philosophical presuppositions and their implications in impressionism in general and in Conrad's impressionism in particular. I will then try to follow through with these philosophical conclusions to discover the effects of Conrad's impressionist concerns on yet larger philosophical issues afoot in his works.

The ultimate goal of this book will be to demonstrate that the implications of Conrad's impressionist narrative technique lead not only to questions about his narratology and artistic representation but also to broader questions concerning his views on western civilization, the nature of the universe, and the meaning of human existence. In the end, I believe that these questions arise as much from the narrative techniques Conrad employs as they do from the subject matter he investigates. Conrad's techniques represent the way human beings obtain knowledge, and therefore his narrative techniques function both in a practical manner to move the narrative along and in a philosophical manner to identify epistemological processes, which then in turn lead to important social, political, and ethical concerns.

To begin, I define literary impressionism and outline its origins, context, and implications, thereby establishing the groundwork for a more extended discussion of Conrad's works themselves. The middle chapters focus on what I call *objects of consciousness*, each chapter investigating different objects of consciousness and their relationship to knowledge throughout Conrad's works. Among these objects of consciousness, I will discuss perception of events, physical objects, and human subjects, as well as the human experience of time and space. During the course of these investigations, I look at the various permutations related to each object of consciousness based upon its appearance in Conrad's works. These central chapters each revolve around one of Conrad's major works ("Heart of Darkness," *Lord Jim*, and *The Secret Agent*) as a kind of touchstone; at the same time, I also discuss the particular issues engaged by each chapter throughout Conrad's works in general. In addition, I look at the implications of these investigations, as each inquiry also considers the relationship between a particular object of consciousness and the popularized view of western civilization. Throughout Conrad's writings, objects of consciousness are either a product of western views or they resemble and function as do western views – or both. Finally, these investigations conclude with a discussion of the nature of Conrad's universe, because it is linked to his ideas concerning western civilization. To arrive at such conclusions, I synthesize my previous discussion of Conrad's impressionism and demonstrate how impressionist technique and epistemology are linked such that they encompass both individual and cultural concerns. I hope to show that Conrad's impressionism leads to a view of western civilization, the nature of the universe, and the meaning of human existence that is consistently connected to and has its origins in Conrad's impressionist theory. In this way, theory and technique merge to form a unified whole.

II

Conrad noted the impossibility of achieving the kind of objective truth many in the nineteenth and early twentieth centuries sought. Throughout his writings, he rejects attempts to universalize truth and demonstrates that human experience is always individual. Both his philosophical concerns and narrative techniques point to an epistemology that presents human experience and knowledge originating from a particular source in space and time.

In defining literary impressionism, I will look to the underlying philosophical presuppositions and issues the movement raises rather than to impressionist representations in the visual arts. Too closely associating literary and visual impressionism, together with difficulties in defining impressionist theory, have produced a long list of impressionist writers that seems to include most well-known authors writing between 1875 and 1925 – and beyond. However, by looking to impressionism's philosophical groundings and by clearly defining impressionist epistemology itself, confusion can be reduced concerning which writers are impressionist and which are not. In short, I will argue that impressionism saw all phenomena filtering through the medium of human consciousness at a particular place and time, thereby representing knowledge as an individual rather than a universal experience. In addition to defining impressionism, I will also look at some of the techniques impressionist writers employ in order to represent their philosophical ideas. In particular, I look at Conrad's impressionism based upon the definition I establish and identify some of the shortcomings of previous commentaries. These shortcomings include the views that Conrad's impressionist literature focused on surface rather than depth, that impressionism was a technique Conrad employed only early on in his career, that his impressionism imitated methods from the visual arts, and that it dealt solely with visual perception. In contrast, I will argue that each of these views does not accurately represent Conrad's impressionism.

I will then look at perception of events, physical objects, and human subjects, as well as the human experience of time and, to a lesser degree, space. Concerning physical objects and events, I investigate human interaction with external objects and events in the form of sensory perception as well as the way these phenomena impress themselves upon consciousness such that each perceptual experience is unique. Conrad sees perception as contextualized, with the perceptual event occurring at a specific point in space and time. Such an event consists of subject and object as well as the physical circumstances of the perceptual event and the perceiver's personal and public past. As a result, perception occurs such that perceiver, perceived, and surrounding circumstances blur to produce an experience that is unique to each perceptual instance. Conrad's view of the interaction between subject and object also has important implications for the way human beings acquire knowledge. Knowledge becomes an individual phenomenon rather than a universal one. Each person gains knowledge through interaction with objects of consciousness, and one person's knowledge is never exactly the same as another's, nor even exactly the same as one's own at a different point in space and time.

Closely associated with perception of events and physical objects is perception of human subjects, and accordingly I will also focus my argument on the phenomenon of human subjectivity; in particular, I consider knowledge of self and others. In so doing, I argue that Conrad blurs the boundaries between self and other (between subject and object as it were) such that knowledge of self can come through knowledge of other and knowledge of other can come through knowledge of self. Human subjectivity exists within the context of self, other, and their surrounding circumstances. No clear distinction exists between self and other for Conrad, and in looking at the other and its relationship to the self, Conrad shows that others help to clarify the self either by similarity or by contrast. In this way, the self learns from others both what it is and what it is not. In addition to knowledge of self through knowledge of others, subjective knowledge may also come through cultural conditions and through investigation into one's self.

Along with subjects, objects, and events, I will also look at Conrad's investigation into the human experience of time and its relationship to knowledge. Conrad considers the way human beings experience time in an individual and contextualized manner. In the process, he blurs distinctions between time and human subjectivity (again between subject and object). In investigating these phenomena, Conrad deals with human time (time as human beings experience it), mechanical time (time as a clock measures it), and narrative time (time as represented in narration). The direct relationship between human time and mechanical time is important to Conrad because he uses the contrast between the two as the clearest example of the individual nature of objects of consciousness. Conrad demonstrates how human time is always at odds with the movement of a clock. Furthermore, each individual's experience of time is unique and cannot be synchronized with that of others except by means of mechanical time's intervention. Conrad also uses narrative time to emphasize the subjectivity of human temporal experience so that his impressionist narrative methods are meant to represent the way human beings actually experience time.

Each of these inquiries leads to two important conclusions. First, Conrad demonstrates that knowledge can never (or almost never) be certain. Second, his emphasis on the individuality of the epistemological process brings into question all attempts to universalize human experience. As a result, western civilization in particular comes under Conrad's scrutiny, and since the popular view of western civilization at the time conceived it to be based upon an absolute foundation, Conrad's epistemology strikes directly at that foundation. Therefore, each investigation of objects of consciousness – whether physical objects, human subjects, events, space, or time – demonstrates the ultimate uncertainty of knowledge and approaches the conflict between this uncertainty and the perceived certainty of western civilization. These questions also lead to two unpleasant logical possibilities for Conrad: epistemological solipsism and ethical anarchy. Uncomfortable with both positions, Conrad rejects moral and intellectual nihilism by focusing on his belief in the certainty of human subjectivity, and in fact employs the very source of the problem – human subjectivity itself – as its solution and in the process creates meaning for human existence.

In this way, my investigation into Conrad's impressionist world will come full circle. I begin with the uncertainty and individuality of human experience in Conrad's works and end with that same phenomenon.

Along the way, though, I try to demonstrate that all facets of Conrad's works are linked. His epistemological inquiries lead to an uncertainty that questions the perceived certainty of western civilization that then leads to questions concerning the nature of the universe and the meaning of human existence. In the end, Conrad arrives at a kind of certainty through uncertainty.

CHAPTER I

Subject/object: science and the epistemological origins of literary impressionism

"Life and the arts follow dark courses, and will not turn aside to the
brilliant arc-lights of science."

"The Ascending Effort"

I

"The fetish of today is neither royalty nor religion... The sacro-sanct
fetish of to-day is science," Mr. Vladimir confidently asserts early in *The
Secret Agent* (*SA* 29). Later, Ossipon concurs: "Science reigns already. It
reigns in the shade maybe – but it reigns" (*SA* 227). During the nineteenth century, science achieved a privileged position in the western
world. For many, it seemed to provide a certainty unavailable elsewhere. Science yielded "facts": information believed to be objectively
verifiable and hence true. Science and scientific methodology also
provided the backdrop for many of the revolutionary challenges to
conventional thinking that arose during the century. Through the work
of Charles Lyell, Charles Darwin, and others, developments in geology,
biology, and other scientific disciplines challenged long-held social beliefs concerning the nature of the Earth and the nature of humanity.[1]
Other thinkers made equally challenging assertions.[2] In the hands of
Auguste Comte, John Stuart Mill, and those who followed them,
such as Herbert Spencer, Cesare Lombroso, Hippolyte Taine, Ernest
Renan, G. H. Lewes, Emile Durkheim, Leslie Stephen, and numerous
others, this new view of the power of science evolved into scientific
positivism, a movement based upon the belief that all knowledge could
be obtained through scientific methodology.[3] Following in the wake of
science, some disciplines adopted scientific methodology, while others
were either influenced by it or reacted against it. Psychology, sociology,
and anthropology, for example, adopted scientific methodology and
strove for the perceived certainty of scientific inquiry, while some

7

branches of theology and philosophy reacted against science's privileged position and influence.

Nor were the arts immune from the effects of scientific positivism; realism, naturalism, and impressionism all responded to science.[4] The fundamental presuppositions and artistic techniques of realism and naturalism are essentially scientific. (Impressionism's relationship to science is more equivocal and will be discussed in more detail later.) Naturalism in particular relied on science as a model, but both naturalism and realism have scientific observation and empirical data at their core. Realists sought to represent everyday occurrences that any observer could recognize, intending to depict life the way people actually experienced it. This aesthetic philosophy is also the source of realist complaints against romantic and sentimental literature. For instance, in Mark Twain's humorous essay, "Fenimore Cooper's Literary Offenses," the common element of Twain's criticisms is that Cooper's novels are unrealistic. Twain argued that many of the events in Cooper's works could never happen in real life and hence Cooper's novels were not only unrealistic but unartistic as well. Furthermore, realists required realism not only of romantic and sentimental literature, but also leveled a similar complaint against Conrad's novel *Lord Jim*. In the "Author's Note," Conrad remarks that certain critics "argued that no man could have been expected to talk all that time, and other men to listen so long. It was not, they said, very credible" (*LJ* vii). For realists, accurately representing reality was a crucial component of an artistic work. To an even greater extent, naturalism adopted scientific methodology. In *The Experimental Novel*, Zola notes that he used Claude Bernard's *Introduction à l'étude de la médecine expérimentale* as a model for his theory of the novel,[5] further arguing that an author should set up a laboratory experiment, creating an environment (based upon real life experience) and then simply place characters in that setting and allow them to respond to the existent stimuli. Zola states that his intention is to

prove for my part that if the experimental method leads to the knowledge of physical life, it should also lead to the knowledge of the passionate and intellectual life. It is but a question of degree in the same path which runs from chemistry to physiology, then from physiology to anthropology and to sociology.[6]

Zola believes that by adopting scientific methodology he can obtain knowledge of human beings and their reactions to various conditions, and this attitude is consistent with the atmosphere of the time.

Even more striking than the influence of science on artistic movements was its influence on how society conceived of human existence. Peter Allan Dale has argued, "[T]he attempt to apply scientific method to human subjects . . . is nineteenth-century positivism's greatest contribution to philosophy as well as its most revolutionary gesture."[7] And in scientific positivism's attempt to explain all reality – even human subjectivity – some began to feel science had overreached its bounds because despite the prominence of science and the certainty it held for many at that time, there were also those who resisted what Dale calls "a religion of science."[8] Science's growing prominence caused some to fear a society based solely on facts, while others felt that applying scientific methodology to all phenomena simply oversimplified reality.

Charles Dickens was one who seems to have feared a society founded upon facts alone, and he ridiculed this idea as it became popularized. Most notably in *Hard Times*, he questioned utilitarian education (a product of the philosophy of Bentham and Mill) whose underpinning was scientific methodology. The novel opens with a speaker insisting,

Now, what I want is, Facts. Teach these boys and girls nothing but Facts. Facts alone are wanted in life. Plant nothing else, and root out everything else. You can only form the minds of reasoning animals upon Facts: nothing else will ever be of any service to them . . . Stick to Facts, Sir! . . . In this life, we want nothing but Facts, Sir; nothing but Facts![9]

In such a system, everything must be based upon demonstrable facts, while all else is rejected. For instance, when the school's instructor, Mr. Gradgrind, asks his student Sissy to define a horse, she thinks of her father's work with circus horses and the pleasant feelings she associates with the memory (4). Her subjective response, however, does not satisfy Gradgrind, who replies, "Girl number twenty possessed of no facts, in reference to one of the commonest of animals!" (5). He then elicits the desired response from another student, Bitzer, who replies, "Quadruped. Graminivorous. Forty teeth, namely twenty-four grinders, four eye-teeth, and twelve incisive. Sheds coat in the spring; in marshy countries, sheds hoofs, too. Hoofs hard, but requiring to be shod with iron. Age known by marks in mouth" (6). For Gradgrind, Bitzer's objective, universally verifiable facts constitute certainty whereas Sissy's subjective, individual experience actually hinders certainty. In fact, Gradgrind forbids his own children from experiencing anything but rational or empirical facts and praises his daughter when she accepts the proposal of a man she loathes because she marries him for rational rather than emotional reasons (131–35). Dickens then makes explicit his concern with this attitude later in the novel when Bitzer, now a grown man, presents a perfectly rational but also perfectly heartless reason for turning over Gradgrind's son to the authorities (382–84). In Gradgrind's society, subjective concepts such as love and compassion take a back seat to facts. Dale argues that such a society mirrors its requirements for art: "[A]rt must become radically realistic; fancy, or imagination, must be suppressed (and with it the romantic aesthetic); taste must be redefined as love of fact."[10] Of course, Dickens exaggerates the pervasiveness of Gradgrind's worldview, but he saw the possibility of such a situation developing because of the degree of confidence society placed in science and its methods. And although Dickens overstates the pervasiveness of Gradgrind's philosophy, he does not overstate the status of science during the nineteenth century.[11]

Similarly, in Conrad's *Victory*, Heyst begins the novel in search of "facts." Like Gradgrind, he tells Mr. Tesman, "Facts. There's nothing worth knowing but fact. Hard facts! Facts alone" (*V* 7; see also 10, 24, 54, 61). Heyst searches for facts devoid of human subjectivity but finds instead human subjectivity in the form of Morrison's friendship and Lena's love. In essence, a fact leads to Heyst's rejection of facts; he tells Lena, "[F]acts have a certain positive value, and I will tell you a fact. One day I met a cornered man" (*V* 197). When Heyst finds Morrison cornered and about to lose his ship to the maneuvering of the Portuguese authorities, he offers to loan Morrison the money to pay the tax the authorities had imposed. Heyst's befriending of Morrison brings about his reentry into the human community, which Heyst had eschewed until then (*V* 198–99). In the end, Heyst discovers that facts cannot bring him to truth and concludes, "I have lost all belief in realities" (*V* 350). In this same vein, the narrator notes of Ricardo's pursuit of facts: "[H]e pursued it [truth] in the light of his own experience and prejudices. For facts, whatever their origin (and God only knows where they come from), can be only tested by our own particular suspicions" (*V* 157). For Conrad, seemingly objective facts cannot be separated from the subjective consciousness experiencing them, and as Gradgrind learns so also does Heyst conclude that facts alone cannot provide fulfillment for human existence.

Conrad also rejects this wholesale acceptance of scientific methodology in determining certainty. Eloise Knapp Hay argues that in *The Secret Agent* Conrad's "eye is severely scornful as it falls on the fetish of science."[12] And Ian Watt notes, "Conrad viewed contemporary attempts to force a marriage between natural science and human culture as misguided."¹³ However, unlike Dickens, Conrad seems not so much concerned with the loss of humanity in a scientific society as he is with showing that the pursuit of facts oversimplifies reality. In *Lord Jim*, Marlow remarks that the magistrates at the *Patna* inquiry "wanted facts. Facts! They demanded facts from him [Jim], as if facts could explain anything!" (*LJ* 29). But Mark Wollaeger notes Conrad's "impatience with the limitations of empiricism and a desire to pierce through material fact."¹⁴ Conrad himself remarks in a letter to William Blackwood, "[F]acts don't matter."¹⁵ The magistrates in *Lord Jim* were interested only in whether Jim had abandoned his post, and they believed that the objective fact – stripped of its subjective context – could provide certainty concerning the event. Like Winnie Verloc, their "philosophy consisted in not taking notice of the inside of facts" (*SA* 120). But, according to Marlow, such an inquiry can never bring about knowledge in any effectual manner because the fact cannot be separated from its context. As Jim struggles with the fact of his desertion, Marlow remarks, "These were issues beyond the competency of a court of inquiry" (*LJ* 93). Marlow summarizes the general efficacy of the court's methodology, suggesting that the examination

was beating futilely round the well-known fact, and the play of questions upon it was as instructive as the tapping with a hammer on an iron box, were the object to find out what's inside. However, an official inquiry could not be any other thing. Its object was not the fundamental why, but the superficial how, of this affair. (*LJ* 56)

What interests Marlow – and what constitutes for him knowledge of the incident – is precisely the opposite of what the inquiry believes to be knowledge. For Marlow, only through understanding its subjective context can he perhaps come to a knowledge of the event. Scientific methodology cannot lead to knowledge of human beings because facts alone can never bring about knowledge of events involving human beings.

By the late nineteenth century, besides its appearance in literature, considerable resistance to the privileging of science had begun to appear elsewhere as well, especially when science moved outside the boundaries of the physical world and entered the sphere of human experience.¹⁶ By the end of the century, Søren Kierkegaard, Wilhelm Windelband, Heinrich Rickert, Wilhelm Dilthey, Friedrich Nietzsche, Henri Bergson, and others had come to question the wisdom of borrowing science and its methods to analyze humanity.[17] Although many were willing to accept that science could explain physical phenomena, they felt it simply could not explain human phenomena with any certainty. Sanford Schwartz has noted that

the apostles of scientism ... did not hesitate to reduce the whole of reality, including human nature, to a system of determinate laws. Bergson, like others of his generation, resisted this militant scientism and attacked the various doctrines that reduce consciousness to a mere mechanism: the materialist view, which treats the mind as an epiphenomenon of the brain's physiological activity, and maintains, in the words of one proselyte, that the brain secretes thought just as the liver secretes bile; the psycho-physical method, which establishes quantitative laws correlating variations in external stimuli with variations in sensory response; and the associationist school, which uses the laws of mechanics to describe the life of the mind.[18]

Those who opposed the "apostles of scientism" felt that scientific methodology could not explain human experience satisfactorily because for them human phenomena are fundamentally different from physical phenomena, which is exactly what scientific positivism failed to acknowledge.

As did others of that time, Conrad also rejected scientism. "Though not formally trained in the new academic disciplines, Conrad's letters reveal familiarity with contemporary science unusual for a literary man,"[19] and he recognized the limitations of scientific methodology. For instance, in "Heart of Darkness," the doctor for the Belgian trading company asks to measure Marlow's head, saying, "I always ask leave, in the interests of science, to measure the crania of those going out there [Africa]" (*Y* 58). This measurement was supposed to tell something about the patient's psychology, but Marlow does not believe a relationship exists between the size or shape of human crania and human psychology, and he remarks of the doctor, "I thought him a harmless fool" (*Y* 58). Even more emphatic, though, the doctor himself acknowledges that he practices pseudoscience. When Marlow asks the doctor whether he measures the crania of those who return, he replies, "Oh, I never see them, and, moreover, the changes take place inside, you know" (*Y* 58). This response demonstrates the contrast between physiology and psychology: the size or shape of the head cannot reveal what occurs within. Conrad also ridicules scientism in *The Secret Agent* when he presents Comrade Ossipon using scientific observation to come to conclusions about human psychology: Ossipon

submitted to the rule of science. He was scientific, and he gazed scientifically at that woman, the sister of a degenerate, a degenerate herself – of a murdering type. He gazed at her, and invoked Lombroso, as an Italian peasant recommends himself to his favourite saint. He gazed scientifically. He gazed at her cheeks, at her nose, at her eyes, at her ears ... Bad! ... Fatal! Mrs. Verloc's pale lips parting, slightly relaxed under his passionately attentive gaze, he gazed also at her teeth ... Not a doubt remained ... a murdering type. (*SA* 222; ellipses are Conrad's)

Ossipon uses physical evidence to come to nonphysical conclusions. He believes he can analyze Mrs. Verloc objectively, but his scientific observation of Winnie's physicality cannot explain her psychology.[20]

Conrad and other literary impressionists responded to scientific positivism by demonstrating that reason and science alone are insufficient for analyzing human problems and human existence.[21] They recognized the role human subjectivity plays – in conjunction with facts – in coming to a knowledge of phenomena, and they sought to access reality while recognizing that reality comes through the medium of human subjectivity.

II

Impressionism is at its core a response to scientific positivism. It saw realism, a child of science, as flawed in its oversimplification of reality. Impressionism's presuppositions, methodology, and product all point to a reality that is very different from that of realism. Much has been written on literary impressionism,[22] but despite this body of commentary the movement remains amorphous, so much so that those definitions of impressionism that do exist are themselves usually "impressionistic." Furthermore, the relationship between impressionist literature and painting remains equally unclear. Certainly, impressionists, both painters and writers, were a loosely knit group of artists who never produced a unifying artistic manifesto nor even a consistently similar product. Nevertheless, I would argue that they were concerned with similar issues and worked from similar philosophical presuppositions. And for all their differences, impressionists, both artistic and literary, viewed the epistemological process as an individual and not a universal phenomenon. In this way, impressionism ran a middle course between science's opponents and proponents and developed a unique relationship to science. Its work is both a product of and a reaction against science. Its methodology is essentially scientific in its attempt to reproduce exactly the way human beings apprehend objects of consciousness; at the same time, though, impressionism recognized that knowledge always comes through the medium of human subjectivity. The problem with the existing work on literary impressionism is that it either restricts the movement's subject matter and methodology thereby ignoring crucial characteristics of impressionist literature, or expands the impressionist canon to include too many dissimilar authors. In contrast, I would like to expand the movement's subject matter and methodology and by so doing restrict the range of authors who could be considered literary impressionists.

Various commentators have identified a wide range of authors as literary impressionists, though rarely agreeing on who is and who is not an impressionist; these critics have argued for impressionism in the works of the Goncourts, Maupassant, Flaubert, Chekhov, Robbe-Grillet, Proust, Hemingway, Woolf, Pater, Joyce, Howells, Conrad, D. H. Lawrence, Stephen Crane, Willa Cather, Henry James, Ford Madox Ford, Jean Rhys, Sarah Orne Jewett, Katherine Mansfield, George Moore, R. B. Cunninghame Graham, W. H. Hudson, Arnold Bennett, Wallace Stevens, and still others.[23] James Nagel tries to clarify this problem by referring to objective impressionists and subjective impressionists.[24] In other words, some impressionists emphasize subjectivity more (i.e., Woolf and Joyce), while others emphasize it less (i.e., Maupassant and Flaubert). Nagel correctly assesses the degree of subjectivity these authors emphasize, but his distinction does not really clear the waters since we are still left with vastly different writers all classified as impressionists of some sort. Of course, circumscribing "isms" of any kind invites disagreement, but with impressionism opinions conflict considerably. Definitions that include such disparate authors as Howells and Bennett on one end of a spectrum and Woolf and Joyce on the other are so broad as to dissolve into nothingness, and this confusion results from inadequate definitions of literary impressionism. In particular, the difficulty in defining literary impressionism lies in two areas: first, determining the relationship between the techniques of impressionist painting and those of impressionist literature; and second, determining the relationship between objects of consciousness and their representation in impressionist art and literature. In other words, confusion concerning literary impressionism causes some critics to draw too close a tie between the techniques of the visual and literary arts, while others fail to identify the nature of impressionist epistemology itself. Contrary to most commentary, I would argue that any similarities between impressionist art and literature result from similarities in philosophy – not technique. Nor do impressionists simply represent visual perception; instead they render a much broader epistemological experience.

Although impressionist art and literature share similar philosophical concerns, their techniques for representing those concerns usually differ considerably because of the differing media they employ. In *Characteristics of French Art*, Roger Fry associates atmosphere and point of view with impressionist painting.[25] Others also identify sharp juxtaposition of colors,[26] innovative use of light,[27] and the use of "empathetic and evocative brushwork"[28] as common techniques in impressionist painting. Furthermore, some commentators have also linked the fragment, or fleeting moment, to impressionist painting.[29] Because impressionism originated in the visual arts and because of the movement's importance in the history of the visual arts, most critics of impressionist literature have looked at it in the light of techniques of impressionist visual arts. James Kirschke, for instance, defines literary impressionism in a fashion "that accords more precisely with the techniques as derived from Impressionism in painting."[30] Problems arise, however, when critics identify the techniques of impressionist painting and then insist on transferring them to impressionist writing. For example, Beverly Jean Gibbs writes, "[T]he impressionistic writers tried to do with color what the impressionistic painters did with the effects of light and shade."[31] Ferdinand Brunetière remarks of Daudet's writing that "you will find that [it] is the method of procedure of none but a painter. The imperfect tense, here, serves to prolong the duration of the action expressed by the verb and stops it – makes it stand motionless – after a fashion, before the very eyes of the reader."[32] Maria Kronegger argues that "the great number of commas" in Jules Laforgue's poem "*Soir de printemps sur le boulevard*" "has its equivalent in the impressionist's broken brush-strokes."[33] Similarly, some critics see representation of light, juxtaposition of colors for emphasis, and hazy atmospheric conditions as characteristics of impressionist writing.[34] In this same vein, Calvin S. Brown sees the fleeting moment as a requirement for impressionist literature and remarks, "Separate fleeting impressions can not be built up into an organic whole of sufficient size, nor can a single fleeting impression be maintained and developed long enough to produce a major work."[35] However, responding to views such as Brown's, H. Peter Stowell counters: "To demand that literary impressionism string out a continuous series of pointillistic impressions is to misinterpret an artistic process that searches for a technique to express a reality within the outer

limits of its own medium... The impressions of perceiving conscious-
nesses in literature must be rendered uniquely. Literature is not painting."[36] The techniques of impressionist painting and literature bear
some similarities, but even greater differences exist. Some of the techniques of painting may occasionally translate into writing, especially
when representing visual perception (for instance presenting physical
objects from limited viewpoints), but the difficulty lies in seeing impressionism's techniques determining its underlying philosophical concerns
rather than impressionism's underlying philosophical concerns determining its techniques.

More important than clarifying the relationship between impressionist
painting and literature, though, is the problem of defining impressionist
epistemology itself. In short, impressionists – whether in the literary or
visual arts – sought to represent the interaction between human consciousness and the objects of that consciousness. Much of this interaction appears as sensory perception, particularly visual perception, but
this process should not be limited solely to visual perception or even to
sensory perception in general, as does Julia van Gunsteren when she
remarks, "What cannot be sensed does not exist for the Impressionist."[37]
Instead, I would argue that impressionists represented the gamut of
objects of consciousness: physical objects, human subjects, events, ideas,
space, and time.[38] For example, in Stephen Crane's "The Open Boat,"
the characters' confusion over whether the man on shore is waving a
coat or a flag,[39] Joseph Conrad's various narrators' views of Jim in *Lord
Jim*, the irregular movement of time in Ford Madox Ford's *Parade's End*,
the variety of views of the revolutionary idea in Conrad's *Nostromo*, Peter
Brench's unreliable perception of events in James' "The Tree of Knowledge," and the contrasting perceptions of the space of Russia in Conrad's *Under Western Eyes* are all examples of impressionist renderings of
objects of consciousness. Regardless of the particular object of consciousness, though, impressionists represent an individual human
consciousness interacting with phenomena at a fixed point in space
and time.

In addition to recognizing the nature of objects of consciousness,
identifying the relationship between subject and object is also important. For many critics, this has proven elusive; some see impressionism
as essentially object-oriented, while others see it as subject-oriented. In
other words, an object-oriented, or objective, view sees impressionists
presenting an object as it projects itself onto human consciousness;

while the subject-oriented, or subjective, view sees impressionists rendering only idiosyncratic, emotional responses to the object. Two early commentators, Jules Laforgue and W. S. Sichel, illustrate these divergent views. Laforgue represents the objective end of the spectrum and argues that impressionism is a "primitive" way of looking at the world. He suggests that the impressionist artist "is one who, forgetting the pictures amassed through centuries in museums, forgetting his optical art school training – line, perspective, color – by dint of living and seeing frankly and primitively ... [paints] as simply as he sees."[40] Laforgue goes on to say that this "primitive eye" reaches "a point where it can see reality in the living atmosphere of forms, decomposed, refracted, reflected by beings and things, in incessant variation."[41] In other words, impressionists merely paint what they see – divorced from personal experience and cultural conventions. On the other hand, W. S. Sichel suggests that the impressionist's "medium is the feelings, his method a style of suggestion rather than of representation."[42] He also argues, "In the personal and plaintive is to be found the method of what we style 'Impressionism.'"[43] Sichel concludes by saying, "Let our modern impressionists bear in mind that what is vulgarly known as 'Realism' has indeed nothing necessarily in common with impressionism at all."[44] For Sichel, impressionism is vivid glimpses of emotion and emotionally charged objects that represent only the artist's own subjectivity – not the object itself.[45]

Both objective and subjective views have also influenced more recent critics, and both are only partly correct. Laforgue suggests that impressionists eliminate cultural influence (particularly artistic conventions), but that is not wholly possible since no one can completely escape cultural influences. More important, though, the objective view excludes the subject's personal experience from the process, and so a physical object, for instance, may be perceived (to a certain extent) divorced from cultural influences but still appear the same to any observer who can forget conventional thinking about visual perception. As a result, the objective view eliminates part of the subject's subjectivity and does not posit an individual epistemological experience. Nevertheless, Laforgue correctly asserts that impressionists do not allow cultural conventions to rule their art and that they make a conscious effort to set aside outside influences and render the object as it actually appears at a specific moment. Similarly, Sichel correctly argues that impressionism represents the artist's subjectivity, but impressionism does not simply present the artist's emotional response to an object. Instead, subject and object are linked, and their relationship is uniquely contextualized – an individual experience that connects subject, object, and surrounding circumstances in an interdependent event.

The divergence of objective and subjective views partly explains why one critic may see Howells and Bennett as impressionists, while another may see Woolf and Joyce as impressionists. (None of whom fit my definition of impressionism – Howells and Bennett because of their objectivity, Woolf and Joyce because of their subjectivity.) This dualist perspective is further problematized because it works from a Cartesian subject/object split. In fact, impressionist representation lies neither solely with the subject nor solely with the object but rather in the space between the two.[46] In this way, impressionism diverges from both positivism and idealism.[47] Positivism saw reality in the object – the external world. Idealism saw reality in the subject – the internal world. Impressionism mediates these extremes and posits the necessary existence of both subject and object – but not from a dualist position; rather, the two merge such that their outlines blur. In Conrad's "Heart of Darkness," for example, Marlow transforms the space of the African wilderness into a dark and brooding expanse that holds the secret to the nature of human existence. At the same time, though, Marlow himself is transformed by his experience with that wilderness, and in this epistemological encounter it is impossible to tell for certain where Marlow's outlines end and those of the wilderness begin.

Positivism, idealism, and impressionism all represent change occurring in the interaction between subject and object. But while positivism and idealism render a one-sided change, impressionism renders a two-sided exchange. For positivism, since reality exists outside the subject, objects may change subjects, but the objects themselves remain the same regardless of who experiences them. On the other hand, for idealism, since reality exists within the subject, subjects may change objects, but the subjects themselves do not change because all objects are part of the subject. However, for impressionism, neither positivism (which minimizes subjectivity) nor idealism (which minimizes objectivity) accurately represents the epistemological process. In contrast to these polarized views, impressionism presents subject and object in constant change through their mutual influence. As in the above example, in Marlow's relationship with the African wilderness, the wilderness projects itself onto Marlow, while Marlow projects himself onto the wilderness. Subject alters object, just as object alters subject – to the reciprocal influence of each. Furthermore, subject and object blur with their surrounding circumstances, whether those be the object's physical setting or the subject's personal and cultural past.[48] These blurred boundaries then locate the object of consciousness at a specific place and time such that the final product is an object limited to its context and inextricable from its surroundings without changing the epistemological event; thus the flux of experience is interconnected. In Marlow's last glimpse of Jim in *Lord Jim*, the increasing darkness of the scene's physical surroundings intensifies the brightness of Jim's appearance, and Jim's brightness intensifies the scene's darkness (*LJ* 336). Removed from that context – the physical background, cultural issues surrounding Jim, as well as Marlow's personal experience with Jim and those cultural issues – Jim would appear differently. In this way, impressionist boundaries are consistently fluid, while positivist and idealist boundaries remain rigid, as does the Cartesian dualist model from which they originate.

As a result of impressionist epistemology, an object of consciousness is different for different subjects. Conrad's *The Shadow Line* provides a good example of this contrast. When the narrator first sees his new command, he says, "I knew that, like some rare women, she was one of those creatures whose mere existence is enough to awaken an unselfish delight. One feels that it is good to be in the world in which she has her being" (*SL* 49). Others may see simply a mode of transportation, but for the new captain the ship is much more: the culmination of many years' work – a reward and emblem of his professional success. The narrator then goes on to say, "An enormous baulk of teak-wood timber swung over her hatchway... When they started lowering it the surge of the tackle sent a quiver through her from water-line to the trucks up the fine nerves of her rigging, as though she had shuddered at the weight. It seemed cruel to load her so" (*SL* 50; cf. *MS* 116). To those loading the ship, it is like any other – no more than a receptacle for cargo. As a result of their shared cultural past, the dock workers and the new captain perceive this physical object to be a ship, but because of different personal pasts, they perceive that same object very differently. Nor does an object necessarily remain the same for a particular subject at different moments in time and different locations in space. In Conrad's "Heart of Darkness," the rivets illustrate this fluidity. Marlow says, "There were cases of them down at the coast – cases – piled up – burst – split! You kicked a loose rivet at every second step in that station yard on the hillside. Rivets had rolled into the grove of death. You could fill your pockets with rivets for the trouble of stooping down" (*Y* 83). While at the

Outer Station, Marlow sees the rivets as simply a useless nuisance, but
when he reaches the Central Station, he sees them very differently:
"What I really wanted was rivets, by heaven! Rivets. To get on with the
work – to stop the hole. Rivets I wanted . . . [A]nd there wasn't one rivet
to be found where it was wanted" (*Y* 83–84). At the Central Station,
those rivets have become Marlow's means to repair his ship and assume
his command. Discovering his ship sunk in the Congo River alters the
way Marlow perceives the rivets such that they appear one way at
the Outer Station and yet another at the Central Station. Always the
subject's individual experience (both personal and cultural), together
with the fluid, changing circumstances of space and time, affect the way
an object is experienced. Recognizing this highly contextualized interaction between subject and object, impressionism tried to recreate the
experience of a single subject at a specific point in space and time. For
impressionism, all experience is individual, and every experience of
objects of consciousness is unique.

Despite the fact that almost exclusively subject-oriented movements
such as surrealism and subject-oriented techniques such as stream
of consciousness appeared primarily after impressionism, their presuppositions already existed in nineteenth-century idealist thought. Impressionism rejected idealism's attempt to produce objects – particularly
external objects – solely from the workings of human consciousness.
Idealism emphasized the subject over the object. But for impressionism,
although subjectivity may alter an object, that object is also altered by its
physical surroundings, and so subjectivity may influence but cannot
single-handedly produce an object. Otherwise, no consensus could exist
concerning the nature of a particular object. For impressionism, a ship,
for instance, would appear differently to different people, but all would
agree it is a ship.

Although impressionism responded to idealist philosophy, its primary
target was positivism, and realism was positivism's artistic and literary
representative. Realism's representation of objects contrasts with that of
impressionism. Realists tried to access the object as free as possible of the
accidents of particular instances – including human subjectivity. In so
doing, they sought to represent an unmediated product. In a sense, this
product was universal because it was supposed to appear the same
regardless of who experienced it; objects were to be recognized from the
subject's own experience, and that experience would concur with the
experience of others. Realism emphasized the object, not the subject. Of

course, differences between realism and impressionism are not always wholly distinct because impressionism did not disagree with the realist attempt to portray the world realistically;[49] it simply disagreed with realism's fundamental assumptions about human experience. Whereas realism's primary emphasis was to represent an object such that everyone experiences the same object, impressionism emphasized that all interaction between consciousness and its objects is, by definition, dependent upon the existence of both subject and object. An object is accessed by someone, and any attempt to represent it in isolation is futile. The object cannot be experienced except at a particular place, at a particular time, by a particular person. To borrow Kant's terminology, realism sought the impossibility of representing noumena, while impressionism sought the possibility of representing phenomena. Therefore, rather than the unmediated representational art and literature realists sought to produce, they in fact present a mediated construct of the object. Because realists tried to eliminate subjectivity from the epistemological process, impressionism believed its works were actually more realistic – more representational – than traditionally termed representational works. In a letter to Arnold Bennett, Conrad wrote, "You just stop short of being absolutely real because you are faithful to your dogmas of realism. Now realism in art will never approach reality."[50] In a sense, realism tried to civilize the interaction between consciousness and its objects, removing individual subjectivity and representing a universal product, while impressionism rendered a primitive and essentially unmediated object. The object appears as it actually appears – at a particular point in space and time and filtered through a particular human consciousness.

In "On Impressionism," Ford Madox Ford contrasts realist and impressionist epistemology. Of Tennyson's lines "And bats went round in fragrant skies, / And wheel'd or lit the filmy shapes / That haunt the dusk, with ermine capes / And woolly breasts and beaded eyes" (*In Memoriam A.H.H.*, 95: 9–12), Ford remarks, "Now that is no doubt very good natural history, but it is certainly not Impressionism, since no one watching a bat at dusk could see the ermine, the wool or the beadiness of the eyes."[51] In effect, Ford argues that Tennyson's bat is not realistic. Rather than representing an unmediated and contextualized visual perception, Tennyson replaces it with one that is mediated and noncontextualized, a perception at odds with epistemological processes. Only a universal observer, divorced from space, time, and all other limiting factors, could discern the bat's woolly breast and beady eyes at the moment it appears in the poem. An individual observer could not detect such details and would see instead a very different bat – one restricted by the circumstances surrounding its appearance. Writing of the impressionist painters, Watt argues, "In one way or another all the main Impressionists made it their aim to give a pictorial equivalent of the visual sensations of a particular individual at a particular time and place."[52] The same is true of impressionist writers as well. In addition to maintaining context, though, impressionism also tries to remove objects of consciousness from the mediating factors of cultural conventions that helped bring about realism's universal product. Of course, cultural conventions are part of an individual's experience, but the difference between impressionism and realism on this point is that impressionism saw culture as only one of many facets of a person's experience. Realism, on the other hand, assimilated the individual into the larger cultural experience, and the resulting representation is one that anyone might have experienced. In other words, for realism cultural context is a priori, while for impressionism it is a posteriori. In essence, E. H. Gombrich refers to this conflict when he argues,

If we trust our eyes, and not our preconceived ideas of what things *ought* to look like according to academic rules, we shall make the most exciting discoveries. That such ideas were first considered extravagant heresies is hardly surprising. We have seen throughout this story of art how much we are all inclined to judge pictures by what we *know* rather than by what we *see*.[53]

When impressionists represented what they actually experienced as opposed to what cultural conventions told them they should experience, the objects of consciousness they rendered became individual rather than universal.

In order to represent this individual point of view through which objects of consciousness filter (the crux of all impressionist theory), impressionist writers have employed a variety of narrative techniques. Some of these techniques include achronology, *in medias res*, central consciousness, limited point of view, and multiple narrators.

Achronological narrative is perhaps best represented in the works of Joseph Conrad and Ford Madox Ford. Ford argues that a novel "is not a sort of rounded, annotated record of a set of circumstances ... [I]t is the impression, not the corrected chronicle."[54] Elsewhere, he outlines this theory more fully, suggesting that the problem with the English novel was

that it went straight forward, whereas in your gradual making acquaintanceship with your fellows you never do go straight forward. You meet an English gentleman at your golf club. He is beefy, full of health, the moral of the boy from an English Public School of the finest type. You discover, gradually, that he is hopelessly neurasthenic, dishonest in matters of small change, but unexpectedly self-sacrificing, a dreadful liar, but a most painfully careful student of lepidoptera and, finally, from the public prints, a bigamist who was once, under another name, hammered on the Stock Exchange... To get such a man in fiction you could not begin at his beginning and work his life chronologically to the end. You must first get him in with a strong impression, and then work backwards and forwards over his past.[55]

According to Ford then, historically, the novel – even the realist novel – had been guilty of unreality; it was a "corrected chronicle" that transformed the immediate epistemological experience into an organized account, taking unorganized incidents projected onto human consciousness at different times and places and organizing them into an ordered, chronological narrative. However, Ford believes human beings do not experience phenomena in such an ordered fashion: "[W]e saw that Life did not narrate, but made impressions on our brains."[56] Human beings piece together experience from one place and another, from one time and another. Through his use of impressionist techniques, Ford consistently demonstrates his desire to accurately represent human consciousness interacting with its objects, to keep the author from getting "between the reader's legs"[57] and to draw the reader into the novel's world.[58] In *The Good Soldier*, Ford's narrator Dowell explains this technique:

[W]hen one discusses an affair – a long, sad affair – one goes back, one goes forward. One remembers points that one has forgotten and one explains them all the more minutely since one recognises that one has forgotten to mention them in their proper places and that one may have given, by omitting them, a false impression. I console myself with thinking that this is a real story and that, after all, real stories are probably told best in the way a person telling a story would tell them. They will then seem most real.[59]

This passage explains why Dowell narrates achronologically: both to represent the manner in which a storyteller sometimes introduces details out of sequence and to make the story real for the reader. Conrad takes achronology to an even higher level in such works as *Nostromo, Lord Jim,* and *Chance*. In these novels, time sequences are radically dislocated and force the reader to put together the events achronologically. H. M. Daleski remarks of *Nostromo*, "Carrying his confusion with him, the reader would seem to be forced, rather, to experience a sense of the general disorder that characterizes the revolutionary times Conrad is depicting."[60] For most of the first part of *Nostromo*, no two chapters chronologically follow one upon the other. Each new chapter is a shift in time, and the reader must gather information about events that can only later be reflected upon, organized, and then sequenced.

In contrast to impressionist narratives, the ordered narration of pre-impressionist novels presents the world of a universal observer. Whether omniscient or nonomniscient, these narrators organize phenomena so that the reader experiences an ordered existence. Omniscient narrators organize phenomena and provide the reader with a breadth of information that is inaccessible in reality. Similarly, the nonomniscient narrators also mediate the epistemological process. Even though they are not omniscient, first-person or limited third-person narrators still employ organizing techniques – that is, rather than presenting phenomena as the subject actually experiences them, they organize that information into a coherent chronicle through the narrator's reflections. Even such first-person narratives as *Jane Eyre* (which includes scenes dealing with the narrator as a child and actually captures the flavor of that earlier time) are still mediated by the later narrator's reflection and by the ordered nature of the narration itself. For impressionism, traditional narrators do not present phenomena the way human beings experience them. The temporal distance such narrators evoke necessarily alters the initial experience, and they lose the immediate workings of consciousness. In contrast, the impressionist novel tries to represent the immediate epistemological experience, so the reader almost becomes the one encountering phenomena, just as the characters do, but not in the after-the-fact reflection of traditional narrators; rather the impressionist novel tries to place the reader into the scene at the actual moment of experience. In so doing, impressionists "invite and control the reader's identifications and so subject him to an intense rather than passive experience."[61] As Ford explains, "We in turn, if we wished to produce on you an effect of life, must not narrate but render impressions."[62] Similarly, Stephen Crane argues, "You must render: never report."[63] In "Heart of Darkness," Conrad creates just such a rendered scene when Marlow overhears a conversation between the Central Station manager and his uncle in which they "made several bizarre remarks: 'Make rain and fine weather – one man – the Council – by the nose' – bits of absurd sentences that got the better of my drowsiness" (*Y* 89). The conversation does not make sense because of Marlow's drowsiness, as only disconnected phrases impinge upon his consciousness. Shortly afterwards, Marlow loses other parts of the conversation: "They moved off and whispered" (*Y* 91). Only afterwards can Marlow partly piece together the meaning of the conversation. In fact, not until he reaches the Inner Station several months later does he fully understand certain parts of the conversation. Consequently, just as Marlow must piece together the meaning of the conversation from the snatches he hears, so also must the reader.

Impressionist *in medias res* narrative techniques are a variation on achronological narration, and again their purpose is to demonstrate that phenomena filter through a single consciousness. Such narratives place the reader in the position of the narrator, and hence the reader encounters phenomena as present occurrences – not the narrator's past experiences of events. For example, in Conrad's "The Brute," as the story opens, the narrator enters a tavern while a conversation is in progress and hears one man say,

That fellow Wilmot fairly dashed her brains out, and a good job, too! . . . I was glad when I heard she got the knock from somebody at last. Sorry enough for poor Wilmot, though. That man and I used to be chums at one time. Of course that was the end of him. A clear case if there ever was one. No way out of it. (*SS* 105–6)

Not until several pages later do both the narrator and reader learn that Wilmot dashed the brains out of a ship – not a woman. In this instance, Conrad represents the way a listener must piece together a story from an unorganized narration. This technique also differs from more traditional *in medias res* techniques in which the fictional characters have knowledge of prior events while the reader does not; instead, in impressionist *in medias res* both the characters and the reader are ignorant of prior events. In "The Brute," the narrator's experience of the events is altered by the fact that the information is gathered without the benefit of encountering the events from their beginning. And so, like the narrator, the reader enters the conversation *in medias res* and must experience phenomena piecemeal, without the aid of a narrator's after-the-fact organizing of the experience. This technique's advantage is its immediacy, as the reader discovers information at the same moment the narrator does.

Central consciousness is another technique literary impressionists sometimes employ and is most closely associated with the later fiction of Henry James. In his works, James employs what may initially appear to be an omniscient narrator; however, it soon becomes apparent that the narration is not omniscient but rather a rendering of the workings of a single or central consciousness. This main character then becomes the medium through which the reader also encounters the events of the narrative. Often, a disparity results between the central character's perception of a situation and that of other characters. For example, in "The Tree of Knowledge," Peter Brench sees actions and events in a particular way. He believes he possesses knowledge that no one else does: that his friend Morgan Mallow is a terrible artist. Brench also feels he makes a great sacrifice by protecting Mallow's wife and son from this knowledge, believing that such knowledge would devastate them. He even thinks Mallow's wife would leave him if she realized how bad an artist he is.[64] Only at the end of the story does Brench discover that Mrs. Mallow has always known that her husband is a terrible artist. With this discovery, it becomes clear that all of the phenomena in the story first filter through Brench's consciousness before the reader encounters them.

Closely related to central consciousness is limited point of view. In fact, the two techniques sometimes overlap. Their difference typically lies, though, in the fact that central consciousness appears only in third-person narratives and usually (if not always) employs a single consciousness to filter phenomena. In contrast, limited point of view can appear as either first- or third-person narration, and when it appears as a third-person narrative it usually does not single out a particular individual's consciousness to filter phenomena, but rather moves from one consciousness to another, as for instance occurs in *Nostromo* or *The Secret Agent*. Limited point of view is similar to traditional first-person and limited third-person narratives, except that while traditional narrators emphasize more what the narrator knows, limited point of view narrators emphasize what the narrator does not know. Ford's narrator Dowell in *The Good Soldier* is a good example: "But, looking over what I have written, I see that I have unintentionally misled you when I said that Florence was never out of my sight. Yet that was the impression that I really had until just now. When I come to think of it she was out of my sight most of the time."[65] Dowell's limited understanding of the novel's events, as well as his biased interpretation of them, reveal that he is the medium through which the information in the novel passes and is altered as a result.

Finally, the multiple narrators technique is similar to first-person limited point of view narration. Multiple narrators was a significant departure from traditional narration in which a single narrator guided the reader through the course of events. In a sense, employing multiple narrators is simply limited point of view multiplied. Instead of a single narrator who relates his or her own individual experience of phenomena, multiple narrators each experience phenomena differently and thus emphatically show that subject and object alter each other and are affected by the context in which they occur. Conrad employed this technique to good effect in such works as "Heart of Darkness," *Chance*, and *Lord Jim*. In *Lord Jim*, for instance, many narrators appear in the novel, and the physical context together with the narrator's subjectivity circumscribe their perceptual experience. Marlow tells us this when he says that Jim "existed for me, and after all it is only through me that he exists for you. I've led him out by the hand; I have paraded him before you" (*LJ* 224). Even more explicitly, Marlow remarks to his privileged listener, "It is impossible to see him [Jim] clearly – especially as it is through the eyes of others that we take our last look at him" (*LJ* 339). Conrad demonstrates that each narrator perceives Jim differently and then interprets that information differently. As a result, none has a complete picture of Jim. For example, Stein says Jim is a romantic (*LJ* 216). Cornelius says he is a fool (*LJ* 397). Jewel says Jim is false (*LJ* 350). These narrators (as well as others) assume they accurately perceive Jim, and in a sense they do in that Jim conforms to their perception. In other words, Jim acts the romantic Stein perceives him to be. He acts the fool Cornelius perceives him to be. He acts falsely as Jewel perceives him to be. However, Jim is not necessarily each of these in essence, but rather the other characters' points of view present different perceptions of Jim. Jewel already perceives Jim to be false when she first meets him because all western men are false. Similarly, Jim acts like a fool, not necessarily because he is one but because Cornelius thinks Jim's code of honor is foolish. As a result of the blurred distinctions between perceiver and perceived, the perceiver's own subjective characteristics and physical point of view, as much as Jim's essential characteristics themselves, present Jim in the light they do. Each is a different Jim, as his outlines blur with those of the perceiver. Both multiple and limited point of view narrators dramatize the limitations of a single consciousness to comprehend phenomena other than individually, and thus knowledge itself is revealed to be limited as well.

All of these narrative techniques depend upon the limitations of the characters' knowledge and understanding for their effect. However, even when impressionists do employ omniscient narrators, either these narrators contrast with other human narrators and thus emphasize the limited nature of human consciousness, or the narrative takes on characteristics of a nonomniscient narrative and presents phenomena in an achronological, piecemeal manner. Such narrators also often withhold information from the reader, so their effect is much like that of any other limited narrator. Watt argues of *Lord Jim* that "Conrad's omniscient narrator here [during the *Patna* incident] pretends to be strictly limited to the point of view of an actual observer at the time of the occurrence."[66] Conrad achieves this effect throughout the opening chapters of *Lord Jim*. Even though an omniscient narrator relates this part of the novel, the reader still remains in the dark about a number of important issues – not the least of which is whether the *Patna* sank (which the reader does not learn until much later) and what caused the accident in the first place (which the reader never does learn for certain). The omniscient narrator also presents information piece by piece in a nonchronological time line, emphasizing human narrative limitations by presenting information that the other narrators cannot know. In fact, this omniscient narrator is as important to the novel in its contrast with the limited point of view of the other narrators as it is in revealing information that is unavailable through the other narrators.

III

Conrad's impressionism, like that of other literary impressionists, employs a variety of these narrative techniques to represent objects of consciousness. However, critics generally concur that Conrad had no systematic philosophy of art. Watt argues, "His consciousness of that craft [of writing] certainly fell far short of any fully conceptualised fictional system."[67] Wollaeger agrees and explains, "Conrad was not a philosophical novelist in the way Camus or even Lawrence was. Rather than espouse an identifiable doctrine, Conrad, like Swift, distrusted system builders or 'projectors,' believing that the dreamer of a comprehensive system was likely to lose touch with reality by becoming imprisoned within his or her own new structure of thought."[68] Conrad echoes this sentiment in a letter to a reviewer of *The Nigger of the "Narcissus"*: "I wrote this short book regardless of any formulas of art, forgetting all the theories of expression. Formulas and theories are dead things, and I wrote straight from the heart – which is alive."[69] He also wrote to Edward Garnett, "My misfortune is that I can't swallow *any* formula."[70] In another letter to Garnett, Conrad reiterates this position: "I don't know what my philosophy is. I was not even aware I had it."[71] As a result, Watt suggests, "Conrad disclaimed, and rightly, that he possessed anything approaching a conscious intellectual system."[72] Nevertheless, although Conrad employed no systematic philosophy, his novels are philosophical. Robert Penn Warren argues, "I run the risk of making Conrad's work seem too schematic and of implying that he somehow sat down and worked out a philosophy which he then projected, with allegorical precision, into fiction. I mean nothing of the sort... I think that even if Conrad is as 'imperfect' philosopher as esthete, he is still, in the fullest sense of the term, a philosophical novelist."[73] I agree with Warren's assessment but would also add that Conrad's works are philosophical not because of a particular system nor solely because of the philosophical questions broached, but because (as I hope will become clear later) certain ideas concerning the way human beings experience phenomena permeate his works. In effect, Conrad begins with the process of epistemology and works outward from there.

Because of his aversion to philosophical systems, Conrad "consciously avoided following the doctrines of any particular literary school."[74] He wrote to Garnett of theories in general that "theory is a cold and lying tombstone of departed truth."[75] More specifically, he argued in his preface to *The Nigger of the "Narcissus"* that the artist

cannot be faithful to any one of the temporary formulas of his craft. The enduring part of them – the truth which each only imperfectly veils – should abide with him as the most precious of his possessions, but they all: Realism, Romanticism, Naturalism, even the unofficial sentimentalism... [A]ll these gods must, after a short period of fellowship, abandon him – even on the very threshold of the temple – to the stammerings of his conscience and to the outspoken consciousness of the difficulties of his work. (*NN* xiv–xv)

Conrad further clarifies his views on literary movements in a letter written to Barrett Clark many years later: "I am no slave to prejudices and formulas, and I shall never be. My attitude to subjects and expressions, the angles of vision, my methods of composition will, within limits, be always changing – not because I am unstable or unprincipled but because I am free."[76] Clearly, Conrad felt that artists cannot enslave themselves to a particular school of thought, but as discussed earlier this is precisely the impressionists' position. They sought to experience individually, contextualized phenomena, essentially divorced from the influence of traditional schools of thought that had homogenized human experience. Far from being a slave to impressionism, Conrad was one of its most creative innovators, consistently stretching its boundaries and augmenting the movement as he did so.

Admittedly, Conrad probably would have disliked being called an impressionist. Hay writes that the label "would have irritated him,"[77] and Watt argues, "Conrad certainly knew something about pictorial and literary impressionism, but the indications are that his reactions were predominantly unfavourable" and "[I]t is very unlikely that Conrad either thought of himself as an impressionist or was significantly influenced by the impressionist movement."[78] Although Conrad never specifically denied the label of impressionist, he did comment – and unfavorably at that – on impressionism. In a well-known letter to Garnett, Conrad wrote of Stephen Crane, "His eye is very individual and his expression satisfies me artistically. He is certainly *the* impressionist and his temperament is curiously unique. His thought is concise, connected, never very deep – yet often startling. He is *the only* impressionist and *only* an impressionist."[79] Most often quoted is the last sentence of this passage, which certainly seems derogatory, but in context the comment is much less harsh. Still, it would be a leap in logic to suggest that Conrad had any great affection for the term *impressionism*[80] (perhaps more because he was averse to "isms" of any sort, though, than because he was specifically averse to impressionism as such[81]). Nevertheless, although Conrad may have disliked the label *impressionist*, much evidence exists in his works to demonstrate that they are impressionistic, and most commentators (including his friend and collaborator Ford Madox Ford) feel the term appropriately describes Conrad's writings. In "On Impressionism," Ford includes Conrad among the impressionist writers,[82] and elsewhere, Ford even more vocally affirms Conrad's impressionism: "We accepted without much protest the stigma 'Impressionists' that was thrown at us."[83] Other early commentators such as Ramon Fernandez, Joseph Warren Beach, Edward Crankshaw, William C. Frierson, and Bruce McCullough concur with Ford.[84] Similarly, most modern scholars also see Conrad as an impressionist.[85] However, as noted earlier, since the inception of the term, defining impressionism has been a slippery endeavor, and this slippery quality applies equally to definitions of Conrad's impressionism as well.

Some critics see his impressionism involved exclusively (or nearly exclusively) with visual perception of physical objects. For instance, Todd Bender argues, "On many levels, Conrad's privileging of sight is characteristic of the impressionist position."[86] And Donald Benson writes, "In its visual aspect atmosphere was of course a veritable fact of Conrad's Malay experience in particular, as the morning mists of the Seine were of Monet's."[87] It is certainly true that visual perception is an important aspect of Conrad's impressionism, but as discussed earlier (and as should become apparent later), visual perception is only one manifestation of literary impressionist technique. Conrad investigates all objects of consciousness, not just visually perceived objects.

Some commentators also associate Conrad's narrative technique too closely with impressionist painting. For example, Benson suggests that Conrad "treats the darkness as the [impressionist] painters treated light."[88] Watt argues that the haze in "Heart of Darkness" "reminds us that one of the most characteristic objections to Impressionist painting was that the artist's obstensive 'subject' was obscured by his representation of the atmospheric conditions through which it was observed."[89] And Bender remarks of "Heart of Darkness," "The verbal collage operates like the pointillist colors in Seurat, when the canvas juxtaposes dots of yellow with dots of blue pigment which merge only on the retina of each viewer's eye in an optical mixture of intense green."[90] Similarly, Adam Gillon argues that "if analogy is broadened to include the musical element of a recurring phrase, the frequent leitmotifs like 'Pass the bottle,' 'Do or Die' 'his opportunity sat veiled by his side like an Eastern bride' ... are like the painter's device of drawing the spectator's eye to a repeated use of a certain color or object in his canvas."[91] But as demonstrated earlier, the techniques of writing and painting are different and attempts to link them too closely often obscure the literature itself and oversimplify it as well, and Conrad's works seem particularly susceptible to this danger.

Other commentators see Conrad's impressionism as dealing only with surface representation. Herbert Howarth argues that Conrad's "pictorialism is subservient to a larger method, which, I would argue, is far removed from Impressionism. He accumulates his 'impressions' only as bricks for an intellectual edifice; they are pieces of evidence with which his judgment must construct a verdict. He has no love for sensation."[92] Hay suggests that Conrad (along with Proust and James)

refuted the impressionists' premise that ideas and secondary reflections derived from lively first impressions are less "real" than sense impressions, that ideas are simply faint recollections of "real" sensory data ... James, Conrad, and Proust led their readers to conceptual questions about a truth or reality *more* real, powerful, and essential than any accessible to simple sensations.[93]

Similarly, Wiesław Krajka argues, "So the narration of *Lord Jim* and the characterization of its main protagonist appear only superficially to be a realization of impressionistic patterns of obscurity, elusiveness and discontinuity. Penetration of the deep semantic strata of the novel has shown its complex narrative machinery, carefully organized and controlled by Marlow, to serve the presentation of Jim in a rather favourable light."[94] These critics reject Conrad as an impressionist writer because they do not see his writings as dealing merely with surface but also with depth. In a sense, I would agree with these critics. One of the most significant features of Conrad's works is their often unrelenting emphasis on "conceptual questions about a truth"; however, these critics see surface and depth as mutually exclusive in impressionist theory, and on this point I would disagree. As should become apparent shortly, in Conrad's works surface and depth are inextricable. Ultimately, the discoveries Conrad makes concerning objects of consciousness lead directly to questions concerning the certainty of western civilization's foundational assumptions and even concerning the nature of the universe and of human existence itself.

Finally, some critics see Conrad's impressionism as merely a phase that he eventually outgrew. For instance, Albert Guerard refers to *Nostromo*'s realism, and he argues that "*Under Western Eyes* is Conrad's best realistic novel."[95] In contrast, I would argue that both novels are impressionistic and not realistic. Guerard also asserts that "*The Secret Agent* is in several ways an astonishing leap into an entirely different kind of art" and that the novel shows "a major change from the impressionist to the realist method."[96] But the narrative techniques in *The Secret Agent* differ only superficially from those employed in earlier works. *The Secret Agent* is unusual among Conrad's works of that time in its directness of language and narrative movement; it lacks an intrusive narrative consciousness through which the reader experiences the world, as is found in "Heart of Darkness" or *Under Western Eyes*. *The Secret Agent* also employs less bewildering shifts of time and place than those employed in *Lord Jim* and *Nostromo*. Furthermore, the direct, concise language of the novel is more in line with realist rather than impressionist fiction and seems to reinforce the assertion of the novel's subtitle that it is "a simple tale." Nevertheless, *The Secret Agent* cannot be classified as realist fiction; Conrad's philosophical preoccupations and most of the narrative techniques that are so representative of his impressionism remain intact in *The Secret Agent*. In fact, many of the overt impressionist techniques of other works remain in covert form. *The Secret Agent* may lack bewildering time shifts, but it is far from a chronological narrative, and, as is true of *Nostromo* and *Lord Jim*, the reader often cannot decipher the meaning of certain facts until others are later revealed. For example, for some time the reader assumes that Verloc – not Stevie – has been blown up. In the same way, although no Marlow or teacher of foreign languages appears in the novel, Conrad still employs the device of piecemeal gathering of information in his use of Winnie Verloc. Her task of gathering information, in large part, resembles Marlow's gathering of pieces of information in order to form a semblance of a whole, and in *The Secret Agent* the reader must also perform this same task. But perhaps the most telling evidence of *The Secret Agent*'s impressionism exists in Conrad's use of time. Throughout the novel, Conrad consistently depicts time as an object of consciousness filtering through individual human minds and representing the individuality of human experience of phenomena.

Even more surprising, although Guerard suggests that "the slighter *Chance* . . . anticipates the full Faulknerian extension of the impressionistic method,"[97] he also sees a strongly realistic aspect of the novel:

The Conrad who conceived the various evocative narrating voices of the early novels fell, at the end, into one of the worst of the realistic traps: to employ narrators or observers who by definition or by profession are unequipped to tell their stories effectively. Some of the imprecise and flabby rhetoric must simply be blamed on . . . a realist's respect for the way a dullard would speak: roughly, bluntly, without grace of style.[98]

If pushed, in the end I believe that Guerard would likely not classify *Chance* as a realist novel, and rightly so since Conrad's technique in *Chance* is probably the most extreme example of impressionist narrative methodology. Still, Guerard seems to see a fairly consistent movement from *The Secret Agent* onward (perhaps even from *Nostromo* onward) toward a realist narrative technique. Even as late as *The Shadow Line* and *The Rescue*, however, impressionist techniques continue to permeate Conrad's works.

In contrast to the foregoing views on Conrad's impressionism, I will argue throughout this book that Conrad's impressionism encompasses all objects of consciousness; that it represents both surface and depth; that it is not an attempt to reproduce the techniques of painting in literature; and that it informed his philosophical concerns and narrative techniques throughout his literary career.

The impressionist narrative techniques of Conrad and other writers share common goals and even occasionally overlap. In addition, impressionist writers often incorporate a variety of techniques into their works.

However, whatever the technique employed the result is the same: literary impressionists sought to represent phenomena as they filter through a single human consciousness at a certain point in space and time such that the resulting representation is one of individual rather than universal experience. In the end, impressionism's individual, fully contextualized epistemology is precisely what previous movements in art ignored, and its return to that idea was a radical departure from most earlier art and literature. At the same time, literary impressionism provides a bridge between realist and stream-of-consciousness literature in the same way it bridges subject and object. Furthermore, impressionism leads to an epistemological and representational process that, because of its highly individual nature, is relative rather than absolute. A process that depends upon individual experience and subjectivity necessarily leads to a theory of knowledge that questions universals. Walter Pater suggested, "Modern thought is distinguished from ancient by its cultivation of the 'relative' spirit in place of the 'absolute'... To the modern spirit nothing is or can be rightly known except relatively under conditions."[99] And this "relative spirit" characterizes the philosophical presuppositions of impressionism. In this way, impressionism anticipated and embodied philosophical issues that would dominate the early twentieth-century intellectual landscape. In this newly relative world, no universal certainty exists, only the certainty of individuals, and for the impressionist the question was how to experience the world without universals as guides.

CHAPTER 2

Objects and events in the "primitive eye": the epistemology of objectivity

"I know that the sunlight can be made to lie."
"Heart of Darkness"

I

In a well-known passage from his preface to *The Nigger of the "Narcissus,"* Conrad writes, "My task which I am trying to achieve is, by the power of the written word to make you hear, to make you feel – it is, before all, to make you *see*. That – and no more, and it is everything" (*NN* xiv; emphasis is Conrad's). Watt suggests that the connotations of the word *see* "obviously include the perception not only of visual impressions, but of ideas."[1] Most readers agree and interpret the word *see* figuratively in this instance. Nevertheless, Conrad also wants to make his readers see literally. In a letter to Blackwood, he is even more emphatic about his intent to represent literal seeing: "I aim at stimulating vision in the reader. If after reading *Part 1st* you don't *see* my man [Lingard] then I've absolutely failed."[2] In fact, literal and figurative "seeing" are inextricably linked in Conrad's works, and his "seeing" is far reaching; it concerns perception of events and physical objects and their relationship to knowledge, as well as its relationship to questions about the nature of human existence and the nature of western civilization.

In order to make the reader "see," Conrad employs impressionist techniques to represent his characters' perception of objects and events and to demonstrate that each perceptual experience is unique. Like other impressionists, he presents perception as contextualized, with the perceptual act located at a fixed point in space and time. To achieve this effect, Conrad employs two primary techniques: limited point of view and blurred boundaries – each with variations. Of course, these techniques overlap and are, as would be expected, two aspects of the same process in that limited point of view occurs because of the context in

35

which subject and object appear, and blurred boundaries occur because of the limited point of view from which the subject encounters the object. Regardless of the particular technique, though, Conrad's impressionist methodology represents objects and events projecting themselves onto human consciousness.

Limited point of view in Conrad can refer to the physical location in space from which perception occurs, but it can also include the influence of the observer's personal and public past on perception. In each case, Conrad's limited point of view presents an individual view of objects by representing both the physical limitations of human perception as well as the way perception occurs within an individual consciousness. Perhaps the clearest instance of physical limitations on perception occurs near the end of *Chance*. When Mr. Powell tries to look at Captain Anthony through the skylight, he says of his point of view:

[M]y angle of view was changed. The field too was smaller. The end of the table, the tray and the swivel-chair I had right under my eyes... The piano I could not see how; but on the other hand I had a very oblique downward view of the curtains drawn across the cabin and cutting off the forward part of it just about the level of the skylight-end and only an inch or so from the end of the table. (*C* 414–15)

Because of his limited perspective, Powell wonders whether he sees the curtain move or just "a trick of imagination" (*C* 416). Marlow then remarks of Powell, "[H]e was startled to observe tips of fingers fumbling with the dark stuff. Then they grasped the edge of the further curtain and hung on there, just fingers and knuckles and nothing else" (*C* 417). Instead of representing the scene in panorama (as a realist writer would), Conrad fixes Powell's perception to a specific location in space, and so Powell sees only the "tips of fingers." This limited angle of presentation also forces the reader to view the scene's phenomena from Powell's individual perspective. The reader can see no more than Powell, and Conrad implies that such is true of all perception. The perceiver can only see what is visible from a particular vantage point in space and time.[3]

"Prince Roman" presents a further variation on limited point of view in which the relationship between perception and knowledge becomes prominent. Conrad writes that Prince Roman "reined in on a knoll and peered. There were slender gleams of steel here and there in that cloud, and it contained moving forms which revealed themselves at last as a long line of peasant carts full of soldiers, moving slowly in double file under the escort of mounted Cossacks" (*TH* 38). In this passage, Prince Roman's inability to clearly discern the objects in the scene results from the physical distance between perceiver and perceived. When he stops on the knoll, he sees "slender gleams of steel" moving in a cloud. Only after a time does he see these objects as soldiers in carts – either because the soldiers move closer to him or through concentrating and allowing his eyes to adjust to the distance. Because of his limited point of view, initially Prince Roman does not see soldiers in carts.

The location of both perceiver and perceived is important in this narrative technique. Limited point of view encompasses subject and object so that while the subject's physical location in space is important, so also is the object's. Mr. Powell can only see a small portion of Captain Anthony's cabin because his angle of view is limited by his physical location in space, but it is also limited because of the angle at which the object of his gaze lies. That is to say, if Powell's physical location changes, then his point of view would also change, and if the perceived objects' physical location changed, then so would Powell's point of view. Similarly, Prince Roman has difficulty discerning the troops both because of his own physical location but also because of the troops' location. In each case, the relationship between subject and object causes the particular perceptual experience – not so much the specific physical location of one or the other.

The incident in "Prince Roman" is also an example of what I will call *primitive perception*.[4] In others words, human beings perceive phenomena either from an individual or a universal perspective – either the immediate sense impression or one that has been more fully mediated by past experience. Primitive perception represents an initial sense impression before the observer organizes it into a meaning that accords with past experience, while civilized perception represents the impression after the observer organizes the initial experience and ascribes meaning to it. This mediating influence of the subject's past experience may appear as public past, private past, or both. In this way, a subject's personal past as well as his or her cultural past alter the initial perceptual experience and convert it into something different from what it first was. In Prince Roman's case, initially he sees slender gleams of steel moving in a cloud; only afterwards does he see soldiers in carts.

Conrad emphasizes primitive perception in his works in order to demonstrate that all phenomena filter through human consciousness, and he records many of these incidents through what Watt terms "delayed decoding."[5] For example, in "Heart of Darkness," during the attack on the steamboat, Marlow remarks, "Sticks, little sticks, were flying about"; shortly afterward, he sees these same objects as, "Arrows, by Jove!" (*Y* 109–10). Later during the same attack, he has a similar experience:

Something big appeared in the air before the shutter, the rifle went overboard, and the man stepped back swiftly, looked at me over his shoulder in an extraordinary, profound, familiar manner, and fell upon my feet. The side of his head hit the wheel twice, and the end of what appeared a long cane clattered round and knocked over a little camp-stool. It looked as though after wrenching that thing from somebody ashore he had lost his balance in the effort ... [M]y feet felt so very warm and wet that I had to look down. The man had rolled on his back and stared straight up at me; both his hands clutched that cane. (*Y* 111–12)

Like the sticks/arrows incident, only after Marlow initially perceives a cane does he see that object differently: "It was the shaft of a spear that, either thrown or lunged through the opening, had caught him in the side just below the ribs; the blade had gone in out of sight, after making a frightful gash; my shoes were full; a pool of blood lay very still, gleaming dark-red under the wheel" (*Y* 112). Watt sees this phenomenon as a kind of perceptual mistake, which the perceiver later corrects; such incidents represent a movement "directly into the observer's consciousness at the very moment of the perception, before it has been translated into its cause";[6] they combine "the forward temporal progression of the mind, as it receives messages from the outside world, with the much slower reflexive process of making out their meaning."[7] However, Bruce Johnson disagrees and argues that such an incident is "not really undesirable temporary misunderstanding so much as an unmediated observation."[8] The term *unmediated* overstates the point somewhat since the idea of a cane or sticks comes from somewhere in Marlow's mind and hence mediates to a minor degree his perception of these objects; otherwise, Marlow could not describe them at all. Johnson recognizes this distinction and later qualifies his definition, suggesting that such incidents are "uninterpreted or minimally interpreted."[9] However, even though both cane and spear are mediated perceptions, a significant gap exists between Marlow's initial perception of a cane and his later perception of a cane occurs after at best minimal mediation by past experience, whereas his denotation of the object as a spear occurs after a much more complete mediation. More important, Johnson correctly argues that Marlow does not see a spear that he initially mistakes for a cane, but instead actually sees a cane and then later sees a spear. Each perceptual event is distinct, and each results in a different object of perception. Marlow's initial perception of a cane is unexpected and incongruous in its contextual surroundings, and so he organizes this primitive perception into something that better accords with previous experience and "is actually the result of complex cultural prejudices."[10] For Conrad, human beings receive initial sense impressions of the flow of phenomena that are without inherent meaning. They then organize, categorize, and transform those impressions into something consistent with past experience. However, Conrad's primitive perception does more than simply identify a perceptual curiosity; it also highlights a significant aspect of the epistemological process. Conrad wants the reader to focus on the initial sense impression in order to show that meaning is not inherent but must be constructed. Most people approach the external world by way of common-sense realism and assume others see the same objects they see. They perceive, for example, "sticks" and immediately transform them into "arrows," but during the process they forget the first impression and assume they have seen only arrows all along. In this way, they constantly reorganize the chronicle – not even realizing that their initial perception was not of an ordered phenomenon but rather of one unordered. In so doing, they represent perception as a universal phenomenon rather than an individual phenomenon.

In addition to those instances found in "Heart of Darkness," primitive perception also occurs in many of Conrad's other works, each time with variations, and this process may involve perception of objects or events – or more commonly the interaction between the two. In several of Conrad's early stories (i.e., "Youth," "The Idiots," and "An Outpost of Progress"), primitive perception occupies an even more prominent place than it does in "Heart of Darkness" because it occurs at the climax of these stories. At the very moment the story reaches its dramatic peak – in a kind of epiphany – a character experiences primitive perception. At that point, the observer is isolated from others and from personal and cultural experience and perceives reality as it actually projects itself onto consciousness. This highest point of revelation is individual and unorganized. The character experiences phenomena stripped of most of the mediating effects of past experience that organize objects of consciousness into a form that conforms to cultural expectations; the characters then perceive reality as it actually appears to them. By introducing the incident at the story's climax, Conrad emphasizes the individuality of human experience as opposed to cultural experience. What appears most certain to human beings is their ordered perception (arrows), and yet that certainty is precisely what comes into question at these moments of unordered perception (sticks).

In "Youth," for instance, Marlow experiences primitive perception at the story's climax, and in this case Conrad further emphasizes the experience by Marlow's past experience mediating the same incident twice. Marlow remarks that he

became aware of a queer sensation, of an absurd delusion, – I seemed somehow to be in the air. I heard all round me like a pent-up breath released – as if a thousand giants simultaneously had said Phoo! – and felt a dull concussion which made my ribs ache suddenly. No doubt about it – I was in the air, and my body was describing a short parabola. (Y 22–23)

Only afterward does Marlow see what happened differently and say, "By Jove! we are being blown up" (Y 23). At first, he believes he experiences "an absurd delusion" because his past experience tells him that being "in the air" is impossible, but in reality he *is* "in the air." Here, Marlow's past experience actually interferes with his ability to organize the event, but once he can no longer deny he is "in the air," his past experience again transforms the event into something that accords with his previous knowledge: being blown up. The initial, primitive sense impression of being "in the air" is what Marlow actually perceived. "Being blown up" is the later, civilized perception.[11] In a similar way, in "An Outpost of Progress," Kayerts also experiences primitive perception at the story's crisis point, but the mediation occurs differently from these other instances. In this case, both past experience and new information provide the mediating material:

He darted to the left, grasping his revolver, and at the very same instant, as it seemed to him, they [Kayerts and Carlier] came into violent collision. Both shouted with surprise. A loud explosion took place between them; a roar of red fire, thick smoke; and Kayerts, deafened and blinded, rushed back thinking: "I am hit – it's all over." (*TU* 112–13)

Kayerts perceives that he has been shot but then reinterprets the situation once he discovers he is not wounded: "Kayerts shut his eyes. Everything was going round. He found life more terrible and difficult than death. He had shot an unarmed man" (*TU* 114). When Kayerts finally sees the dead man, he uses both past experience and new information (the corpse) to transform his primitive perception into civilized perception. He transforms his initial, individual perception into a universal perception and sees the incident differently than he had originally.

Primitive perception plays an important role in Conrad's later works as well. For example, several incidents of primitive perception appear in *The Shadow Line*. The most striking of these occurs at a crucial point in the novel. The narrator remarks,

I became bothered by curious, irregular sounds of faint tapping on the deck. They could be heard single, in pairs, in groups. While I wondered at this mysterious devilry, I received a slight blow under the left eye and felt an enormous tear run down my cheek. Raindrops. Enormous... Suddenly – how am I to convey it? Well, suddenly the darkness turned into water. This is the only suitable figure. A heavy shower, a downpour, comes along, making noise. You hear its approach on the sea, in the air too, I verily believe. But this was different. With no preliminary whisper or rustle, without a splash, and even without the ghost of impact, I became instantaneously soaked to the skin. (*SL* 113–14)

The storm's suddenness forces the narrator to perceive the rain, and the event as a whole, with minimal mediation. As he suggests, a storm "comes along, making noise," so noise is a precursor to storms and is part of the narrator's past experience that provides the mediating material for perceiving storms. Without that precursor, the narrator experiences the immediate sense impression of the storm. Furthermore, the storm is unexpected because a deadly calm has engulfed the ship for so long. The calm's appearance made no sense, nor does its disappearance at this moment. This event is particularly unusual in its employing both primitive and civilized perception to reflect upon an initial perceptual experience. Even after the fact, the narrator cannot account for the storm's sudden onset. Past experience here only provides part of the event's meaning. It is a storm – but unlike any he has experienced before, and the incident demonstrates the difference between the flow of phenomena and its cultural interpretation. The event also emphasizes the limitations of past experience to provide certainty concerning phenomena, and it highlights human inability to fully comprehend the world. In a sense, this incident also mirrors the problem of the novel as a whole: the fragility of human existence set against its inability to control or predict nature.

These incidents of primitive perception occur either at the narrative's climax or at some other crucial juncture.[12] The characters transform their initial perception – organizing, universalizing, and "correcting" the chronicle to conform with past experience, drawn primarily from shared cultural experience. In this way, primitive perception moves from a relative, individual experience to one that is shared and socially sanctioned, and thus the perceiver seems to see the same thing everyone else sees. In so doing, the observer loses that initial perception of the flow of phenomena in the process of organizing the experience. In this movement from minimal mediation to full mediation, Conrad delineates and integrates impressionist individual perception and the way it becomes contextualized. Organizing primitive perception into civilized perception can be useful, because it helps individuals to function in a social group where consensus exists concerning the identity of a particular object or event. However, the problem with mediating these initial sensory impressions is that civilized perception obscures primitive perception and implies that a particular meaning for the flow is inherent, whereas primitive perception demonstrates that such a meaning is not inherent but constructed. For Conrad, primitive perception focuses our attention on how human beings experience the external world. Far from being universal and accessible to all, the world is perceived from an individual point of view. Culture mediates perception by taking a fluid, continuous human experience and dividing it into discrete segments and assigning meaning to them. Consequently, Conrad's epistemology suggests that our knowledge of the objective world is one that encounters the sensory stream and then organizes it to create its meaning. In representing these incidents of primitive perception, Conrad implies that the seamless flux of human experience may be a phenomenon that is very different from the one culture constructs for it.

In addition to the roles of personal and cultural past in primitive perception, personal past also has another crucial role in contextualizing perception. Conrad himself experiences the effects of personal past on perception. In *A Personal Record*, he writes,

The Red Ensign!... [I]t was, as far as the eye could reach, the only spot of ardent colour – flamelike, intense, and presently as minute as the tiny red spark the concentrated reflection of a great fire kindles in the clear heart of a globe of crystal. The Red Ensign – the symbolic, protecting warm bit of bunting flung wide upon the seas, and destined for so many years to be the only roof over my head. (*PR* 137–38)

The red ensign is an object of comfort that reminds Conrad of his days at sea. Others seeing the same red ensign would have a different response. In particular, those unacquainted with life at sea would see the object differently. And just as the personal past of *The Shadow Line*'s narrator causes him to perceive his ship differently from the dock workers (*SL* 49–50), in "Falk" different characters perceive a white cotton umbrella differently. Hermann sees the umbrella as a useful tool against the elements (*T* 180); Falk sees it as simply an item to be retrieved for Hermann (*T* 196); but the narrator sees it as something much more significant. Because Hermann had forgotten the umbrella at Schomberg's, Falk goes to retrieve it. Had Hermann not forgotten the umbrella, the narrator would not have unexpectedly met Falk there and thus would not have had the opportunity to clear up their misunderstanding. With the problem solved, the narrator exults, "Oh! blessed white cotton umbrella!" (*T* 207). The umbrella, then, appears different to each character. Similarly, Edward Said notes that Koh-ring, "which had been a source of hope for Leggatt and for his secret sharer, is just the opposite for" the narrator of *The Shadow Line*.[13] For him, the island is the center of a "fatal circle" from which the ship seems unable to escape (*SL* 84). Perhaps the clearest example of this phenomenon, though, occurs in *Nostromo*, in which all seem to perceive the silver differently. Charles Gould's father saw it as a curse and a manifestation of the government's corruption (*N* 57). Mrs. Gould also sees the silver as a curse, one that has corrupted her husband and their marriage (*N* 521–22). Dr. Monygham views it as simply another manifestation of political oppression (*N* 511). Charles Gould, on the other hand, sees the silver as a symbol of political success and economic wealth (*N* 214). Finally, Nostromo vacillates in his view of the silver. He sees it as a means to wealth (*N* 503), but he also sees it as destroying his carefully constructed self-image and ultimately making him its slave (*N* 424, 526–27, 561). In each instance, despite the fact that they all see the same silver ingots, the different personal pasts of the characters influence their perceptions of the silver such that each sees the silver differently.

A similar situation occurs in the characters' perception of the revolution. Charles Gould sees the event as a fight for economic freedom (*N* 245). Giorgio Viola sees it as an "outbreak of scoundrels and leperos, who did not know the meaning of the word 'liberty'" (*N* 21) and thinks, "These were not a people striving for justice, but thieves" (*N* 20). Dr. Monygham sees it as another in a long line of repressive governments, different only in appearance from the others (*N* 511). Father Corbelàn sees it as an opportunity to restore church property and power (*N* 188–99). Decoud sees the revolution as simply a means to further his relationship with Antonia (*N* 215, 236), and other characters experience yet a different event. As with the silver, the context of the individual's personal past alters the revolution, and so it appears different to each perceiver. Even though they all experience the same event, it is markedly different for each. In essence, the entire novel is an investigation into the way phenomena filter through the consciousness of various characters and are altered as a result. Perhaps an even more emphatic instance of this phenomenon occurs in Conrad's unfinished "The Sisters": "[Stephen] made his own the fleeting beauties of sunrises and sunsets with the avidity of a thief, with the determination of a buccaneer. He thought nobody could see in them what he saw, and the snatching before the eyes of men of profound impressions had for him all the harsh joy of unlawful conquest."[14] In this case, Conrad specifically refers to Stephen actually making the events of sunrises and sunsets his own. Stephen himself recognizes that the events he sees are different from what others see. The sunrises and sunsets are altered as they filter through Stephen's consciousness such that they become incidents unique to his experience.

Conrad also demonstrates that one's personal past can change one's perception of an object or event from one time to another as a result of additional experience. For example, in *The Shadow Line*, Koh-ring seems to change for the narrator. He has passed the island before in his travels without attaching any particular significance to it. However, when it continues to appear day after day while his ship languishes in the dead calm, it becomes an odious object – a continual reminder of their precarious predicament (*SL* 84). Likewise, just as Marlow's view of the rivets in "Heart of Darkness" changes as Marlow changes (*Y* 83–84), so also does Razumov's view of his notes, lamp, and books change as Razumov changes. Razumov's perception of the accouterments of his essay alters as a result of additional experience. Initially, Razumov perceives his notes, the lamp, and the books on his desk as a means to success in his studies. He hopes these objects will lead to the silver medal and with it a position in society. But Haldin's visit changes those prospects. Later, when Razumov again looks at those objects, they appear different: "He looked at the lamp which had burnt itself out. It stood there, the extinguished beacon of his labours, a cold object of brass and porcelain, amongst the scattered pages of his notes and small piles of books – a mere litter of blackened paper – dead matter – without significance or interest" (*UWE* 68). Razumov believes he will be linked to Haldin's crime, despite his own innocence in the bombing, and so Haldin's visit has nullified Razumov's future. Consequently, the lamp, books, and notes are "without significance" because they can no longer bring Razumov success.

This same process can occur with events as well. As noted earlier, in

Sulaco, Decoud perceives the revolution in *Nostromo* not as an opportunity to advance his political agenda but rather as an opportunity to advance his romantic agenda (*N* 215, 236). However, Decoud's perception of this event changes while he waits for Nostromo on the Great Isabel. The additional information he acquires there concerning (from his perspective) the senselessness of "all exertion" (*N* 498) influences Decoud's perception of the revolution such that it changes from an opportunity for greater communion with Antonia into simply one more senseless event in an existence of ultimate isolation.

Whether limited physical point of view, primitive perception, the influence of public and private past experience on the perception of objects and events, or the physical circumstances in which they appear, the result is the same: the boundaries between subject and object blur as each is altered by the other and by the context in which they appear. Conrad's characters may try to isolate phenomena from the stream of experience, but Conrad continually emphasizes that such an attempt is an artificial gesture. Just as the outlines blur in the perceptual experience, so also do distinctions between objects blur.

In addition to the permutations of limited point of view, one of the primary characteristics of much impressionist work is that distinctions and boundaries between subject and object or between one object and another are fluid as an observer perceives an object in the context of a seamless flow of experience. In Conrad's works, this process of contextualization occurs in several ways. The most straightforward of these techniques simply places an object in a physical setting and demonstrates how that context affects the object. For instance, in *Lord Jim*, Marlow notes,

There is something haunting in the light of the moon; it has all the dispassionateness of a disembodied soul, and something of its inconceivable mystery. It is to our sunshine ... what the echo is to the sound: misleading and confusing whether the note be mocking or sad. It robs all forms of matter ... of their substance, and gives a sinister reality to shadows alone. (*LJ* 246)

The context of moonlight affects the perception of an object; the same object appears different in sunshine. In *The Rescue*, context similarly affects Hassim's view of his native land: "[A]t every dazzling flash, Hassim's native land seemed to leap nearer at the brig – and disappear instantly as though it had crouched low for the next spring out an impenetrable darkness" (*Re* 79). Without the intermittent flashes of lightning, Hassim would see the land's nearness grow more slowly or perhaps even imperceptibly. However, because of the intervening periods of darkness, when the lightning appears, he sees the land as radically different each time. In "The Inn of the Two Witches," Byrne also experiences this phenomenon when he first encounters the inn:

[S]uddenly he felt rather than saw the existence of a massive obstacle in his path. What was it? The spur of a hill? Or was it a house? Yes. It was a house right close, as though it had risen from the ground or had come gliding to meet him, dumb and pallid, from some dark recess of the night. It towered loftily. He had come up under its lee; another three steps and he could have touched the wall with his hand. (*WT* 146–47)

In this case, the context of the darkness affects Byrne's ability to discern the inn and causes the boundaries of the inn to blur with those of its surroundings, and so Byrne cannot easily distinguish the inn when he encounters it.[15] If Byrne had encountered the inn at a different time of day, under different atmospheric conditions, or even at a different location, the inn would have appeared different.

Context can also cause objects to blur such that different objects may appear much more similar than they would if viewed in isolation. For instance, in *The Secret Agent*, the narrator remarks,

The very pavement under Mr. Verloc's feet had an old gold tinge in that diffused light, in which neither wall, nor tree, nor beast, nor man cast a shadow. Mr. Verloc was going westward through a town without shadows in an atmosphere of powdered old gold. There were red, coppery gleams on the roofs of houses, on the corners of walls, on the panels of carriages, on the very coats of the horses, and on the broad back of Mr. Verloc's overcoat, where they produced a dull effect of rustiness. (*SA* 15)

Concerning this scene, J. Hillis Miller argues, "The diffused light makes everything look alien. Instead of seeing houses, walls, carriages, and people as distinct objects, the spectator also sees the identical gleams which the diffused light casts on each indiscriminately."[16] Context affects the objects here such that they almost appear to be a single entity.

In "Heart of Darkness," Conrad further emphasizes this contextualized perception by showing that objects and other phenomena cannot be extricated from their physical context without altering their appearance. An early instance occurs while Marlow travels down the African coast; he notes that day after day the shoreline looked exactly the same (*Y* 61). The primitive wilderness appears as a fluid, homogenous whole, and little distinguishes these daily scenes from one another. Later, as Marlow travels up the Congo, he emphasizes not only the homogeneity of the wilderness but also the interconnectedness of the flow of experience: "Sometimes I would pick out a tree a little way ahead to measure our progress towards Kurtz by, but I lost it invariably before we got abreast" (*Y* 100). In this case, Marlow tries to extricate an object from its context but cannot do so in this primitive setting. The context of the individual tree links the tree to all those surrounding it as they form the African jungle. In a sense, the individual tree loses part of its individuality as its identity blurs with that of those around it, and so Marlow cannot simply select it out from its context. Finally, Marlow notes the necessary ties between human beings and their surroundings. He says the Africans "wanted no excuse for being there [in Africa]. They were a great comfort to look at" (*Y* 61). In contrast, Marlow says of the Europeans, "We were cut off from the comprehension of our surroundings... We could not understand because we were too far and could not remember, because we were travelling in the night of first ages, of those ages that are gone, leaving hardly a sign – and no memories" (*Y* 96). These passages are particularly important – first because Marlow again emphasizes the interconnectedness of human beings and their context, along with how that context alters them, and second because Conrad links literal and figurative perception here. In looking at the relationship between human beings and their surroundings, Conrad shows how western civilization is out of place in the wilderness. In short, the Africans belong, whereas the Europeans do not, and as should become clear later, this fact results directly from Conrad's view of western civilization itself.

Not only does physical context affect the nature of objects or events, but its absence can also affect their nature. In *The Shadow Line*, the narrator remarks,

I moved forward too, outside the circle of light, into the darkness that stood in front of me like a wall. In one stride I penetrated it. Such must have been the darkness before creation. It had closed behind me. I knew I was invisible to the man at the helm. Neither could I see anything. He was alone, I was alone, every man was alone where he stood. And every form was gone, too, spar, sail, fittings, rails; everything was blotted out in the dreadful smoothness of that absolute night. (*SL* 112–13)

The men in *The Shadow Line* are "alone" in the "dreadful smoothness of that absolute night." Without context, it is as if the men and the objects around them have lost part of their own existence; such is Conrad's view of the interconnectedness of the flow of phenomena. Conrad's "The Tale" presents an important variation on the effect of absence of context:

The ship was stopped, all sounds ceased, and the very fog became motionless, growing denser and as if solid in its amazing dumb immobility. The men at their stations lost sight of each other. Footsteps sounded stealthy; rare voices, impersonal and remote, died out without resonance. A blind white stillness took possession of the world . . . At the moment of anchoring the fog was so thick that for all they could see they might have been a thousand miles out in the open sea. (*TH* 67–68)

Watt remarks that "[m]ist or haze is a very persistent image in Conrad,"[17] and it usually plays an important role when it appears. In "The Tale," the fog causes an absence of context, and in this absence the sailors are isolated from the rest of reality. By the same token, the fog also causes a blending of boundaries, and visible objects seem to flow into one another, so the fog both isolates the objects and merges them together at the same time, and both aspects emphasize the inevitable effect of context on phenomena.

Absence of context also appears prominently in "An Outpost of Progress." In this case, though, the context is not physical but cultural. The narrator remarks that Carlier trailed "a sulky glance over the river, the forests, the impenetrable bush that seemed to cut off the station from the rest of the world" (*TU* 88). The "impenetrable bush" cuts off Carlier and Kayerts from the context of the outside world, and therefore its ability to influence the objects and events in the African wilderness diminishes substantially. As the story progresses, the traders' isolation from their European context becomes more and more pronounced. When Makola trades servants for ivory, the European traders are scandalized (*TU* 104–5). Said suggests that "their wish to gather ivory according to the mercantile laws of European civilization – laws whose motivation they have never examined – reveals to them the startling fact that in primitive society trade can be based only upon the buying and selling of human beings."[18] As time passes, though, the traders become inured to the contradictions between what occurs in the African wilderness and what would be acceptable in Europe. This lack of a European context culminates in Kayerts' murder of Carlier over a dispute about sugar rations (*TU* 110–13).[19]

The best example, though, of Conrad's metaphoric (and metonymic) use of blurred boundaries and their ability either to integrate or isolate phenomena occurs in the white fog incident in "Heart of Darkness." Just before the final few hours' journey to the Inner Station, the steamboat becomes buried in a white fog, which Marlow says was "more blinding than the night" (*Y* 101). He then goes on to say: "What we could see was just the steamer we were on, her outlines blurred as though she had been on the point of dissolving, and a misty strip of water, perhaps two feet broad, around her – and that was all. The rest of the world was nowhere, as far as our eyes and ears were concerned" (*Y* 102). The image of fog is a particularly appropriate one in the story. Its misty and hazy quality is a physical representation of the blurring between subject and object and between object and object.[20] The fog permeates everything like a kind of connective tissue, binding things together.[21] Nothing can be separated from its surroundings because everything is interconnected. At the same time, though, the fog cuts off the immediate experience from everything outside it, and so the immediate experience cannot be influenced by anything outside it. Again, this scene of isolation demonstrates, by its absence of context beyond the immediate experience, the necessity of context in the epistemological process and the problem of segmenting phenomena from the stream of experience. In each case, the isolating effect of absence of context is disorienting, just as those on the steamboat are wholly disoriented by the fog's effect. During this incident, the pilgrims cannot even determine the direction of the sounds they hear, alternately thinking they come from one bank and then from the other (*Y* 106). Marlow further emphasizes this point when he remarks, "Were we to let go our hold of the bottom, we would be absolutely in the air – in space. We wouldn't be able to tell where we were going to – whether up or down stream, or across – till we fetched against one bank or the other, – and then we wouldn't know at first which it was" (*Y* 106). Without context, they cannot orient themselves and in fact run a serious risk if they attempt to move without a surrounding context. This incident becomes a microcosm of Marlow's entire experience. Everything is interconnected, and trying to remove phenomena from their context risks disorientation and delusion. The objects he observes are shifting and indistinct. Furthermore, this incident resists the usual means of organization and forces those on board the steamboat to experience the external world with minimal mediation by past experience. But this is only the most prominent example of blurred distinctions and boundaries in the story. Marlow's entire journey is one of uncertainty resulting from experiencing phenomena in unfamiliar contexts.

In Conrad's investigations of context, not only do the boundaries between objects blur, but so do boundaries between perceiving subject and perceived object. As discussed earlier, impressionist epistemology is such that subjects alter objects and objects alter subjects. Jim's

disappearance from Marlow's view in *Lord Jim*, in which the darkness of
the surrounding landscape and the whiteness of Jim's appearance emphasize each other (*LJ* 336), as well as the way the wilderness and
Marlow alter each other in "Heart of Darkness" are both examples of
the mutual influence of objects and subjects and the way their boundaries become fluid. So also are the various incidents of primitive perception, which show how the public past of cultural experience mediates
the perceptual process so that cultural past influences the nature of an
object's appearance. Similarly, an individual's private past also affects
the perceptual process. Such blurring of subject and object occurs, for
example, in *Nostromo*. The novel revolves around the image of the silver,
and the boundaries between the silver and many of *Nostromo*'s characters become unclear. This is particularly true of Charles Gould and
Nostromo. The narrator remarks, "[T]he mine preserved its identity,
with which he [Gould] had endowed it as a boy; and it remained
dependent on himself alone" (*N* 82). Gould projects himself onto the
mine and "felt that the worthiness of his life was bound up with success"
(*N* 85; see also 214, 245, 521). Gould and the mine blur in these passages.
Gould has altered the nature of the mine by projecting himself onto it,
but at the same time the mine has altered Gould. The mine changes
from an agent of his father's death to one of political and economic
success, while Gould, among other things, changes from a loving husband to a distant one. The mine becomes the center of Gould's life and
in fact in many ways governs his existence. Each alters the other. As
Gould's existence is bound to the mine, so also is Nostromo's bound to
the silver. The narrator comments, "The existence of the treasure
confused his [Nostromo's] thoughts with a peculiar sort of anxiety, as
though his life had become bound up with it" (*N* 424) and "[T]he silver
of San Tomé was provided now with a faithful and lifelong slave"
(*N* 501). In the end, Nostromo's existence and that of the silver become
so intertwined that it becomes impossible to separate them, and
Nostromo's once seemingly free and independent existence disappears:
"And the feeling of fearful and ardent subjection, the feeling of his
slavery – so irremediable and profound that often, in his thoughts, he
compared himself to the legendary Gringos, neither dead nor alive,
bound down to their conquest of unlawful wealth on Azuera – weighed
heavily on the independent Captain Fidanza" (*N* 526–27). Nostromo's
slavery to the silver demonstrates the difficulty of extricating objects
from their surrounding phenomena and the impact this context has on
both perceiver and perceived. Once the silver becomes contextualized

with Nostromo, their existences are linked and altered. In this way, the silver changes from an object of wealth to one of enslavement, while Nostromo changes from an honorable man to a thief. Neither Gould nor Nostromo can separate themselves from the silver of the San Tomé mine. The mine and Gould almost become a single entity, as do the silver and Nostromo. Unfortunately for both, their existences become so altered by their tie to the silver that it actually consumes them (N 245, 521–22, 561). Of course, not all subjects and objects so completely merge, but blurred boundaries usually occur such that it becomes impossible to tell where the margins of subject end and those of object begin.

Perhaps the most striking instance of blurred boundaries in Conrad's work occurs in "Heart of Darkness." The story's brooding, somber, dark, hazy feeling is its pervasive quality. In fact, this mood permeates the entire story and is not merely a product of the mood of the events in the story but also of Conrad's portrait of the external world itself, as well as the larger social and philosophical issues with which the story is concerned. From the story's outset, the frame narrator highlights the haziness and uncertainty of Marlow's experience when he says, "[T]he meaning of an episode was not inside like a kernel but outside, enveloping the tale which brought it out only as a glow brings out a haze, in the likeness of one of these misty halos that sometimes are made visible by the spectral illumination of moonshine" (Y 48). The way the tale is told – the haze around the kernel as it were – emphasizes Marlow's "inconclusive experiences" (Y 51) and the uncertain world he encounters. Watt suggests that the story "is essentially impressionist in one very special and yet general way: it accepts, and indeed in its very form asserts, the bounded and ambiguous nature of individual understanding."[22] Marlow himself notes this uncertainty:

It seems to me I am trying to tell you a dream – making a vain attempt, because no relation of a dream can convey the dream-sensation, that commingling of absurdity, surprise, and bewilderment in a tremor of struggling revolt, that notion of being captured by the incredible which is of the very essence of dreams. (Y 82; see also 105 and 138)

The haziness and dreamlike quality of the episode are crucial aspects to understanding "Heart of Darkness" because they highlight the uncertainty and irrationality of Marlow's experience outside the comfortable context of European civilization.

Associating Marlow's experience with that of a dream is important in that even more than with waking experience, distinctions and boundaries between dream phenomena appear fluid and indistinct. Separating phenomena from the surrounding flux of dream experience is difficult, as one thing seamlessly flows into the next. This blending of one object with the next in a dream also mirrors the blurred boundaries that run throughout the story. In addition to hyper-blurred boundaries, the objects and events in a dream can also be shifting, unpredictable, and irrational. Human beings cannot get beyond the essentially unmediated quality of a dream, because it does not conform well with past experience and defies our usual methods for organizing experience. Only when we consider dreams outside past experience do they cease to appear absurd. Consequently, because of its dreamlike quality, Marlow's initial perceptual impression of his African experience becomes difficult to mediate. Instead, his listeners must accept Marlow's experience as it first appears, in effect unmediated and unorganized. Conrad establishes this chaotic flow of a dream in contrast to the seemingly organized flow of reality. Through personal and cultural experience, the ordinary waking flow of phenomena may appear inherently ordered and comprehensible. A dream's flow, however, is not subject to order or meaning. A significant aspect of "Heart of Darkness" is that sleeping and waking experience blur. Marlow's African experience is a waking one, but the flow of phenomena acts like that of a dream. Consequently, he learns that the organization and meaning he associates with waking reality is not inherent but is constructed from his personal and cultural experience. The "commingling of absurdity, surprise, and bewilderment" does not result from an actual dream, but rather from Marlow's encounter with the primitive wilderness, where he discovers order is an attribute of civilization and not necessarily of reality.[23]

This link between the uncivilized wilderness and a dream experience exists elsewhere in Conrad's works. For instance, in "The Sisters" Stephen sees the mountainous landscape as "a disorderly mob of peaks whose shapes were as fantastic and aimless as a fevered dream."[24] Uncivilized space contrasts with civilized space in its irrationality and disorganization; both of which have the effect of a dream. Similarly, the narrator of *Nostromo* remarks, "Nostromo cleared the shelving shore with one push of the heavy oar, and Decoud found himself solitary on the beach like a man in a dream" (*N* 301). After Nostromo leaves the island, the last link to the civilized world is gone. Decoud then encounters the unorganized wilderness, where the ordered, meaningful existence of his civilized world disappears, and as he confronts the wilderness his existence comes to appear as disordered and illogical as a dream. He no longer has a frame of reference for mediating and interpreting the world and comes to believe that the uncivilized world is without inherent meaning and that the civilized social structure he knew is merely a construct.

In "The Duel," dream imagery appears somewhat differently, but the end effect is much the same. Unlike "Heart of Darkness" and *Nostromo*, the dreamlike action of the story occurs in the heart of European civilization, ostensibly within the course of normal social interactions. However, the duel itself consistently runs counter to normal social values, so much so that D'Hubert several times associates it with a dream. He remarks, "It was all like a very wicked and harassing dream" (*SS* 182). The dreamlike quality of the experience reaches a climax when D'Hubert must fully enter the irrationality of the dream and realizes that "[t]he problem was how to kill the adversary. Nothing short of that would free him from this imbecile nightmare" (*SS* 251). D'Hubert must in a sense enter the dreamworld and act in opposition to social values, that is murder Feraud, in order to exit the dream existence he cannot otherwise escape. That such irrational and antisocial behavior occurs in the midst of civilization emphasizes the fact that for Conrad nothing supports western values but society's mutual consent. Nothing inherently holds those values in place. Similarly, in "Youth" Marlow refers to his experience as "an absurd dream" (*Y* 24). As was true of "The Duel," once reality becomes irrational, Marlow can only interpret events in terms of a dream. To do otherwise would require Marlow and D'Hubert to question the rationality of human experience, but by perceiving the event as a dream they can maintain social stability by placing the irrationality they experience outside of social reality. However, Decoud and the older Marlow of "Heart of Darkness" cannot make this transformation, and as a result must instead recognize a shifting foundation for western civilization.

Ultimately, Conrad's impressionist representation of objects and events has implications for the way his characters obtain knowledge of these phenomena. For Conrad, knowledge is based in large part upon perception, and this is particularly true of knowledge of objects and events. "Heart of Darkness" and other works emphasize the indistinguishability of boundaries between subject and object and between object and object, and in so doing they represent the uncertainty of objective knowledge. The conceptualization of this perceptual process emphasizes Conrad's view of the individual and relative nature of objective knowledge. As Marlow suggests, "We live, as we dream – alone" (*Y* 82), and the ultimate uncertainty and irrationality of the dream experience throughout "Heart of Darkness" and elsewhere invariably results from the Europeans' removal from the context of western civilization in one form or another. Outside that context, order and reason appear not as inherent qualities of human existence but rather as constructed qualities for social convenience. As a result, Conrad's investigation into the epistemological processes by which human beings perceive objects and events uncovers not only his uncertainty concerning the perceptual process itself, but also the cosmology underlying and influencing that process.

II

Throughout "Heart of Darkness," Conrad links literal and figurative seeing by associating the uncertainty of knowledge of objects and events, the dreamlike narrative and setting, and the contextualization of subject and object with the larger concern of the nature of western civilization. For instance, in addition to its relationship to epistemology, Conrad also uses primitive perception to comment on civilization. He does this in three ways. First, as demonstrated earlier, characters use their cultural past to organize primitive perception, and so society influences the characters' perception of objects and events. Second, primitive perception serves as a model for Conrad's comments on civilization such that civilized values mediate human experience the way civilized perception mediates sensory impressions. Third, Conrad links primitive perception to the dissolution of western civilization by presenting them as occurring simultaneously. Whether appearing at the climax or at some other crucial juncture in a literary work, primitive perception's privileged place in Conrad's writings demonstrates its importance to the movement of those works and its relationship to the larger issues that Conrad also addresses. Ultimately, these incidents show how his characters construct meaning for both the external world and for their system of values.

Conrad further links by analogy the role cultural past plays in organizing primitive perception. In the same way his characters use cultural past to mediate the flow of human perception, they also use cultural values to mediate the flow of human experience. Just as cultural past provides order and meaning for perceived phenomena, cultural values provide order and meaning for human existence. In so doing, Conrad ties the question of how we perceive to the role of western society. Rather than seeing society's values as concepts brought to bear on the world as we experience it, Conrad's Europeans go directly to a western-conceived notion of the world, unaware of the intervening step – the way Conrad sees human beings going directly to "arrows," unaware of the "sticks" step in between. These characters also transform their primitive perception of objects by making them conform to cultural experience just as they transform their primitive perception of human existence by making it conform to western cultural values. The climax of "Heart of Darkness," for example, occurs when Marlow discovers that his cultural values are simply constructs that transform an initial and immediate impression of the world into western civilization. His realization is a kind of primitive perception of the nature of the world. Having made this discovery, he must then come to recognize the meaning of his existence. Without cultural ideals as givens, he must accept his immediate perception of a primitive world without inherent meaning. But even in discovering that his cultural values are constructs, as should become clear later, Marlow wants to maintain those values as a shelter from such disturbing knowledge, so Marlow removes the postscript from Kurtz's essay on the suppression of savage customs and lies to the Intended.

As Marlow peels away layers of civilization, the gap between European and African diminishes, and rather than emphasizing their differences, Marlow continually notes their similarities. He parallels the Congo and the Thames (Υ 50), the Intended and Kurtz's African mistress (Υ 160), the Roman and European colonists (Υ 49–50), the European colonists and the Africans (Υ 96, 142). Bender argues of the Congo/Thames relationship that

the fictive present scene on the Thames with the ominous red glow of a modern city in the dusk is juxtaposed to the journey into the "primitive" remembered horrors of Africa. This collage can exist only in the mind of the storyteller and from such oppositions the texture of the story as a whole is woven back and forth from past to fictive present, from Europe to the Congo.[25]

In each instance of paralleled opposites, the differences between civilized and savage gradually disappear, and with them also go western absolutes because an important aspect of western cosmology of that time was the belief that the civilized is inherently – not arbitrarily – superior to the primitive. The primary assumption justifying colonial activities is that the colonized need colonization and are improved by it.

However, at each instance of civilization's direct appearance in the story, the primitive world is not improved. In fact, Conrad often portrays the civilized as detrimental to the uncivilized. The clearest example of this phenomenon is "the grove of death" at the Outer Station. Marlow says of its inhabitants,

They were dying slowly – it was very clear. They were not enemies, they were not criminals, they were nothing earthly now, – nothing but black shadows of disease and starvation, lying confusedly in the greenish gloom. Brought from all the recesses of the coast in all the legality of time contracts, lost in uncongenial surroundings, fed on unfamiliar food, they sickened, became inefficient, and were then allowed to crawl away and rest. These moribund shapes were free as air – and nearly as thin. (*Y* 66)

In this case, the civilized actually destroys the uncivilized. Among those in the "grove of death" is a man with a white cloth tied around his neck. Marlow remarks, "It looked startling round his black neck, this bit of white thread from beyond the seas" (*Y* 67). The symbolic strangulation of African by European is unmistakable and represents for Conrad the problem of treating a relative system as if it were absolute.

Even when the civilized does not destroy the uncivilized, it is still clearly out of place, just as the Europeans themselves are out of place in an African setting (*Y* 96). In a European setting, western values are at home because everything is constructed around them, but in the African wilderness such values become absurd. Both Kurtz and Marlow discover this. Kurtz had gone into the wilderness "equipped with moral ideals" (*Y* 88) and intent on improving the inhabitants based upon those ideals (*Y* 79, 91), but he finds nothing underlying those ideals and nothing to enforce them, and hence they have no power over his life. On the other hand, Marlow makes a similar discovery, most surprisingly in the cannibals' "restraint." From Marlow's cultural perspective, because the cannibals were not civilized, they "had no earthly reason for any kind of scruple" (*Y* 105). European restraint, with its absolute ideals, would not have surprised him, but this same restraint in a primitive people does surprise him. Marlow says, "But there was the fact facing me ... like a ripple on an unfathomable enigma" (*Y* 105), and their restraint remains a riddle until Marlow gradually lets go of the idea of an absolute foundation for western values. At that point, the cannibals' restraint is no more ludicrous nor sensible than European restraint.

Finally, the connection between perception and the construction of western civilization occurs when the two are linked in the same incident.

Conrad hints at this link in "An Outpost of Progress," when he conflates the two. At the story's climax, Kayerts has what amounts to an unmediated perceptual experience while that same instant he also demonstrates an almost complete dissolution of western values. At the very moment that Kayerts' perception proves to be an individual experience, his perception also blends with the disintegration of civilized values. When he shoots Carlier in a dispute over sugar (*TU* 110–13), his perception of the event is essentially unmediated by either cultural experience or cultural morality. This incident signals a complete breakdown of his cultural values. Even the irony of the story's title highlights this movement toward dissolution. Far from progressing, the characters regress to a point where nearly all traces of civilization disappear.

Not until "Heart of Darkness," however, does the link between the two become inextricably interconnected. Early in the story, several incidents demonstrate a lack of western morality, but the attack on the steamboat underscores this lack because Marlow experiences primitive perception several times during the attack and because Kurtz, the representative European (*Y* 117), orders the attack. Watt argues, "Kurtz is obviously intended as the climactic example of the inner moral void which Marlow has found in all the representatives of Western progress."[26] What the Russian passes off as a kind of indiscretion (*Y* 139) was in fact a deadly encounter. Kurtz's ordering of the attack was a wanton disregard for civilized morality and shows how his cultural norms no longer mediate his behavior. And so, as he did in "An Outpost of Progress," Conrad presents both the perception of the event and the morality of the event in effect unmediated by the influence of western civilization.

Conrad further emphasizes the link between literal and figurative seeing by associating Marlow's dreamlike experience in "Heart of Darkness" with images of absurdity. Invariably these images are directly associated with western cultural ideas, as they demonstrate both the image's absurdity and its dislocation in the African wilderness. As suggested earlier, dreams usually run counter to the organized chronicle and rational expectations of civilized experience. In this way, the absurdity of dream phenomena becomes analogous to the absurdity of European culture as it appears in Africa. For Conrad, looking at the inherently unorganized wilderness in light of images of organized western civilization can only result in absurdity, and numerous incidents bear this out.

The French gunboat carrying out a war against the Africans does so to suppress savage customs and to civilize the Africans, but as Marlow notes the whole procedure makes no sense:

In the empty immensity of earth, sky, and water, there she was, incomprehensible, firing into a continent. Pop, would go one of the six-inch guns; a small flame would dart and vanish, a little white smoke would disappear, a tiny projectile would give a feeble screech – and nothing happened. Nothing could happen. There was a touch of insanity in the proceeding, a sense of lugubrious drollery in the sight. (*Y* 61–62)

Set against the backdrop of the entire African continent, this "attack" has no effect and no rational purpose. Yet it is in perfect harmony with European ideas about the relationship between western and non-western cosmology. Similarly, just after arriving in Africa, Marlow encounters what he calls "objectless blasting": "A heavy and dull detonation shook the ground, a puff of smoke came out of the cliff, and that was all. No change appeared on the face of the rock. They were building a railway. The cliff was not in the way or anything" (*Y* 64). The fact that the blasting has no effect on the cliff reveals the impotence of modern civilization against the primitive wilderness, while the cliff's not being in the way demonstrates the absurdity of imposing civilization on a wilderness that is "not in the way of anything." And in case the listener missed the point, Marlow remarks, "Another report from the cliff made me think suddenly of that ship of war I had seen firing into a continent" (*Y* 64). The gunboat firing into the continent was ineffectual and absurd, as is this attempt to create an unnecessary railroad in the primitive wilderness.

The company's chief accountant provides yet another important instance of the incongruity of western civilization in the African wilderness. Marlow recounts, "I met a white man, in such an unexpected elegance of get-up that in the first moment I took him for a sort of vision. I saw a high starched collar, white cuffs, a light alpaca jacket, snowy trousers, a clean necktie, and varnished boots" (*Y* 67). Such a character would not appear out of place in Europe, so much so that he would likely go about completely unnoticed. And despite Marlow's admiration for this man's ability to maintain his civilized appearance, the accountant appears completely out of place. With his dress and his books "in apple-pie order" (*Y* 68), he represents the western idea of order, but imposed on the wilderness, he simply appears farcical. The incongruity of his European dress in the African jungle is the incongruity of western civilization in this primitive setting.

But perhaps the clearest example of this kind of absurdity and dislocation of European culture in an African setting appears in the employment contract of the cannibals:

[The company] had given them every week three pieces of brass wire, each about nine inches long; and the theory was they were to buy their provisions with that currency in river-side villages. You can see how *that* worked. There were either no villages, or the people were hostile . . . So, unless they swallowed the wire itself, or made loops of it to snare the fishes with, I don't see what good their extravagant salary could be to them. I must say it was paid with a regularity worthy of a large and honourable trading company. (*Y* 104; emphasis is Conrad's)

The company transacts business as if it were in the heart of Brussels rather than the heart of Africa. An economic system based upon monetary exchange is the norm in Europe, and it functions relatively efficiently there, but on the Congo river the cannibals' salary has no use and hence no value. The whole system then is senseless in that context. But this business transaction also has larger implications. Money has no value except by mutual consent, and only social consensus empowers money with any value at all. Otherwise, it is merely paper (or metal). Consequently, this whole transaction represents Marlow's view of how European social transactions function: western truths are truths by the mutual consent of society's members, not by the existence of any inherent truth.[27]

Like the dream quality of Marlow's narrative, Conrad himself also links the blurring of distinctions between physical objects to the indeterminacy of western ideals. Kurtz goes into the wilderness with the idea of civilizing the Africans (*Y* 79, 88, 91), but at the same time he exploits their resources. Marlow's aunt expresses much the same idea when she talks of Marlow's "weaning those ignorant millions from their horrid ways" (*Y* 59). Marlow himself refers to these ideals and their blurring when he notes that Fresleven, who was killed after beating an African chief in a dispute over some hens, was also supposed to have been "the gentlest, quietest creature that ever walked on two legs. No doubt he was; but he had been a couple of years already out there engaged in the noble cause" (*Y* 54). Kayerts has a similar experience in "An Outpost of Progress": "He seemed to have broken loose from himself altogether. His old thoughts, convictions, likes and dislikes, things he respected and things he abhorred, appeared in their true light at last! Appeared contemptible and childish, false and ridiculous. He revelled in his new wisdom while he sat by the man he had killed" (*TU* 114). Removed from civilization, society's values and customs hold little of the power they once did. Only at the end of the story, when the steamboat's whistle announces the return of civilization to the outpost, does Kayerts recognize the consequences of his actions in terms of European justice. At that point, Kayerts kills himself, knowing that justice is at hand. But as long as the supporting social structure is absent, the truth of his cultural values is not self-evident. Even until Kurtz's final revelation, he tries to maintain his cultural ideals: "Of course you must take care of the motives – right motives – always" (*Y* 148). In the end, though, those ideals cannot withstand the incongruity. In Conrad's works, civilization's values were not mere shams; they provided for an ordered social interaction in Europe, but they also were not absolutes and became blurred with exploitation. Conrad assessed the situation as "the vilest scramble for loot that ever disfigured the history of human conscience and geographical exploration."[28] The members of "the new gang" who are emissaries "of pity, and science, and progress" (*Y* 79) were supposed to both civilize and trade with the primitive peoples, but the juxtaposition of the two intentions became too incongruous to maintain, precisely because civilized values were not based upon absolutes. Had they been so, they would not have appeared absurd in the primitive setting.

In the end, through impressionist theory and technique, "Heart of Darkness" and Conrad's other writings clearly bring into question nineteenth-century assumptions of universal reality, suggesting instead that our perceptual experience and objective knowledge are both individual and relative and that knowledge of objects and events cannot be universalized. Wollaeger argues that in "The Return" Alvan Hervey calls "into question the visible as a final source of knowledge."[29] However, throughout his works, Conrad continually demonstrates that his characters initially experience the world individually and only later organize it to conform to the universal experience of society. This process reveals that even the seeming certainty of perception – of knowing exactly what one perceives – is in fact uncertain. For Conrad, certainty is tenuous, whether it be knowledge of objects and events or the values of western civilization.

CHAPTER 3

Other-like-self and other-unlike-self: the epistemology of subjectivity

> "One's own personality is only . . . something hopelessly unknown."
> "Letter to Edward Garnett"

In representing objects of consciousness, Conrad does not limit himself simply to physical objects, but also considers human subjects. Knowledge of objects begins with impressionist perception, as does knowledge of subjects, as Conrad focuses on both self and other – and more particularly on their interrelationship. In an article on "Heart of Darkness," Eric Tretheway refers to "the question that Conrad never ceased to worry throughout his career, that of the possibility of shaping a 'substantial,' coherent self."[1] Various other commentators have also looked at Conrad's conception of the self.[2] A common feature of these investigations is that they look to the self for knowledge of the self. Similarly, commentators on perception of other human beings look to the other for knowledge of the other.[3] These commentaries on self and other consistently imply that self and other are distinct and self-contained entities.[4] In contrast to this separation of self and other, I would argue that Conrad presents a necessary link between the two, between subject and object, in coming to any knowledge – however limited – of human subjectivity. The self alters the other, just as the other alters the self, and in the space between them exists the possible epistemology of subjectivity.

I

Conrad is concerned with subjective knowledge throughout his works, but *Lord Jim* provides perhaps the best example of his inquiry into human subjectivity and its relationship to western civilization. And as is true of knowledge of objects, Conrad's impressionism is the means by which he investigates knowledge of human subjects. Similarly, just as Conrad's investigation of objective knowledge begins with the

61

perceptual act, so also does he begin his investigation into subjective knowledge. Conrad's inquiry into subjects proceeds somewhat differently, however, from that of objects. Perception of subjects relies on both the perceiver of the subject as well as on other perceivers of the same subject. Whereas narration is a relatively minor component in the perception of objects, it is a major factor in the perception of subjects. Human beings have more confidence in their ability to assess physical objects than they do human subjects. In assessing human subjects, the narration of others both confirms our own perception and also supplies unperceived facets of a perceived subject. Furthermore, narration plays a significant role because human subjects are both objects and subjects at the same time. They are physical objects in the eyes of others, since they have extension and occupy space, but at the same time these objects are themselves perceiving subjects and therefore inherently different from other physical objects.

Besides the increased role of narration, another important difference exists between the perception of objects and subjects in Conrad's works. In a sense, perception of subjects involves two levels: first the perception of subjects as physical objects and second the perception of those physical objects as human subjects. Archie Ruthvel's experience in *Lord Jim* provides a good distinction between the two. Like Marlow's encounter with the cane/spear in "Heart of Darkness" (*Y* 111–12), Archie encounters an initially incomprehensible object that then filters through his past experience and is transformed into something comprehensible. He first perceives "something round and enormous, resembling a sixteen-hundred-weight sugar-hogshead wrapped in striped flannelette, up-ended in the middle of the large floor space in the office" (*LJ* 38). Only after the captain of the *Patna* "had managed to tug and jerk his hat clear of his head, and advanced with slight bows" and had begun talking "little by little it dawned upon Archie that this was a development of the *Patna* case" (*LJ* 38). Initially, Archie perceives something unexpected and inexplicable; as the captain approaches and addresses him, however, this incident becomes explicable through the mediation of Archie's past experience. In other words, as the captain exhibits cultural gestures and begins speaking, Archie first interprets the object in front of him to be a person and then identifies who that person is and makes an assessment concerning him.

In *Victory*, Shomberg's inability to move past the human subject as physical object accounts for the difference between his treatment of people and Heyst's. The narrator comments that Shomberg "was no great judge of physiognomy. Human beings, for him, were either the objects of scandalous gossip or else the recipients of narrow strips of paper, with proper bill-heads stating the name of his hotel. – 'W. Shomberg, proprietor; accounts settled weekly'" (*V* 98). Heyst on the other hand moves beyond the mere perception of human beings as physical objects and gains some understanding of their subjectivity. Similarly, in *Lord Jim*, Conrad's investigation into human subjectivity focuses on Marlow's study of Jim. Marlow perceives Jim as he does any other physical object, but he also perceives Jim's subjectivity through his own eyes and through those of other observers. Tamb' Itam, Gentleman Brown, Stein, Jewel, Cornelius, Doramin, and others all narrate their perceptual experience of Jim. In addition, Jim narrates his own perception of himself. Marlow then uses these various sources of information to try to gain a clearer picture of Jim. Throughout the novel, Marlow also presents his own perception of Jim, which he then interprets in an attempt to obtain knowledge of Jim as a human subject. Several times, he comments on Jim's appearance (i.e., *LJ* 40, 43, 46), by which means he assesses Jim as "one of us." As he does in "Youth" and "Heart of Darkness," Marlow filters his initial sensory perception through past experience to assess Jim. The difference, though, is that with the perception of objects Marlow moves from an essentially unmediated object to a mediated one, that is, for example, from a cane to a spear. In perceiving Jim, however, Marlow seems to move in the opposite direction; he begins with a mediated object but ends with one that is not mediated.

The point at which cultural mediation appears in the perceptual and narrative processes brings about this difference between Marlow's perception of object and subject. Marlow perceives an unexpected object when he sees the helmsman grasping a cane. His experience then mediates this perception, translating the cane into something else (a spear). In his perception of Jim, though, Marlow initially perceives an expected image because, in a sense, he narrates his perception of Jim *in medias res* (in this case, its traditional form rather than impressionist form); he narrates his perception of Jim part way through the process. Marlow has perceived Jim as a physical object, and then, based upon his cultural experience, Marlow interprets this physical object to be a westerner and a seaman like himself. The picture of Jim that Marlow narrates is not an initial impression at all but rather one already mediated by cultural experience. As a result, Jim looks the way Marlow expects him to look. But Jim's appearance and his actuality are incongruous, and so Marlow must reassess his perception of Jim and peel away the layers of cultural experience. He then discovers a perception that is in effect unmediated. In both instances, the object of perception appears to be one thing when mediated by cultural experience and another when unmediated by cultural experience. For Conrad, this cultural experience alters the being of the perceived.

Along with their own perception of subjects, the characters also perceive subjects through the perceptual experience of others, and narration is the vehicle for communicating these differing views of human subjects. Many narrators appear in *Lord Jim*, and narration presents much of the perception of subjects. The narrative process itself, though, is a mediation. In fact, the narrative process in Conrad is very much like perception in general, in that contextual factors limit both. Marlow tells us this when he says of Jim, "He existed for me, and after all it is only through me that he exists for you. I've led him out by the hand; I have paraded him before you" (*LJ* 224). In other words, Marlow's narration mediates the reader's perception of Jim. Furthermore, as discussed earlier, the multiple narrator technique that Conrad employs in *Lord Jim* and elsewhere demonstrates the limited point of view from which each narrator experiences Jim. The outlines of these narrators merge with the outlines of Jim and the context in which they appear. Therefore, the inability of these narrators to recognize that their perception is limited severely limits their ability to perceive Jim. Of the various narrators who assess Jim, only Marlow considers the possibility of a gap between his perception of Jim and an actual knowledge of Jim. Marlow recognizes his own perceptual limitations and solicits the experience of other perceivers in order to supplement and confirm his own perception and to come, perhaps, to a more complete knowledge of Jim.

II

Perception and knowledge of subjects occurs in relation to both self and other. In considering the relationship of the other to the self, Conrad investigates two kinds of other: the other-*unlike*-self and the other-*like*-self. Both are important because both help to define the self. The other-like-self defines what the self is; the other-unlike-self defines what the self is not.

When investigating the other-unlike-self, Conrad represents it in two forms: former community members whom the community has rejected, and those who have never been part of the community. Regarding the first, Jim's fellow officers on the *Patna*, for instance, are among those the community rejects. Both Marlow and Jim make this point clear. Marlow remarks that Jim "wanted me to know he had kept his distance; that there was nothing in common between him and these men" (*LJ* 103; see also 24 and 154). Marlow himself says, "They were nobodies" (*LJ* 46). (Later, he also rejects Cornelius and Gentleman Brown.) Superficially, these men look like members of the European maritime community, but they harbor crucial differences in both appearance and character. In fact, their appearance represents their character. Marlow and others of the community consistently describe these men in an unpleasant light. The *Patna*'s captain is fat and unsightly (*LJ* 21, 23–24); the chief engineer is sunken and emaciated (*LJ* 23–24); Cornelius is "unsavoury" (*LJ* 285); and Gentleman Brown is dying in squalid surroundings (*LJ* 344–46). In this way, Marlow symbolically links perception and knowledge. Those who are "one of us" look respectable and upstanding, while those who are not look unsightly and unsavory – except Jim, who looks the part but acts otherwise. Together with unattractive physical descriptions, the community often describes these others-unlike-self using nonhuman imagery; Marlow comments on Cornelius' "slow laborious walk [that] resembled the creeping of a repulsive beetle" (*LJ* 285; see also 286). He also describes the *Patna*'s skipper as "a trained baby elephant walking on hind-legs" (*LJ* 37). Similarly, Jim refers to the *Patna*'s other officers as "three dirty owls" (*LJ* 123), and Captain O'Brien calls the *Patna*'s officers "Skunks" (*LJ* 194). By dehumanizing these men, the community effectually eliminates them from their society. Speaking of Jim's fellow officers, Tony Jackson argues that "tossing out a scoundrel . . . would be an act of negation that would effectively validate the self-representation of the Merchant Marine."[5] These officers have significant negative character traits, and the westerners wish to exclude them from their community because they do not want to see those characteristics in themselves. By removing evil elements from their midst, the community reaffirms itself as a worthwhile entity.

The community responds similarly to the other-unlike-self whom it perceives as always existing outside the group, that is the traditional other. Many of Conrad's Europeans view all non-westerners in this manner. Despite many differences among Arabs, Chinese, Malaysians, and other non-westerners, the westerners lump them together as others-unlike-self. When the *Patna*'s chief engineer mistakenly tries to knock down Jim during the panic to abandon ship, he says, "I thought you were one of them niggers" (*LJ* 91). The only significant characteristic the westerners see in the non-westerners is their difference from westerners. In this difference, they also perceive non-westerners as inferior. For example, the *Patna*'s captain refers to the Arab pilgrims as "cattle" (*LJ* 15), not only insulting them but, more important, dehumanizing them; by so doing, he tries to ensure that these others-unlike-self could not be confused with himself. An even clearer explanation of this attitude appears in Marlow's letter to his privileged listener:

You said also – I call to mind – that "giving your life up to them" (*them* meaning all of mankind with skins brown, yellow, or black in colour) "was like selling your soul to a brute." You contended that "that kind of thing" was only endurable and enduring when based on a firm conviction in the truth of ideas racially our own, in whose name are established the order, the morality of an ethical progress. (*LJ* 339; emphasis is Conrad's)

This perception of superiority is a product of superior technology and what the Europeans also perceive to be superior morals and customs. For them, superior technology indicates an inherently superior cosmology. The non-westerners further complicate the issue by reinforcing this belief, linking a superior technology to a superior society.[6] To the Arab pilgrims, "[t]he ship of iron, the men with white faces, all the sights, all the sounds, everything on board to that ignorant and pious multitude was strange alike, and as trustworthy as it would for ever remain incomprehensible" (*LJ* 85–86). Even more surprising, during the *Patna* inquest, the ship's Asian helmsman "declared it never came into his mind then that the white men were about to leave the ship through fear of death. He did not believe it now. There might have been secret reasons" (*LJ* 98). This attitude of awe only confirms the westerners' belief in their superiority and serves to define them as an entity.

This view of non-western inferiority occurs throughout Conrad's works. In "Typhoon," MacWhirr says to Jukes, "The Chinamen! Why don't you speak plainly? Couldn't tell what you meant. Never heard a lot of coolies spoken of as passengers before. Passengers, indeed!" (*T* 31; see also 55, 58, 88, 101). In *The Shadow Line*, the Chief Steward of the Officers' Sailors' Home says of Hamilton, "He swears at me and tells me I can't chuck a white man out into the street" (*SL* 10). In "The Planter of Malata," Professor Moorsam's sister becomes incensed when Renouard compares the apparitions his Asian plantation workers claim to see with those some Londoners claim to see (*WT* 67). In "Freya of the Seven Isles," Nelson says that Heemskirk "was as savage with me as if I had been a Chinaman" (*TLS* 176). In *Almayer's Folly*, Almayer thinks to himself, "Trusting to Malays was poor work – but then even Malays have some sense and understand their own interest" (*AF* 13). And in *The Nigger of the "Narcissus,"* the narrator comments, "The feverish and shrill babble of Eastern language struggled against the masterful tones of tipsy seamen" (*NN* 4). In each instance (along with others in Conrad's works), the common factor is the characters' belief that westerners are superior to non-westerners, regardless of the individuals involved. Marlow emphasizes this attitude when he says, "Beloved, trusted, and admired as he [Dain Waris] was, he was still one of *them*, while Jim was one of *us*" (*LJ* 361; emphasis is Conrad's). Despite his merits, Dain Waris is still the other-unlike-self; westerners and non-westerners alike perceive him only in his difference from Europeans. For many of Conrad's characters, any merits in non-westerners or similarities between them and westerners are either ignored, seen as poor imitations, or deemed insignificant compared with their differences.

Conrad also addresses this perceived difference in "Heart of Darkness," but in this story he problematizes the issue by introducing various conflations of modern Europeans and other peoples. He seems to intend these conflations to be unsettling in order to undermine such differences and to demonstrate the westerners' need for the other-unlike-self to define what the self is not. Marlow links the British and Romans (*Y* 49–50), but such a link is not particularly troubling since the westerners see their own colonial endeavor as more enlightened whereas that of the Romans "was merely a squeeze... They were conquerors... They grabbed what they could get for the sake of what was to be got. It was just robbery with violence, aggravated murder on a great scale" (*Y* 50). On the other hand, Kurtz is quoted as saying, "Each station should be like a beacon on the road towards better things, a centre for trade of course, but also for humanizing, improving, instructing" (*Y* 91; see also 79, 88). In the end, though, Conrad exposes the fallacy that these two colonial endeavors differ in any substantive manner, as he shows European colonialism to be little different from Roman conquests. In so doing, he undercuts the Africans' role as the other-unlike-self and also emphasizes their purpose for the westerners' knowledge of self.

Even more unsettling conflations occur when Marlow challenges notions of the other-unlike-self by linking European and African. For Marlow, Africans and Europeans are similar and their differences are the accident of different cultures.[7] Marlow experiences this similarity himself and says of the Africans, "Well, you know, that was the worst of it – this suspicion of their not being inhuman... [W]hat thrilled you was just the thought of their humanity – like yours – the thought of your remote kinship with this wild and passionate uproar" (*Y* 96). Later, Marlow remarks, "I remember I confounded the beat of the drum with the beating of my heart, and was pleased at its calm regularity" (*Y* 142).[8] Marlow's interview with Kurtz's Intended further yokes European and African. He says at one point that the Intended "put out her arms as if after a retreating figure ... a tragic and familiar Shade, resembling in this gesture another one, tragic also, and bedecked with powerless charms, stretching bare brown arms" (*Y* 160). In this moment, Marlow brings together the powerful human emotions of love and grief common to both the Intended and Kurtz's African mistress, as they merge into one figure. Throughout the story, Marlow consistently presents similarities rather than differences between the two cultures and in this way undermines not only the superiority of western civilization but also its distinctness.

In "Heart of Darkness," arbitrary cultural differences determine the westerner's perception of the other-unlike-self's difference and inferiority. And despite the moral implications and the abuses of colonialism that result from this perception of non-westerners (i.e., *Y* 50–51),[9] the other-unlike-self provides a crucial function in Conrad's works. Evaluation must be based upon a point of comparison. By representing non-westerners as degraded, immoral, and ignorant, westerners can make comparisons that allow them to see their own society as advanced, moral, and enlightened. Without this object of comparison, they could not evaluate their society. Perhaps more important, though, without the other-unlike-self, individuality or heterogeneity cannot exist, and boundaries between self and other not only blur but become essentially nonexistent. As discussed earlier, impressionist epistemology presents blurred boundaries between subject and object's and between one object and another, but the phenomenon of blurred boundaries differs from indistinguishability. As should become clear shortly, it is one thing for the subject's boundaries to blur with the object's, but another thing entirely for the subject to be subsumed by the object. With no individuality of self, there could be no knowledge of self. Consequently, both collectively and individually, the other-unlike-self provides distinctions that define what the self is not, and thereby the other-unlike-self can provide some knowledge of self.

Together with knowledge of the other-*unlike*-self, the other-*like*-self also aids in obtaining knowledge of the self. Whereas the relationship between self and other-unlike-self is one of dissimilarity, that between self and other-like-self is one of similarity, as the other-like-self confirms shared communal characteristics.

The blurred distinctions between subject and object in Conrad's works are particularly apparent in the relationship between self and other-like-self. In *Lord Jim*, for instance, Marlow consistently enlists his audience in confirming that they, Marlow, and Jim are part of the same community, that Jim is "one of us" (*LJ* 43, 78, 93, 106, 224, 325, 331, 361, 416). They not only belong to the community, though, they also represent it. Marlow says of Jim, "I liked his appearance; I knew his appearance; he came from the right place; he was one of us. He stood there for all the parentage of his kind" (*LJ* 43). Unlike the other *Patna* officers, Jim looks like a member of the community. Even more telling is Marlow's statement, "I tell you I ought to know the right kind of looks. I would have trusted the deck to that youngster on the strength of a single glance" (*LJ* 45). Jim reminds Marlow, and most of the community, of themselves. Therefore, as Wollaeger argues, "[T]he cognitive aim of understanding Jim is also motivated by Marlow's emotional *need* for those experiences, as if by living through Jim's crisis vicariously he might find within himself the strength Brierly evidently lacked." Marlow's relationship with Jim is analogous to his relationship with Kurtz: "[I]n both instances Marlow is able to cross over into the experience of another, yet still withdraw his 'hesitating foot' [*Y* 151]."[10] But more than this, Marlow is altered by his experience with Jim, just as Jim is altered by his experience with Marlow's perception and that of various other narrators as they view Jim through the medium of their own subjectivity. Because Jim is "one of us," knowledge of him can lead to knowledge of westerners in general and of Marlow in particular, and this is precisely Marlow's interest in him. "Jim appears as what philosophers call a 'best case': if Marlow should be able to 'know' anyone, it is Jim; and if he can't know Jim, what can he know?"[11] The same influences that make up Jim also exist in Marlow. As a result, perception of Jim is in part perception of Marlow. Recognizing this relationship, Marlow asks himself, "Was it for my own sake that I wished to find some shadow of an excuse for that young fellow?" (*LJ* 51). Marlow's investigation of Jim's subjectivity then becomes a search for self. For this reason, he says, "It was the fear of losing him that kept me silent, for it was borne upon me suddenly and with unaccountable force that should I let him slip away into the darkness I would never forgive myself" (*LJ* 180). His desire to rescue and rehabilitate Jim is born partly out of friendship, but it is more of a form of self-preservation, since the boundaries between Marlow and Jim have blurred.

This relationship between self and other-like-self produces even more immediate results in "The Secret Sharer." Before the young captain meets his "secret sharer," he comments, "But what I felt most was my being a stranger to the ship; and if all the truth must be told, I was somewhat of a stranger to myself" (*TLS* 93). As the young captain confronts his new surroundings and untested role as captain, he questions his knowledge of self. However, after communing with Leggatt, he identifies with this other-like-self and learns something of his own self.[12] Daleski argues that the young captain "has ceased to be 'somewhat of a stranger' [*TLS* 93] to himself, and that, having learnt to know his own resources, he has also taken full possession of himself."[13] And according to Said, "By seeing an image of himself in another person, [the young captain] can ascertain his own identity."[14] By the time Leggatt leaves, the young captain has in fact learned much of himself from this experience; he learns he can command his ship and crew effectively, respond appropriately to danger, and make moral judgments based upon his own conscience. Each of these abilities directly results from his interaction with his other-like-self.

In addition to those others-like-self which we perceive around us, the other-like-self from the past can also provide knowledge of the self. In *The Shadow Line*, the narrator remarks,

A succession of men had sat in that chair. I became aware of that thought suddenly, vividly, as though each had left a little of himself between the four walls of these ornate bulkheads; as if a sort of composite soul, the soul of command, had whispered suddenly to mine of long days at sea and of anxious moments. "You, too!" it seemed to say, "you, too, shall taste of that peace and that unrest in a searching intimacy with your own self – obscure as we were and as supreme in the face of all the winds and all the seas, in an immensity that receives no impress, preserves no memories, and keeps no reckoning of lives." (*SL* 52–53)

The new captain perceives himself in the others-like-self from the past as their outlines merge with his. The previous captains give the new captain knowledge of his role and his self, defining him and his circumstances. In part, their experience becomes his experience, and even though their physical presence has long since disappeared, they continue to fulfill their role as others-like-self.

Despite the knowledge the other-like-self provides, though, problems can sometimes arise because of this blurring between self and other-like-self. Jim is a good example in that he perceives himself through fictional characters. He reads of romance heroes, accepts them as the other-like-self, and then perceives himself to be like them:

[H]e would forget himself, and beforehand live in his mind the sea-life of light literature. He saw himself saving people from sinking ships, cutting away masts in a hurricane, swimming through a surf with a line; or as a lonely castaway, barefooted and half naked, walking on uncovered reefs in search of shellfish to stave off starvation. He confronted savages on tropical shores quelled mutinies on the high seas, and in a small boat upon the ocean kept up the hearts of despairing men – always an example of devotion to duty, and as unflinching as a hero in a book. (*LJ* 6)

Jim seems unable to distinguish between real and ideal actions. He simply accepts that romance characters represent real human beings rather than imaginary ideals, and by perceiving these characters as actual others-like-self, he then begins to perceive his own self on their terms.

Furthermore, not all westerners are others-like-self, and in some cases this too becomes problematic. As suggested earlier, Jim's fellow officers on the *Patna* are examples of those who are not "one of us." The community rejects these men and tries to do the same with Jim; Marlow refers to "the serried circle of facts that had surged up all about him [Jim] to cut him off from the rest of his kind" (*LJ* 31). However, Jim's case is more difficult because he does not appear unsavory, as do the others. Jim bears more in common with the community and in fact resembles the best among them. Jackson suggests that Jim is "a node of intolerable and ineluctable contradiction for the Merchant Marine."[15] But this contradiction is precisely what Marlow wants to solve. He says that Jim "looked as genuine as a new sovereign, but there was some infernal alloy in his metal. How much? The least thing – the least drop of something rare and accursed" (*LJ* 45–46). Jim looks and (for the most part) even acts like a representative member of society, but a flaw exists. Marlow's difficulty is determining whether this flaw is unique to Jim (outweighing all other communal characteristics) or whether the flaw itself is a communal characteristic. This investigation becomes crucial because ultimately it will affect Marlow's conception of himself and of European civilization as a whole.

The Shadow Line provides yet another kind of contradiction between the appearance and reality of the other-like-self. The new captain remarks of his predecessor, "That man had been in all essentials but his age just such another man as myself. Yet the end of his life was a complete act of treason, the betrayal of a tradition which seemed to me as imperative as any guide on earth could be" (*SL* 62). The previous captain has the trappings of a representative European, but inexplicably he betrays communal values and tries to destroy his ship and its crew. The former captain appears to be "one of us" but acts otherwise (*SL* 61–62). Like Jim, the former captain cannot simply be dismissed as the other-unlike-self. In fact, his greater authority and experience make him even more representative than Jim. As in Jim's case, unexpectedly the former captain acts at odds with accepted conventions. The new captain acknowledges his ties to his predecessor (*SL* 52–53) but also confronts the former captain's treachery. In the end, the new captain merely dismisses the contradiction as something inexplicable, while Marlow actively pursues a solution to the problem of Jim in order to come to terms with its implications.

Even when accurately identifying the other-like-self, however, problems can arise. Although investigating the other-like-self can provide some knowledge of self and other, Conrad recognizes that knowledge is often based upon experienced phenomena and that Marlow's and the other narrators' limited perception of Jim then influences the degree to which they can know him. The other narrators believe they know Jim, but Marlow knows neither he nor they have a clear knowledge of Jim. Paul Armstrong remarks, "Instead of advancing Marlow's clarity or certainty about Jim, the rival readings he discovers make the young man increasingly enigmatic."[16] Marlow is certain of his knowledge of Jim's collective self, that Jim is "one of us," but he consistently remarks that Jim's individual subjectivity is unclear. For example, he says, "I cannot say I had ever seen him distinctly – not even to this day, after I had my last view of him" (*LJ* 221; see also 177, 223, 306, 330–31, 339). And although at times he feels Jim begins to become clear (i.e., *LJ* 216, 246), this confidence never lasts, and the novel ends on a note of uncertainty:

[T]here are days when the reality of his existence comes to me with an immense, with an overwhelming force; and yet upon my honour there are moments, too, when he passes from my eyes like a disembodied spirit astray amongst the passions of this earth, ready to surrender himself faithfully to the claim of his own world of shades. Who knows? He is gone, inscrutable at heart. (*LJ* 416)

At the close of the novel, Marlow's knowledge of Jim remains uncertain, but since Jim represents the community, Marlow's being "fated never to see him clearly" (*LJ* 241) has broader implications for knowledge of the other-like-self because not only is Jim unclear but Marlow also says,

It is when we try to grapple with another man's intimate need that we perceive how incomprehensible, wavering, and misty are the beings that share with us the sight of the stars and the warmth of the sun. It is as if loneliness were a hard and absolute condition of existence; the envelope of flesh and blood on which our eyes are fixed melts before the outstretched hand, and there remains only the capricious, unconsolable, and elusive spirit that no eye can follow, no hand can grasp. (*LJ* 179–80)

Marlow realizes that he can know only so much of other subjects, as does the editor in "The Planter of Malata," who was "without great sympathy for a certain side of that man [Renouard] which he could not quite make out. He only felt it obscurely to be his real personality" (*WT* 6). The narrator of "Karain" concurs: "It is impossible to convey the effect of his [Karain's] story. It is undying, it is but a memory, and its vividness cannot be made clear to another mind, any more than the vivid emotions of a dream" (*TU* 26). In Conrad's works, limited by our physical point of view and individual subjectivity, others are forever inaccessible except in a limited way. As a result, knowledge of subjectivity through investigation into others is partial and uncertain.

In "The Return," Alvan Hervey makes just such a discovery, and the knowledge that he can gain only limited access to the others destroys him. Married for several years, Hervey suddenly learns he knows little of his wife and thinks, "What was she? Who was she?" (*TU* 183). She is about to leave him when she changes her mind, and Hervey is surprised to note that she looks the same whether she is true or false to him:

[H]e was shocked to see it [her appearance] unchanged. She looked like this, spoke like this, exactly like this, a year ago, a month ago – only yesterday when she ... What did she think? What meant the pallor, the placid face, the candid brow, the pure eyes? ... And he would never know what she meant. Never! Never! No one could. Impossible to know. (*TU* 171–72)

Hervey discovers that perception of his wife can never provide the clarity necessary for knowledge of her to any significant extent; she will always be partly inaccessible to him. Of his wife's reasons for leaving him and then returning, he thinks, "And of all this he would never know the truth. Never. Not till death – not after ... [T]he secret of hearts alone shall return, forever unknown" (*TU* 174). Yet Hervey feels he must obtain a knowledge of others and thinks, "Faith! – Love! – the undoubt-ing, clear faith in the truth of a soul – the great tenderness ... It was what he had wanted all his life" (*TU* 178). But he cannot obtain this knowl-edge and realizes his wife "had no love and no faith for any one. To give

her your thought, your belief, was like whispering your confession over
the edge of the world. Nothing came back – not even an echo" (*TU* 183).
Because of his inability to wholly know the other-like-self, Hervey feels
himself alone in the world and cannot confirm his self in light of others
like himself.

   In addition to the difficulty of obtaining a clear knowledge of others,
knowledge of self through knowledge of the other-like-self can sometimes even lead to a loss of self. Knowledge of the other-like-self helps
define what the self is, but the other-like-self represents only a partial
self. Knowledge of self becomes problematic when the self cannot be
defined outside the other-like-self. For instance, Jim encounters difficulties when he identifies with the fictional characters of "light literature"
(*LJ* 6). Daleski argues, "On the lower deck of the training-ship, as he
lives adventures 'in his mind' [*LJ* 6], he becomes detached not only from
his surroundings but also, as it were, from himself; he 'forgets himself'
[*LJ* 95], giving himself up to his dreams and losing himself in them."[17]
Jim perceives himself in terms of romantic heroism and often daydreams about the heroic exploits he envisions for his future (*LJ* 6, 20,
95). Consequently, his own self becomes subsumed by these fictional
characters.[18] Suresh Raval argues that Jim "relinquishes the truth of
experience, the contingency that threatened his confidence in himself in
Patna, and molds and defines his reality by an unswerving commitment
to the ideal."[19] When he does not measure up to "the ideal," however,
Jim spends the rest of his existence trying to refute the possibility that his
self is different from those fictional characters and in so doing never
gains a knowledge of self. Marlow says, "[I]t is my belief no man ever
understands quite his own artful dodges to escape from the grim shadow
of self-knowledge" (*LJ* 80). In Jim's case, rather than looking elsewhere
for self-knowledge, he makes excuses when he does not live up to the
standards of romance (*LJ* 9, 123). On the other hand, in "Heart of
Darkness," the Russian's complete devotion to real adventures and later
to Kurtz effaces his subjectivity:

If the absolutely pure, uncalculating, unpractical spirit of adventure had ever
ruled a human being, it ruled this be-patched youth. I almost envied him the
possession of this modest and clear flame. It seemed to have consumed all
thought of self so completely, that even while he was talking to you, you forgot
that it was he . . . who had gone through these things. (*Y* 126–27)

The Russian says that he set off alone into the African wilderness to "see
things, gather experience, ideas; enlarge the mind" (*Y* 123). Although his
adventures are not fictional, like Jim's, their source is the same and their

result is the same: they "consumed all thought of self." This behavior continues when he meets Kurtz. Unlike Kurtz's other admirers, the Russian knows of Kurtz's crimes but ignores them, disregarding thoughts of self and running significant risks in remaining near Kurtz. By the time Marlow meets him, the Russian has become so devoted to Kurtz that he excuses Kurtz's excesses, even those that threaten the Russian and run counter to all his social truths. He simply says, "You can't judge Mr. Kurtz as you would an ordinary man. No, no, no!" (*Y* 128). But such an attitude betrays the Russian's lack of self-knowledge in his inability to perceive the world except through Kurtz's eyes.

Kurtz experiences a similar loss of self, but this loss occurs when he transforms the other-*unlike*-self into the other-*like*-self. He allows the Africans to worship him and becomes part of their community, defining himself in terms of the godlike figure they perceive him to be. Kurtz is not a god, though, and as long as he perceives himself as one, he can grow no closer to a knowledge of self. Kurtz would "go off on another ivory hunt; disappear for weeks; forget himself amongst these people – forget himself" (*Y* 129), and he cannot retrieve his self until it is too late. Daleski argues that "having let go to a degree that he has no self left to hold on to, reduced to his own nullity, Kurtz is but the first exemplar in Conrad of the moral nihilism which is the concomitant of such disintegration."[20] Kurtz's rejecting of his western other-like-self, coupled with his inability to extricate himself from his new other-like-self, ultimately destroys him, as he is caught between these two worlds. Kurtz's Intended also loses her self by identifying too closely with the other-like-self. In this case, though, the loss occurs through her love for Kurtz. Her feelings are based upon Kurtz's embodying western ideals of that time. She identifies with these ideals, and, in a sense, when he dies she also ceases to exist. When Marlow meets her over a year after Kurtz's death, she is unchanged since she heard the news. Steve Ressler suggests that Marlow loses his self as well and "in a sense becomes Kurtz,"[21] but I would argue instead that Marlow does what the Intended cannot. Despite remaining loyal to Kurtz, Marlow refuses to let Kurtz subsume him and finally relinquishes Kurtz: "There remained only his memory and his Intended – and I wanted to give that up, too, to the past, in a way – to surrender personally all that remained of him with me" (*Y* 155). Marlow has gained some knowledge of self through his experience with Kurtz, but he also recognizes that Kurtz can only provide partial knowledge of the self, and so he moves beyond the other-like-self in search of self-knowledge.

In contrast, in *Victory* the consumed self takes yet a different and more problematic turn. Lena's life has been so oppressed that she shows little if any individual self: "I am here with no one to care if I make a hole in the water the next chance I get or not" (*V* 78). In this case, her lack of interaction with the other-like-self leaves her without confirmation of self. After communing with Heyst, she says, "Why, I could face him [Shomberg] myself now that I know you care for me... Only it isn't easy to stand up for yourself when you feel there's nothing and nobody at your back" (*V* 85). Initially, Heyst's interest in Lena seems to provide the necessary confirmation of self. Of their relationship, Daleski argues, "Attachment may thus be viewed as leading to the establishment of self, but this would appear to be dependent on a readiness to lose the self."[22] However, I believe that rather than establishing her self, their relationship becomes another means of losing her self; Lena's life has been so bereft of human communion that when she meets Heyst she swings completely in the opposite direction and allows him to subsume her self so that she simply replaces one negated self for another. Her situation is in many ways better with Heyst, but both before and after meeting him she is bereft of self. Once Heyst carries her off, Lena surrenders any self she had to the being Heyst creates, asking Heyst for a new name (*V* 88) and claiming, "[I]t seems to me, somehow, that if you were to stop thinking of me I shouldn't be in the world at all!... I can only be what you think I am" (*V* 187). She further reinforces this sentiment, when Heyst says of Mr. Jones and Ricardo, "Upon my word now that I don't see them, I can hardly believe that those fellows exist" and Lena responds, "When you don't see me, do you believe that I exist?" (*V* 247).[23] In her own mind, she has been transformed into what she believes Heyst thinks her to be, and in the process her self is effaced. Like Lena, Nostromo also replaces one negated self for another, but unlike her, he does not change from a state of isolation to one of communion; instead, Nostromo first perceives himself through a fixed idea and then through a physical object. Royal Roussel remarks that Nostromo "had endeavored to embody his ideal conception of his self in the eyes of those around him."[24] Throughout much of the novel, he submits to the Europeans' fixed idea of him, but their knowledge of Nostromo does not so much represent his subjectivity as it does their own projection onto him. Nevertheless, he accepts this projection, while at the same time losing his self to it. When he finally breaks away from the Europeans' perception of him, he simply replaces the fixed idea with an object. Whereas earlier the Europeans' perception of him had subsumed his

self, during the latter part of the novel the silver subsumes his self
(N 526–27, 561).[25] Ramchander Singh argues, "[T]he power of silver still
compels him [Nostromo] not to betray its concealment because it is now
his own life, having superseded his idea of the self."[26] Warren goes even
further and suggests that Nostromo "commits a kind of suicide: he has
destroyed the self by which he had lived."[27] However, even Nostromo's
original conception of self had been a fiction that "superseded" his true
self, as he tried to conform to the Europeans' perception of him.

In various interactions between self and other-like-self, Conrad demonstrates that knowledge of the self – though always limited – partly
depends upon knowledge of the other-like-self (which is also limited).
Nevertheless, a fine line exists between a relationship that helps to
provide self-knowledge and one that negates the self when the other-
like-self is not recognized as only a partial representation of the self.

III

In Conrad's works, the relationship between western civilization's ideals
and knowledge of the self is often similar to the problem of loss of self to
the other-like-self. For instance, as suggested earlier, throughout the
novel Jim sees himself in light of the fictional other-like-self of romance,
but that creation is a product of society's ideals of conduct. Marlow says
of Jim's predicament, "He was indeed unfortunate, for all his reckless-
ness could not carry him out from under the shadow. There was always
a doubt of his courage. The truth seems to be that it is impossible to lay
the ghost of a fact" (*LJ* 197). Once Jim fails to live up to these ideals, this
"fixed standard of conduct" (*LJ* 50), he can never regain his unqualified
footing in society. These ideals are Jim's reason for being, but they also
create circumstances that make it is impossible for him to be. In the end,
he must leave civilization in order to try to regain his place in it. When
he leads the attack on Sherif Ali's stronghold, he proves himself equal to
the ideals, but even that success is not good enough. Having once failed
is enough to sow seeds of doubt, and despite Marlow's insisting, "It is
not I or the world who remember. It is you – you, who remember"
(*LJ* 236), the world *does* remember. Even Marlow remembers Jim's
failing and betrays this lingering feeling during his visit to Patusan.
Although Marlow affirms Jim has done well there, Jim says, "But all the
same, you wouldn't like to have me aboard your own ship – hey?"
Marlow tries to deflect this accusation by saying, "Confound you! Stop
this." But Jim responds, "Aha! You see" (*LJ* 306). So despite Jim's

successes, Marlow still sees him as falling short of the ideals of conduct.

Ultimately, Jim's inability to shake his memory of the past leads to his downfall; Gentleman Brown intuits precisely this sore spot and establishes a subtle tie between them. In this way, Brown becomes Jim's other-like-self: "And there ran through the rough talk a vein of subtle reference to their common blood, an assumption of common experience; a sickening suggestion of common guilt, of secret knowledge that was like a bond of their minds and of their hearts" (*LJ* 387).[28] Could Jim have simply forgotten the *Patna* incident or even seen his Patusan successes as counterbalancing it, Brown could not have manipulated him, but because the standards of conduct do not allow for failure, Jim is always seeking the impossible and is never able to obtain a knowledge of the self.[29] At the close of the novel, Marlow comments, "He goes away from a living woman to celebrate his pitiless wedding with a shadowy ideal of conduct" (*LJ* 416). Raval says of Jim's final choice, "Instead of giving him moral stability, the ideal has now lost its intersubjective value and become detached and inhuman. It is put in the service of death rather than of life… [H]e has purchased his ideal at a spiritual price that involves nothing less than a dehumanization of that self."[30] Even in death, Jim seeks this ideal at the expense of self, and Marlow's juxtaposing the "living woman" against "shadowy ideal" emphasizes Jim's loss of self to the demands of ideals.

This relationship between western civilization and the self is a consistent concern for Conrad and helps explain Marlow's unusual – perhaps even obsessive – interest in Jim. Marlow often refers to Jim as "one of us," but more than simply that Jim is the other-like-self, Marlow is primarily concerned with society's role in directing Jim's existence because Jim loses his self to it. Marlow says of Jim, "I ought to know the right kind of looks. I would have trusted the deck to that youngster on the strength of a single glance, and gone to sleep with both eyes – and, by Jove! it wouldn't have been safe. There are depths of horror in that thought" (*LJ* 45). These "depths of horror" are not only that Marlow could not safely entrust his ship to Jim's care, but also that Jim seems so much to represent their community and yet lacks a crucial element. Later, even more explicitly, Marlow comments, "[H]e was too much like one of us not to be dangerous" (*LJ* 106). Jim's danger is his incongruous appearance and reality; a flaw exists, "some infernal alloy in his metal" (*LJ* 45), but it is enough to compromise the whole. This conflict disturbs Marlow: "He had no business to look so sound. I thought to myself – well, if this sort can go wrong like that … and I felt as though I could fling down my hat and dance on it from sheer mortification" (*LJ* 40; ellipsis is Conrad's). Douglas Hewitt suggests, "Jim has also raised doubts of the finality of the very standards themselves."[31] And Watt remarks,

Like Brierly, Marlow finds the thought that even someone of "this sort can go wrong like that" (*LJ* 40) deeply disturbing; it means that "not one of us is safe" (*LJ* 43). Inescapably confronted with the exposed vulnerability of the moral guarantee of his whole way of life, Marlow finds all kinds of latent doubts arising about "the sovereign power" [*LJ* 50] of the established code.[32]

Armstrong concurs: "Because this sovereignty [of the standard of conduct] can be counterfeit, it is a convention, not given by divine right."[33] Marlow is afraid that if this "infernal alloy" is a part of someone like Jim – one with the right background and lineage – it could be part of all westerners. If so, then the whole edifice of society's absolutes crumbles as a source for self-knowledge.

Brierly's fate reinforces the implications of Jim's failure because although Jim looks the part, Brierly actually embodies the ideals; some dislike and envy Brierly because of his seeming infallibility. Marlow says of him, "He had never in his life made a mistake, never had an accident, never a mishap, never a check in his steady rise, and he seemed to be one of those lucky fellows who know nothing of indecision, much less of self-mistrust" (*LJ* 57). All agree that Brierly is as close to a living manifestation of the ideal as one can get, and yet he commits suicide when confronted with Jim's failure. It is unclear whether his suicide results from an earlier undisclosed failing of which Jim's case reminds him or whether he simply recognizes that given the right circumstances he also has the capacity to fail. Either way, however, Brierly found himself wanting and would not risk either exposure or failure. Marlow says, "[T]he matter was no doubt of the gravest import, one of those trifles that awaken ideas – start into life some thought with which a man unused to such a companionship finds it impossible to live" (*LJ* 59). But if even Brierly cannot live up to the standards, then who can? Perhaps one could live with absolutes even in light of personal shortcomings, as long as someone can meet those standards, but if no one can meet them, then the standards themselves must be questioned, along with their ability to aid in the knowledge of human subjectivity.

Brierly's position is similar to that of the young captain in "The Secret Sharer," because he recognizes a similarity between himself and one who has violated social codes. According to the facts, Jim acted crimi-

nally by abandoning ship and endangering its passengers, but Jim feels
there was not "a hair's-breadth" (*LJ* 131) between the right and wrong of
the affair.[34] For him, bare facts alone cannot explain the incident's
meaning; certain conditions exist that require an individual rather than
a universal judgment. But for Brierly, the facts *do* explain the affair, and
his only conclusion is Jim's guilt – and his own by affinity. In so doing,
Brierly sides with absolutes, allowing his self to be lost to those universals. Unlike Brierly, though, the young captain in "The Secret Sharer"
identifies with the other-like-self and remains loyal to him rather than to
absolutes. According to the facts, Leggatt, like Jim, has acted criminally
and failed to live up to social ideals. Instead of accepting Captain
Archibold's universal judgment, however, the young captain accepts
Leggatt's individual judgment. For both Jim and Leggatt, circumstances
suggest a necessary relativity as opposed to the absolute standards of the
law. Like Archibold, who is very anxious to give up Leggatt "[t]o the
law" (*TLS* 118), Brierly can only perceive Jim's situation from an absolute perspective. But for the young captain, Archibold's "obscure tenac-
ity on that point [giving up Leggatt to the law] had in it something
incomprehensible and a little awful" (*TLS* 118), and rather than allowing
absolutes to subsume his self, the young captain chooses to side with his
other-like-self. In so doing, he achieves some knowledge of himself.
Despite this discovery, though, the young captain does not allow his self
to be subsumed by Leggatt and says, "I hardly thought of my other self,
now gone from the ship" (*TLS* 142). Once Leggatt leaves, the young
captain is again alone but with added knowledge of himself through
communion with his other-like-self.

As a result of Jim's representative nature, as well as the relationship
between his cowardly act and society's standards, Marlow remarks that
"the knowledge of his [Jim's] weakness – made it a thing of mystery and
terror – like a hint of a destructive fate ready for us all whose youth – in
its day – had resembled his youth" (*LJ* 51). Because Jim represents the
possibility that under certain circumstances any member of the community could fail, his failure becomes a universal rather than an individual
phenomenon:

The occasion was obscure, insignificant – what you will: a lost youngster, one in
a million – but then he was one of us; an incident as completely devoid of
importance as the flooding of an ant-heap, and yet the mystery of his attitude
got hold of me as though he had been an individual in the forefront of his kind,
as if the obscure truth involved were momentous enough to affect mankind's
conception of itself. (*LJ* 93)

However, Jim's situation *is* as important as Marlow believes, because it reveals a "ghost of doubt" (*LJ* 51) about the community's ability to measure up to its ideals. In fact, Marlow argues that no one measures up. After Marlow tells Jewel that Jim will not leave Patusan because "he is not good enough" (*LJ* 318), he adds, "Nobody, nobody is good enough" (*LJ* 319). Marlow experiences "the doubt of the sovereign power enthroned in a fixed standard of conduct" (*LJ* 50) and realizes that society has established unreachable standards of conduct, and yet he is unwilling to abandon them because they are all that holds the community together. Furthermore, these standards are part of the make up of the community members and must be acknowledged as such.

In Conrad's works, two factors problematize the relationship between western civilization and obtaining subjective knowledge. First, western ideals of conduct are impossibilities human beings can never fully embody. Second, failing to recognize human limitations leads to loss of self and the inability to obtain knowledge of human subjectivity. To be subsumed by ideals is not only to lose one's self but also to be subsumed by a standard of conduct whose impossibility makes it illusory. Consequently, although a degree of self-knowledge may be gained through recognition of others (both like and unlike self) and through perception of social values and norms, these can only provide partial knowledge of the self, and to view them as the sole source of subjective knowledge is to risk never obtaining such knowledge. Ultimately then, the self also becomes a primary source for subjective knowledge, both through investigation into its relationship with the other and through investigation into itself.

In "Heart of Darkness," Marlow says of life, "The most you can hope from it is some knowledge of yourself" (*Y* 150), but elsewhere Conrad remarks, "Men have but very little self knowledge."[35] For Conrad, this knowledge of self is important because the existence of the self is the only certainty and the only thing that is uniquely one's own. In *A Personal Record*, he remarks, "[T]he fact is that I have a positive horror of losing even for one moving moment that full possession of myself" (*PR* xix). The self is also something others can only know in part. Just as Marlow argues that knowledge of others is limited for the self, that they are "incomprehensible, wavering, and misty" (*LJ* 180), so also is knowledge of self limited for the other. In "Heart of Darkness," Marlow says, "I don't like work – no man does – but I like what is in the work, – the chance to find yourself. Your own reality – for yourself, not for others – what no other man can ever know. They can only see the mere show, and never can tell what it really means" (*Y* 85). Work helps create the reality of the self by bringing about what is uniquely individual. Responding to the fatigue, danger, or ennui of work, human beings discover their capabilities and can come to some knowledge of themselves. However, self-knowledge is not self-evident; it must be sought out and may never be complete.

Such knowledge is based upon perception of self, but perception can sometimes be at odds with reality, and when that happens self-knowledge is impossible. Jim's situation exhibits just such a disparity: while on the *Patna*, Jim's thoughts

> would be full of valorous deeds: he loved these dreams and the success of his imaginary achievements. They were the best parts of life, its secret truth, its hidden reality. They had a gorgeous virility, the charm of vagueness, they passed before him with a heroic tread; they carried his soul away with them and made it drunk with the divine philtre of an unbounded confidence in itself. (*LJ* 20)

Despite this perception of himself, during Jim's schooldays' rescue incident and during the *Patna* crisis, he fails to act according to that perception. Conrad emphasizes the disparity between perception and reality by presenting the schooldays' rescue immediately after Jim's daydreams about performing heroic deeds (*LJ* 6). Jim, however, refuses to accept the possibility that his perception of self is false and instead locates blame for each missed opportunity on things beyond his control.[36] After the first incident, "He felt angry with the brutal tumult of earth and sky for taking him unawares and checking unfairly a generous readiness for narrow escapes" (*LJ* 9), while after the *Patna* affair, he says of his fellow officers, "It was their doing as plainly as if they had reached up with a boat-hook and pulled me over" (*LJ* 123). But Fate and the *Patna*'s crew do not cause Jim to act other than his perception of self. Instead, Jim *is* other than his perception. In fact, Jim's perception is not really a perception at all; imagination rather than experience forms its basis. His perception is a priori not a posteriori. Marlow identifies this contradiction:

> [W]hen yet very young, he became chief mate of a fine ship, without ever having been tested by those events of the sea that show in the light of day the inner worth of a man, the edge of his temper, and the fibre of his stuff; that reveal the quality of his resistance and the secret truth of his pretences, not only to others but also to himself. (*LJ* 10)

Because of his inexperience, Jim has nothing to compare to the perception he acquires from his reading and incorrectly assumes imagination can fill the void. So after ascribing blame elsewhere for his failures, Jim then confidently reasserts his self-perception and never relinquishes it, feeling that if he can have just one more chance he can show society that his perception of self is consistent with his actuality of self, and thus his illusory perception prevents him from ever obtaining self-knowledge.

On the other hand, the young captain in "The Secret Sharer" finds himself in a similar situation but responds very differently. Like Jim, he is "untried as yet by a position of the fullest responsibility" (*TLS* 93) and wonders "how far I should turn out faithful to that ideal conception of one's own personality every man sets up for himself secretly" (*TLS* 94). But while the young captain wonders whether he will act according to his imagination, Jim simply assumes he will. The young captain's self-assurance comes only after being tested, whereas Jim begins self-assured – even though he had not first experienced crisis situations and then projected a perception of self based upon those experiences.[37] Instead, Jim sought to construct a reality from society's expectations and then fit himself into that mold. Perhaps he simply could have ignored the discrepancy between his self and the absolute standards he perceives, as Marlow says, "I have come across a man or two who could wink at their familiar shades" (*LJ* 197). But for Conrad such individuals simply exist in ignorance; their attitude, according to J. Hillis Miller, is contrary to Conrad's aim "to destroy in the reader his bondage to illusion, and to give him a glimpse of the truth, however dark and disquieting."[38] Those who "wink at their familiar shades" deceive themselves as to the true nature of the self and of society's absolutes, and they remain as ignorant of the self as those who lose their self to another entity.

Even true knowledge of self, however, is not without pitfalls; Guerard summarizes Conrad's views on the subject: "The soul left to its own devices scarcely bears examination, though examine it we must."[39] Although Conrad believes knowledge of self is positive, something for which to strive, he also believes its revelations to be disturbing. In fact, Conrad wrote to his aunt, "One must drag the ball and chain of one's selfhood to the end."[40] Similarly, Marlow refers to "the grim shadow of self-knowledge" (*LJ* 80), and of himself in particular, he says, '[A]s though – God help me! – I didn't have enough confidential information about myself to harrow my own soul till the end of my appointed time" (*LJ* 34). Such knowledge is disturbing because it reveals that none can bear the light of western ideals and because it is often tied to the indeterminacy of human existence and of civilization itself. Society

establishes ideals, but for Conrad if human beings grow in knowledge
of themselves, they discover that a human being "is not a masterpiece"
(*LJ* 208) and that western ideals are at odds with human experience;
such individuals learn not only of their own selves, in all their weak-
nesses and limitations, but also that their system of beliefs is at odds with
reality. Kurtz provides perhaps the best example of such realizations
through self-knowledge; Marlow remarks, "Did he live his life again in
every detail of desire, temptation, and surrender during that supreme
moment of complete knowledge? He cried in a whisper at some image,
at some vision – he cried out twice, a cry that was no more than a breath
– 'The horror! The horror!'" (*Y* 149). The difference between Kurtz and
Jim then is that Kurtz gains some knowledge of self – however fleeting –
whereas Jim never does. Seemingly paradoxical, Marlow refers to
Kurtz's revelation as both "a moral victory" and "the appalling face of a
glimpsed truth" (*Y* 151), but this is exactly Conrad's attitude toward
knowledge of the self. Kurtz's experience is "a moral victory" because
he finally achieves a degree of self-knowledge (even though only momentarily), but it is also "the appalling face of a glimpsed truth" because
that knowledge reveals his own nature and that of the ideals he had
accepted – as well as the contrast between his perception and reality.
For Conrad, this same relationship exists for all human beings: knowledge of self is an achievement, but it comes at the cost of discovering
truths that may be "appalling."

Even more troubling than the truth that knowledge of self may reveal,
such knowledge is also uncertain. As knowledge of subjects through
knowledge of others is uncertain, so also is knowledge of subjects
through knowledge of self. Marlow remarks that he cannot say that he
had ever seen Jim distinctly. He goes on to say that "it seemed to me that
the less I understood the more I was bound to him in the name of that
doubt which is the inseparable part of our knowledge. I did not know so
much more about myself" (*LJ* 221).[41] Similarly, Marlow says Jim was
not "clear to me. He was not clear. And there is a suspicion he was not
clear to himself either" (*LJ* 177). In each passage, both self and other are
unclear because doubt always exists about subjective knowledge. And
although knowledge of self may be more certain than knowledge of
others, it may also be incomplete and is never guaranteed. If for no
other reason then, since self-knowledge comes partly from knowledge of
others as well as knowledge of communal customs and ideas, the
uncertainty Marlow experiences concerning these sources influences his
knowledge of self as well. But Conrad's doubts concerning our ability to

achieve complete self-knowledge go beyond the uncertainty of social beliefs and knowledge of others; he wonders even whether one can fully know that part of the self not determined by communal ideals and other human beings.

As he investigates impressionist perception, Conrad comes to similar conclusions concerning knowledge of both objects and subjects: that knowledge is relative and tied to the individuality of the human consciousness. Even that which is most familiar to us – our own self – remains shifting and opaque. Raval argues, "Clarity, self-understanding – the goals of an epistemology of the self – are thus put beyond the possibility of attainment."[42] And yet, I would argue that through perception of self and perception of the interaction between self and other Conrad holds out the possibility that human beings can gain a degree of subjective knowledge if they are willing to accept the possible uncertainty and unsettling results of their search.

CHAPTER 4

"Sudden holes" in time: the epistemology of temporality

"Eternity is a damned hole. It's time that you need."

The Secret Agent

Throughout his works, Conrad is concerned with various objects of consciousness. In addition to events, physical objects, and human subjects, he also investigates the human experience of time and its relationship to knowledge of the external world. J. M. Kertzer argues, "For Conrad, time is always in some sense 'human time'... The world empty of human activity and judgment is a timeless void."[1] As was true of objects, subjects, and events, Conrad identifies a gap between objectivity and subjectivity when experiencing time because time can only be accessed through human consciousness.[2] Using impressionist techniques, Conrad considers how human beings experience time in an individual and contextualized manner. Furthermore, he inquires into the relationship between western civilization and the human experience of time. In his inquiry, Conrad considers three different temporal representations: human time, mechanical time, and narrative time. He investigates each of these – and more important how they interrelate. In particular, the relationship between human time and mechanical time attracts much of his attention. Conrad associates human time with the primitive and mechanical time with the civilized, and as is true of primitive and civilized perception in general, primitive time is time experienced without cultural influence, while civilized time is time experienced with cultural influence.

I

Human time appears in two forms in Conrad's works: personal time and cyclical time, and both blur the boundaries between subject, time, and context. Personal time is time as human beings experience it. For

Conrad, regardless of how objective time may be in essence, human beings cannot experience it as such. They never experience objective, regularized time; instead time may speed up, slow down, move forward, backward, or even stop, but however it appears its common feature is that it proceeds irregularly. With personal time, the context of physical setting and surrounding events influences how time is experienced, but human subjectivity itself also provides a crucial context for its experience. In this way, the distinctions between time and the person experiencing it blur.

The Secret Agent presents several examples of personal time as part of Conrad's general investigation into the relationship between human and mechanical time in the novel. After murdering her husband, Winnie decides that drowning is better than hanging and determines to throw herself into the Thames. On the way, a few minutes on the clock lengthen into many hours in her mind: "'I'll never get there before morning,' she thought. The fear of death paralysed her efforts to escape the gallows. It seemed to her she had been staggering in that street for hours. 'I'll never get there,' she thought" (*SA* 203; see also *SL* 106). Adriaan de Lange argues, "From the earliest novels, through to *Suspense*, the fiction invariably deals with a bewilderment caused by discontinuities in the experience of space and time."[3] Winnie experiences such bewilderment as she staggers toward the Thames and experiences personal time and space. Despite the shortness of the objective time and distance involved, both seem endless because the context of Winnie's fear of death causes time to slow and space to elongate. Were the context to differ, her temporal and spatial experience would also differ.

Shortly before this event, Winnie has a similar experience with time slowed and finds it equally disconcerting: she "looked up mechanically at the clock. She thought it must have stopped. She could not believe that only two minutes had passed since she had looked at it last. Of course not. It had been stopped all the time. As a matter of fact, only three minutes had elapsed" (*SA* 202). Winnie cannot accept the idea of personal time and instead believes the clock has stopped because she "seemed to have heard or read that clocks and watches always stopped at the moment of murder for the undoing of the murderer" (*SA* 202). For Winnie, Verloc's murder has taken a long time, but when the clock registers a lapse of only three minutes she realizes something is amiss. Winnie attributes the nonregularized experience of human time to the one aberration she can identify in the normal fabric of life: Verloc's murder. Instead of recognizing human time as subjective, she sees her crime affecting time. In a sense, her crime does affect time; however, it does not affect mechanical time but rather human time. In the aftermath of her discoveries about Stevie's death and her murder of Verloc, Winnie's despair, anger, and grief merge with the time in which they occur, and she experiences time moving much more slowly than it does on the clock.

Chief Inspector Heat experiences an unusually graphic discrepancy between personal and mechanical time when he places himself into Stevie's consciousness and imagines Stevie's temporal experience at the moment he was blown to pieces:

The man . . . had died instantaneously; and yet it seemed impossible to believe that a human body could have reached that state of disintegration without passing through the pangs of inconceivable agony . . . Chief Inspector Heat rose . . . above the vulgar conception of time. Instantaneous! He remembered all he had ever read in popular publications of long and terrifying dreams dreamed in the instant of waking; of the whole past life lived with frightful intensity by a drowning man as his doomed head bobs up, streaming, for the last time. The inexplicable mysteries of conscious existence beset Chief Inspector Heat till he evolved a horrible notion that ages of atrocious pain and mental torture could be contained between two successive winks of an eye. (*SA* 71)

From this scene, Heat realizes the existence of both human time and mechanical time – and the difference between them. In mechanical time ("the vulgar conception of time"), only "two successive winks of an eye" elapse, but in human time "ages of atrocious pain and mental torture" pass. As Heat imagines himself in Stevie's place, he experiences an eternity compressed into a moment. He knows the objective temporal interval for the explosion was instantaneous, but he also knows personal time cannot be synchronized with mechanical time. Unlike Winnie's experience in which her own psychology provides the context that alters her perception, the physical context of Stevie's scattered body in addition to Heat's own subjectivity alter his perception of time, and so he comes to believe that such complete destruction of the human form cannot occur except through extended human suffering.

Elsewhere, an even more striking example of personal time occurs, as Conrad demonstrates not only the human inability to synchronize personal time with mechanical time but also with the personal time of others. During Verloc's death scene, his personal time is at odds with mechanical time and with Winnie's personal time, but in this case time does not simply slow down or speed up but actually modulates between the two with an irregular and unpredictable movement: Winnie's movements "were leisurely enough for Mr. Verloc to elaborate a plan of defence involving a dash behind the table, and the felling of the woman to the ground with a heavy wooden chair. But they were not leisurely enough to allow Mr. Verloc the time to move either hand or foot. The knife was already planted in his breast" (*SA* 197). Time first "leisurely" slows for Verloc so that he has ample time to subdue Winnie; it then accelerates at the moment of the blow, which happens so quickly that time seems to jump directly from past to future, never stopping in the present. Before Verloc can prevent Winnie's future attack, it has already occurred in the past. Because of his individual point of view, Verloc's apprehension of the time required to strike the blow is at odds with what actually occurs. In essence, Verloc and Winnie move at different rates of time in this scene. Verloc can neither synchronize the time he experiences with the clock's time nor with Winnie's, and this inability causes his death.[4]

Conrad further emphasizes the irregularity of personal time in this scene by setting it against the backdrop of mechanical time. He links and then contrasts the flow of Verloc's blood with the flow of mechanical time:

> Mrs. Verloc raised her head slowly and looked at the clock with inquiring mistrust. She had become aware of a ticking sound in the room. It grew upon her ear, while she remembered clearly that the clock on the wall was silent, had no audible tick. What did it mean by beginning to tick so loudly all of a sudden? ... Dark drops fell on the floorcloth one after another, with a sound of ticking growing fast and furious like the pulse of an insane clock. At its highest speed this ticking changed into a continuous sound of trickling... It was a trickle, dark, swift, thin... Blood! (*SA* 198–99; final ellipsis is Conrad's)

Winnie confounds the clock's objective, mechanical ticking with the irregular flow of lifeblood out of Verloc's body. However, the ticking of Verloc's blood only marginally resembles that of the clock. The regular intervals between the ticks of the clock contrast with the irregular intervals between the ticks of the dripping blood, which begin slowly and then speed up "like the pulse of an insane clock." As the flow of blood grows stronger, the distinct ticks become indistinguishable from one another, finally growing into a seamless flow. In this image, Conrad emphasizes human temporal irregularity in the dripping blood as it moves from slow ticks to an unbroken flow, and then contrasts this movement with the regular, segmented progression of mechanical time. Furthermore, as the dripping blood evolves into a flow, it becomes like the flow of blood through Verloc's body and resembles the seamless flow of time human beings experience in contrast to the clock's segmented time. In a sense, the segmented, dripping blood that signifies Verloc's death is associated with mechanical time and hence suggests its nonhuman, nonliving qualities while the nonsegmented flow of blood that coursed through Verloc's body before his death is associated with human time and implies its human, living qualities. Conrad further underscores the fact that the circumstances surrounding Verloc's death are only accessed through the medium of human consciousness by presenting this scene as an example of primitive perception. Winnie first perceives a clock ticking but only afterwards organizes the sound into dripping blood as she recognizes the discrepancy between the regularity of a clock's ticking and the irregularity of the ticking she hears.

Personal time appears in Conrad's other works as well. In *Under Western Eyes*, for instance, Razumov experiences personal time. Between the time Haldin leaves Razumov's room and the time appointed for his capture, time slows for Razumov: "Razumov stood looking down at the little white dial. It wanted yet three minutes to midnight. He took the watch into his hand fumblingly. 'Slow,' he muttered, and a strange fit of nervelessness came over him" (*UWE* 63–64). Like Winnie, Razumov wants to attribute the discrepancy between personal time and clock time to some kind of mechanical failure, but when the clock tolls one after what seems an eternity (*UWE* 64–65), it becomes clear that the discrepancy was merely Razumov's personal experience of time resulting from his agitation over the Haldin affair; Razumov's anticipating Haldin's capture caused time to slow for him. As he did in *The Secret Agent*, Conrad again juxtaposes human time against the backdrop of mechanical time by causing Razumov to question the time he experiences in contrast to the time registered on his watch.

The narrator of *The Nigger of the "Narcissus"* experiences the opposite effect. As they sail out to sea, he remarks, "The smiling greatness of the sea dwarfed the extent of time. The days raced after one another, brilliant and quick like the flashes of a lighthouse, and the nights, eventful and short, resembled fleeting dreams" (*NN* 30). For the narrator, time moves faster than the movement of the clock. Unlike Razumov or Winnie, who experience time passing infinitely more slowly than the time registered on the clock, the narrator experiences time passing remarkably quickly. In this case, though, the context of personal past does not so much affect the way the narrator experiences time as much as physical context does. For him, the vastness of the sea "dwarfed the extent of time." In this scene, time and space are closely connected. As the narrator looks out over the seemingly endless and unsegmented expanse of water, the segmentation of time through the appearance of days and nights seems very short. In a sense, the narrator experiences time in its almost unsegmented form, as an endless expanse of space is linked to an infinite duration of time.

Early in *Lord Jim*, discrepancies between personal time and mechanical time constantly beset Jim. In the rescue at school and the *Patna* incident, Jim is each time "too late" (*LJ* 8). At these moments, he cannot synchronize his personal time with either mechanical time or the time that others experience. Robert Jacobs suggests that on the *Patna* Jim "exists in a different time from detail external to himself – the action of the rust-flake has been fantastically speeded up."[5] Rust usually flakes off bulkheads gradually, but in this case it is as if Jim views a movie in fast forward. Events take him unawares and initially move faster than he perceives them to be moving. At the same time, though, a curious reversal soon occurs. The initial accident and the bulging bulkhead happen more quickly than Jim can respond to them, but later the situation reverses. Jim complains that

there was no time. No time! No time!... Before he could shout three words, or make three steps, he would be floundering in a sea whitened awfully by the desperate struggles of human beings, clamorous with the distress of cries for help... He imagined what would happen perfectly; ... he went through it to the very last harrowing detail. (*LJ* 86; see also 90)

Unlike Winnie and Razumov, here Jim perceives events to be moving faster than they actually are. Despite his assertion otherwise, in fact there *was* time – essentially all the time in the world because the bulkhead holds and the *Patna* never does sink. However, Jim's personal time speeds up in the context of the ensuing panic he imagines, and he cannot keep up with the speed with which events seem to occur. Like Winnie and Razumov, Jim attributes the time discrepancy to outside forces: "He had been taken unawares... Everything had betrayed him! He had been tricked into that sort of high-minded resignation which prevented him lifting as much as his little finger" (*LJ* 95). Jim thinks fate causes his failing rather than the gap between human and mechanical time. As a result, he always feels that if he can change forces outside himself, the consequences will also change, and although perhaps partly true, he fails to see that his own subjectivity is a major factor in the outcome of events.

In the end, Jim's reasoning becomes disastrous, because he thinks he can repair the damage with another chance. So Jim rejects the opportunity to move on with his life, leaving the *Patna* incident behind, and

instead goes to Patusan to gain control over his existence. Jacobs argues,
"[I]n Patusan, where Jim is commanded to 'fix the clock,' he has control
[over time]."[6] But Jim's control is short lived, and his inability to fully
control time leads directly to his death. Initially, Patusan is a timeless
place, and this suits Jim's purpose well; as Kertzer suggests, Jim seeks "to
escape from time altogether by retreating into the timeless oblivion of
the East."[7] Conrad reinforces this idea of Patusan's timelessness with the
image of Tunku Allang's broken clock, signifying that western chronological time does not function in Patusan. Essentially isolated from
western influence, Patusan remains in cyclical time – time measured
only by changes in the sun, moon, and seasons – and in this state of
nonlinear time Jim escapes his past for a while. Unfortunately, he can
only partly relinquish linear time, and precisely because he allows
Gentleman Brown to draw him back into linear time (where Jim's
shameful past returns to haunt him), his destruction becomes complete.
He believes his death atones for abandoning the *Patna*, and the contrast
between the time sequences of these events reinforces his view. When
Jim jumps ship, time appears to speed up for him, leaping directly from
past to future, as it had for Verloc. Jim says, "I had jumped . . . It seems"
(*LJ* 111; ellipsis is Conrad's). To Jim, he is standing on the deck and then
suddenly in the lifeboat. He experiences no intervening moment. In his
death, however, Jim supplies those missing moments by experiencing
time slowed. His entire death scene appears in slow motion and for him
reverses the movement of his earlier failing (*LJ* 415–16). Nevertheless,
Marlow leaves the reader with the distinct impression that Jim remains
convinced that outside forces and not his own subjectivity have caused
the temporal discrepancies he experiences.

   Besides time slowed and time sped up, characters may also experience time stopped, either momentarily or for an extended period. In
"The Inn of the Two Witches," the narrator remarks,

A moment of suspended animation followed Byrne's words. The sorceress with
the spoon ceased stirring the mess in the iron pot, the very trembling of the
other's head stopped for the space of a breath. In this infinitesimal fraction of a
second Byrne had the sense of being really on his quest, of having reached the
turn of the path. (*WT* 148)

Time stops briefly at this point of revelation for Byrne before continuing
its flow, but during that instant when all else around him seems to stop,
Byrne's stream of consciousness continues to function as he takes in the
entire scene before a moment passes.

While Byrne experiences time stopped momentarily, Razumov experiences it stopped for an extended period. After Haldin's arrival and betrayal, Razumov remains fixed at the moment of betrayal. In fact, Razumov's watch becomes symbolic of this phenomenon:

[T]he watch and chain slipped through his fingers in an instant and fell on the floor. He was so startled that he nearly fell himself. When at last he regained enough confidence in his limbs to stoop for it he held it to his ear at once. After a while he growled – "Stopped," and paused for quite a long time before he muttered sourly – "It's done." (*UWE* 64)

Conrad yokes together time and betrayal by juxtaposing the stopped watch with Razumov's comment "It's done" and by so doing again contrasts human and mechanical time. Although other characters experience time continuing to flow, for Razumov it remains stopped.[8] Time is altered for him as it was for Winnie because of a significant event. For Winnie, it is Verloc's murder; for Razumov, it is Haldin's betrayal. Later, when the moment of Haldin's betrayal seems to appear again for Razumov, he moves to break out of his frozen existence, in a sense cycling back to the moment of betrayal:

[H]e sat down with the watch before him. He could have gone out at once, but the hour had not struck yet. The hour would be midnight. There was no reason for that choice except that the facts and the words of a certain evening in his past were timing his conduct in the present . . . He was the puppet of his past, because at the very stroke of midnight he jumped up and ran swiftly downstairs. (*UWE* 362)

Midnight is the moment of betrayal and also the moment of restitution when Razumov confesses his crime. He wishes to alter the events that have stopped time, and once he confesses and exorcises the ghost of Haldin's betrayal, time then begins to flow again. Razumov does not care how heavy the recompense is for his confession because any life is better than the frozen death in which he now exists. For him, the fact that betrayal and expiation occur at midnight is significant because each event is the gateway into a new existence. Just as midnight signifies the shift from one day to another, from night to day, from darkness to light, Razumov's frozen existence begins to thaw ever so slightly in the warmth of a new day. Although crippled because of his confession and its aftermath, Razumov welcomes his new existence, in which he can experience time flowing once again and in a sense begin to live once again.

As well as experiencing irregularity in the movement of personal time, certain characters appear outside time altogether. In *The Secret*

Agent, Stevie exists outside time. William Bysshe Stein refers to his "atemporality,"[9] and the narrator of *The Secret Agent* remarks, "Stevie usually established himself of an evening with paper and pencil for the pastime of drawing those coruscations of innumerable circles suggesting chaos and eternity" (*SA* 179). Because of his diminished abilities, Stevie does not respond to time as do the other characters and instead only perceives its movement through recognizable cycles. In *A Personal Record*, Conrad also suggests that one of his examining officers existed outside time: "'This ancient person,' I said to myself, terrified, 'is so near his grave that he must have lost all notion of time. He is considering this examination in terms of eternity'" (*PR* 113). In this instance, the man's nearness to death removes him from time. His future appears outside time, and he perceives time in terms of an eternity without beginning or end. Both Stevie and the examining officer exist in part outside society and hence outside time as well. This separation from society emphasizes the role both cultural and personal context play in the experience of time.

Ultimately, regardless of how much attention human beings pay to the regular intervals of mechanical time, their experience will always be relative and individual. Even one as attentive to mechanical time as Sir Ethelred can only experience time through his own subjective point of view. During his interview with the Assistant Commissioner, Sir Ethelred "gave a haughty oblique stare to the ponderous marble time piece with the sly, feeble tick. The gilt hands had taken the opportunity to steal through no less than five and twenty minutes behind his back" (*SA* 111). Despite his wish otherwise, time proceeds faster than Sir Ethelred experiences it, and he is annoyed that he cannot synchronize his individual time with the clock's universal time. His inability to synchronize personal time with mechanical time, though, is simply the same inability all human beings experience. For Conrad, each of these conflicts between personal and mechanical time shows that the human experience of time is at odds with the movement of the clock.[10]

Along with personal time, Conrad investigates cyclical time as a form of human time. Cyclical time is a temporal flow with only the cycles of nature as demarcations. In some ways, cyclical time is even more dependent upon context than personal time, since not only is human subjectivity a context but so also is the physical space in which the temporal experience occurs. In addition to human subjectivity, heavenly bodies, seasonal changes, and physical setting influence the experience of time, and in this way, space contextualizes time as the two intersect. For instance, in "Heart of Darkness," Marlow remarks, "Going up that river was like travelling back to the earliest beginnings of the world" (*Υ* 92) and "We were wanderers on a prehistoric earth, on an earth that wore the aspect of an unknown planet" (*Υ* 95; see also 96, 103). Time and space merge in this setting as the unbroken expanse of wilderness and the unceasing flow of time join in presenting an unsegmented whole, untouched and undivided by civilization. Primitive time is linked to primitive space as it were, and the setting contextualizes the experience by determining the nature of the time that Marlow encounters; for Marlow, time cycles back upon itself rather than moving forward chronologically. Elsewhere, as Marlow traveled down the African coast, he experienced cyclical time even more fully: "Every day the coast looked the same, as though we had not moved" (*Υ* 61). Marlow links space and time as the cyclicality of time and space converge. In this case, not only the primitive setting but also its seemingly unchanging appearance present a homogeneity of time and space, making it impossible to extricate time from its context. Furthermore, the sameness or seamlessness of space reinforces the seamless flow of time. Just as space here holds none of the artificial boundaries of civilized activity – houses, streets, walls, and so forth – that mark civilized space, Marlow experiences time without the demarcations of hours, minutes, and seconds that form western linear time.

Lord Jim and *The Shadow Line* include similar incidents, each with variations on cyclical time. In *Lord Jim*, the narrator comments on the *Patna*'s journey:

Every morning the sun, as if keeping pace in his revolutions with the progress of the pilgrimage, emerged with a silent burst of light exactly at the same distance astern of the ship, caught up with her at noon . . . glided past on his descent, and sank mysteriously into the sea evening after evening, preserving the same distance ahead of her advancing bows. (*LJ* 16)

The only temporal divisions in this scene are the appearance and disappearance of the sun, but even in these distinctions a sense of seamless flux exists as one day exactly resembles another so that the cyclical nature of time merges into an unending flow. Even more than in "Heart of Darkness," Conrad links time here with the context of space. Every day the ocean looks the same, and without the backdrop of the sun's movement, the characters cannot distinguish one day from another. In this case, those on the *Patna* are even further removed from civilized space than was Marlow traveling down the African coast. On the open ocean, with no land in sight, every space of the ocean appears exactly the same.[11] Distinguishing one part of space from another is impossible, so that space becomes an unbroken expanse, a homogenous entity without segmentation. Such a setting serves as a particularly apt context for the passengers' and crew's experience with cyclical time. The very nature of the water itself, its fluidity that so successfully resists segmentation, becomes analogous to the homogenous nature of cyclical time, which also resists segmentation, and even with the sun's cycle, the ocean's expanse looks the same, as if the same day appears over and over again.[12]

In *The Shadow Line*, the narrator experiences cyclical time as the ship languishes in the dead calm: "[T]he nights and the days wheel over us in succession, whether long or short, who can say? All sense of time is lost in the monotony of expectation, of hope, and of desire" (*SL* 97). As with other instances of cyclical time, time and space converge in the narrator's experience; in this instance, however, the reappearance of the physical context emphasizes the tie between time and space and the homogeneity of the two: "The Island of Koh-ring ... seemed to be the centre of the fatal circle. It seemed impossible to get away from it. Day after day it remained in sight" (*SL* 84). The narrator expects a linear movement of time, which he associates with physical progress on his journey through space. But Koh-ring's continual reappearance forces the narrator out of his culturally determined expectations of chronological time, and he experiences cyclical time instead. Koh-ring's continual reappearance represents an essentially seamless flow of experience. The narrator links the unchanged landscape to his unbroken temporal experience. Each morning when he sees Koh-ring again, time cycles back upon itself. The narrator also hints at another important aspect of human experience with time: the inability to measure time accurately without external aids. As was apparent in the incidents in "Heart of Darkness" and *Lord Jim*, without spatial indicators a linear conception of time becomes insupportable.

Another manifestation of cyclical time could be called *the cyclical event*. This phenomenon resembles the seeming repetition of the same day in the scenes from *Lord Jim* and *The Shadow Line*. It also resembles Razumov's reliving the night of Haldin's betrayal on the night of his confession. However, cyclical events are different from other examples of cyclical time in that the same event does not actually repeat or even seem to repeat as such; instead an altogether new event occurs – but one that differs qualitatively little from other similar events. *Nostromo* provides the best example of this phenomenon. Countless revolutions have occurred throughout Costaguana's history, all with the same result: a powerful government that benefits the few while repressing the many. Guerard suggests that Conrad's narrative method itself may emphasize this view of history: "It could be argued, again, that the chronological dislocations and distortions of emphasis may reflect a theory of history as repetitive yet inconsecutive, devoid of reason, refusing to make sense."[13] Although each revolution occurs differently and engages different participants, little substantive difference exists among the individual revolutions. Gareth Jenkins argues, "We have in Part One a miniature version of what the book as a whole, in a series of circular movements, brings out: that the future does not move away from the past but is doomed to repeat it. No real progress is possible; a change is merely an illusion that masks a fundamental reality of disorder."[14] Even the Sulaco secession, seemingly so different from other revolutions, will eventually end the same way. Dr. Monygham comments, "[T]he time approaches when all that the Gould Concession stands for shall weigh as heavily upon the people as the barbarism, cruelty, and misrule of a few years back" (*N* 511). Despite Monygham's general cynicism, his words are in fact prophetic, because at the close of the novel the seeds of yet more revolution have been sown in the quickly growing labor unrest. Jenkins agrees with Monygham and concludes that

however many revolutions there are and no matter how well intentioned the actors are there can be no real change for the better. Even the secessionist revolution, conducted without barbarity or stupidity (the characteristic of most previous revolutions) does not really alter matters, for it will end up as repressive and exploitative as any previous régime.[15]

Hay goes even further, referring to "economic demands which are more inhuman and arbitrary than any human despot of the past."[16] The principal actors, specific battles, and surrounding events change with each new revolution so that each is a different event, but their results so resemble one another that the same period of history seems to occur over and over again, as more remains the same than actually changes.

Despite these examples of cyclical time, for most westerners, nonlinear time seems wrong. In "An Outpost of Progress" and "Heart of Darkness," Conrad contrasts the Africans' conception of time with that of the Europeans. In "An Outpost of Progress," he notes, "Those fellows, having engaged themselves to the Company for six months (without having any idea of a month in particular and only a very faint notion of time in general), had been serving the cause of progress for upwards of two years" (*TU* 100). Using nearly the same language, Marlow remarks in "Heart of Darkness" that the cannibals "had been engaged for six months (I don't think a single one of them had any clear idea of time, as we at the end of countless ages have. They still belonged to the beginnings of time – had no inherited experience to teach them as it were)" (*Y* 103). Marlow argues that the Africans experience a different, nonlinear time because of their lack of a western worldview. "Inherited experience" implies chronological time – not cyclical time, and therefore the Africans' sense of achronological time results from their immediate temporal experience, as opposed to the westerners' experience, which is determined by the cultural artifact of linear time. For the Africans, past, present, and future contain none of the distinctions of western time, and chronological temporal intervals in particular have no meaning.[17] For them, cyclical time is at once arrested and in motion. It has movement, but not simply forward movement; instead, it moves both forward and backward. In a sense, cyclical time is past, present, and future all at once, as it moves away from and then back toward any particular moment.

Cyclical time and personal time are not wholly isolated phenomena in Conrad's works. They intersect and overlap at various points (i.e., *NN* 30), and both demonstrate the uniqueness of human temporal experience. Time as human beings experience it is not a universal phenomenon that can be systematically represented as it is in mechanical time, but rather it is a unique and personal phenomenon. Sue Tyley has suggested that Conrad "demonstrates that time is not a finite quantity capable of being possessed, but that it exists elusively in relation to the quality of its content, and should be apprehended accordingly."[18] Tyley correctly argues that Conrad questions the conventional western perception of time, but it is not so much the content of time that determines its duration; instead Conrad questions the assumption that time is objectifiable or, more important, that human beings can experience it as such. In other words, although time may be objectifiable in essence (as evidenced by clocks and other mechanical measuring devices), human beings cannot experience it as objective, and thus regularized time has little meaning for them. As Kertzer suggests, "It is only in the mind of man that time is given any significant order and hence meaning."[19] Of course, to a certain extent past experience of temporal intervals may aid in future estimates of a given interval, but for Conrad regardless of how often human beings experience a certain time interval, in numerous instances they cannot synchronize their temporal experience with the movement of a clock. The clock's objective movement then becomes irrelevant to human time because one character always experiences an hour's passing more quickly or slowly than does another; they only experience time as it relates to themselves and as they filter it through the context of physical setting, surrounding events, and personal subjectivity.

Furthermore, more than simply being unable to experience regularized time, Conrad's characters experience time in an essentially unmediated manner. In this way, Laforgue's "primitive eye"[20] is not limited to perception of objects and subjects but is characteristic to all impressionist experience. Together with those who experience personal time, those who experience cyclical time in a sense perceive with a primitive eye. The Africans, who live on a "prehistoric earth" (Υ 95) and whom Marlow calls "prehistoric man" (Υ 96), maintain a primitive eye in their experience of time, one that is unmediated by the "countless ages" (Υ 103) of civilization. For those experiencing human time, theirs is the direct experience of time without cultural mediation (in the form of mechanical time), depending solely upon the physical and subjective contexts in which it occurs. Consequently, with the experience of time, even more than with the perception of objects and subjects, the relationship between initial experience and later organization is tenuous. In perceiving objects and subjects, the observer can rely on past experience to bring initially incongruous perceptual incidents in line with organized existence. With time, however, a character can only rely on a glance at the clock, and as such a regularized system for organizing time appears even more arbitrary and even further removed from actual human experience than systems for organizing objects and subjects. As a result, in each appearance of human time in Conrad's works, cultural views come into question. With personal time, human beings cannot synchronize their lived time with the system of mechanical time that civilization has established. With incidents of cyclical time, in addition to the inability to synchronize personal time with mechanical time, western settings are absent. For example, the scenes from "Heart of Darkness" and "An Outpost of Progress" are set in the African wilderness, while those from *Lord Jim*, *The Nigger of the "Narcissus,"* and *The Shadow Line* occur on the open ocean. Removed from society's influence, Conrad's characters perceive time not as a universal phenomenon but rather as an individual one that cannot be extricated from its context. Conrad consistently shows that time for human beings is not the regularity of the metronome but rather the irregularity of human experience. But whether it is the inability to synchronize personal time with mechanical time or the appearance of cyclical time in the absence of a western setting, the point of intersection for all representations of human time is their dislocation from western civilization.

II

In addition to human time, Conrad investigates mechanical time, and as we have seen, he juxtaposes human time and mechanical time and considers their relationship. Mechanical time is objective, linear, segmented, and regular – in contrast to human time, which is subjective, nonlinear, unsegmented, and irregular. In his inquiry into mechanical time, Conrad demonstrates that mechanical time is primarily a system of convenience for social interaction. Human beings cannot actually experience mechanical time because its objective characteristics exist outside human consciousness. If mechanical time were an accurate representation of time for human beings, then time would be objective in that an hour, for example, would have the same duration regardless of when, where, or how it appeared. However, not only does temporal duration vary from person to person, but (as with Marlow's perception of the rivets) even when the same person experiences different instances of a certain time interval, the duration varies as the context varies. (And in a post-Einstein world, even removing human subjectivity, time is determined by the context in which it is experienced and hence is relative and not absolute.)

As was true of human time, mechanical time also appears in two forms: linear time and standard time. Linear time is both chronological and segmented, time divided into regular intervals and moving sequentially, for instance, one hour leading to another hour and then another and so on, and each hour of equal duration. One of the most uniquely western phenomena is linear time. Westerners are so used to this concept that they often accept it as an absolute truth. Western civilization, though, is one of the few cultures that conceives of time as linear. Most developed societies, particularly industrialized nations, have adopted linear time not because of its inherent truth but because of its social convenience. In contrast, most primitive cultures conceive of time as cyclical. *The Secret Agent* provides a good distinction between civilized, mechanical time and primitive, human time. At one end of the spectrum is Sir Ethelred, with his close attention to linear time, and at the other is Stevie, with no conception of linear time at all.[21]

One of the important side effects of linear time is the concept of past, present, and future. When presented as linear and segmented, this concept argues for a time antithetical to human experience because in human time past, present, and future have a very different meaning. For Conrad's characters, past, present, and future retain a kind of cyclical relationship such that time flows less from beginning to middle to end than it does simply durationally. Even cyclical time flows – just not chronologically. Furthermore, in human time, as past, present, and future merge into a single entity, their linearity becomes muted, and a single, unbroken whole emerges. Bergson argues for just such a view of time, suggesting that an unsegmented relationship should exist between past, present, and future such that the past is linked to and influences the present and future, the present contains the past and is influenced by it, and the future contains and is influenced by both present and past. He illustrates this idea with a chiming bell: "I retain each of these successive sensations [the sounds of the chimes] in order to combine it with the others and form a group which reminds me of an air or rhythm which I know: in that case I do not *count* the sounds, I limit myself to gathering, so to speak, the qualitative impression produced by the whole series."[22] If one counts the sounds, then the experience becomes segmented, and each chime is isolated from the others and has no influence on them. If one "gathers" the sounds, however, then each influences and merges with the others and an effect from the whole – not just the parts – results. Similarly, some thinking about linear time presents past, present, and future as relatively separate entities, in which case they become segmented and limited in their interaction. However, as Bergson suggests, past, present, and future – or in other words time itself – is more cumulative than segmented, more of a whole than of parts. In fact, Conrad demonstrates that precisely this attempt to segment past, present, and future proves disastrous for certain characters, who fail to experience time's flow and lock themselves into a particular segment of time. These characters' experience with either past, present, or future expands such that they seem to exist in only one segment of time. By so doing, they impose a state of stasis on time's flow and in this state cease to experience the flow of human time and in a sense cease also to be human.

Of *Under Western Eyes*, Harriet Gilliam argues, "Lacking a personal past which can be made publicly significant and not even knowing who his own father is, Razumov can find meaning in the present only as it becomes a vehicle with which to propel himself into an imagined but far more significant future."[23] As Gilliam points out, in part, Razumov cannot help but live for the future. Since he has little past with which to influence the present, the present is simply an opportunity to create a past upon which to build the future. As a result, as Daleski argues, "Like Jim he [Razumov] gives himself to daydreams of the glories that await him, seeking to fix an identity in ambitious projections of his future. But in the present his hold on himself (as is soon shown) is dependent on his hold on routine."[24] Because Razumov can only in a sense live in the future, when Haldin arrives in Razumov's room and disrupts his future, the effects are extreme. Razumov believes all is lost, the silver medal gone and his life ruined: "[H]is solitary and laborious existence had been destroyed – the only thing he could call his own on this earth" (*UWE* 82). Gilliam argues, "[R]eality resides for him only in his planned future."[25] Had Razumov also been able to exist in the present instead of just in the future, other alternatives might have appeared, but with his future locked into one existence, Haldin's arrival disrupts what Razumov believes to be his only course of life. Others who possess a past that merges with present and future can recover from such a blow because various future alternatives can exist, but because of Razumov's particular circumstances Haldin's arrival destroys his present existence by altering his only future. Consequently, his life becomes devoid of meaning, and he embarks on a course of events that can only end in the effectual destruction of his life, notwithstanding his final expiation for Haldin's betrayal.

Stein argues a similar course for Almayer's life.[26] Like Razumov, Almayer's existence is focused almost exclusively on the future: "He absorbed himself in his dream of wealth and power away from this coast where he had dwelt for so many years; forgetting the bitterness of toil and strife in the vision of a great and splendid reward. They would live in Europe, he and his daughter" (*AF* 5). Such a life sharply contrasts with his present and past existence, in which he lives in a squalor that he endures not because he can expect no better but because he is waiting for his imagined future existence. As a result, the present has no meaning for Almayer: "He killed time wandering sadly in the overgrown paths round the house" (*AF* 23). The great house Almayer begins to build (aptly labeled Almayer's Folly) becomes the central symbol of Almayer's foolish expectations for the future because it will never be completed, just as Almayer's imagined future existence will never arrive. When the revolt against the Dutch fails, the search for gold becomes illusory, and Nina leaves with Dain Maroola, Almayer's imagined future also disappears, and without that future in which he has spent his existence, Almayer's life is emptied of meaning. Once that happens, the narrator's comment early in the novel becomes prophetic: Almayer "often envied his near neighbor the Chinaman Jim-Eng, whom he could see stretched on a pile of cool mats – a wooden pillow under his head, an opium pipe in his nerveless fingers" (*AF* 23). Of this passage, Stein argues, "Here Conrad does more than simply foreshadow the resolution of the action. He hints at the only certain cure for modern man's chilling sense of deracination – the extinction of consciousness."[27] At the novel's close, having moved into the ruins of Almayer's Folly, Almayer seeks the oblivion of opium and death to escape the loss of his imagined future (*AF* 151, 153–56).

Perhaps the most striking example of a character who exists solely in the future is Captain Hagberd of "To-morrow." For the captain, his son Harry is always returning "to-morrow" (*T* 248, 250–51, 254, 258–60, 274, 277). The captain has advertised, waited, and hoped for his son's return, and his whole existence is attuned to Harry's return "to-morrow." The front garden is a good example of the captain's focus: "He turned it over and over several times every year, but was not going to plant anything 'just at present'... 'Not till our Harry comes home to-morrow'... Everything was put off in that way, and everything was being prepared likewise for to-morrow" (*T* 250). The narrator refers to the captain's focus on "to-morrow" as "that idea which blinded his mind to truth and probability" (*T* 255). The captain's delusional fixation on the future culminates when his son actually does return, but the captain does not recognize him (*T* 259). His mind has been so turned to the future that he does not even recognize the future when it actually appears in the present, and the story ends with the captain's "trust in an everlasting to-morrow" (*T* 277), a tomorrow that of course can never come.

Other characters also perceive time as segmented, but rather than existing in the future, they exist in the past. Of such characters, Guerard comments, "The typical Conradian protagonist of the early work is haunted by the past and either longs for or dreads the future. Therefore he betrays the present."[28] As discussed earlier, Jim's inability to escape his past leaves him prey to Gentleman Brown and causes Jim's death.

Also, after Razumov's future is destroyed, time stops for him, and instead of living in the future, he then begins living in the past, unable to move from the moment of Haldin's betrayal. Kurtz's Intended also remains frozen in the past. For her, present and future do not exist. Marlow remarks, "It was more than a year since his [Kurtz's] death . . . I perceived she was one of those creatures that are not the playthings of Time. For her he had died only yesterday" (*Y* 157). Rather than the past merging with the present and future, the Intended segments it and isolates it from present and future. She will live forever in the past, as she says, "And now I am unhappy for – for life" (*Y* 160). In *Chance*, de Barral also exists in the past – with disastrous consequences. Robert Hudspeth comments, "To de Barral his trial was only yesterday, to Flora it was deep in the past. De Barral, in being imprisoned, was taken 'out of time.'"[29] Roussel concurs: "[I]n de Barral's time the past seven years constitute only a 'long yesterday' [*C* 357] and, therefore, he has no sense of the passage of time in Flora's world."[30] De Barral cannot move past his trial and imprisonment and therefore cannot recognize the progression of time in Flora's life – her development into a woman, her marriage to Captain Anthony, and the other changes in her life. In a sense, de Barral's life stops with his incarceration, and his inability to escape the past and enter the present with Flora constitutes the primary tragedy of the novel. Similarly, Verloc also exists in the past. He has lived so long with the conception of himself as "the celebrated agent Δ" (*SA* 26) that when Mr. Vladimir abruptly tries to thrust Verloc into the present it proves fatal. Verloc's inability to escape from his past ways of operating ultimately causes the botched attempt on the Greenwich Observatory. He is used to passing secret information, stirring up meetings, infiltrating the enemy camp. He does not perceive himself to be a saboteur, and yet this is precisely what he must become in order to move out of the past and become a secret agent of the present. Verloc's inability to escape the past is most graphically exemplified in his death scene, when he is unable "to move either hand or foot" (*SA* 197) before his wife stabs him. Frozen in the past, he is paralyzed and unable to do anything about present events.

Finally, some characters exist only in the present, isolated from both past and future. Stein argues that this is true, in a sense, of many Asians in Conrad's novels.[31] In part, this becomes Decoud's problem as well; Kertzer refers to Decoud's "loss of past and future."[32] Physically isolated on the Great Isabel, Decoud becomes temporally isolated from past and future, and so his despair appears to have no end since no future exists.

Decoud lives in a perpetual present in which he will remain forever alone on the island. Even the idea of his beloved cannot dispel his despair; neither his past with Antonia nor an imagined future together exist any more, as the present consumes Decoud's past experience and future expectations. The narrator further emphasizes the presentness of Decoud's consciousness by specifically referring to the first day of his time on the island, the third day, the tenth day, and so on. So while the clock's time moves, Decoud's remains fixed in the present moment (*N* 496–501).

The common experience of each of these characters is that past, present, and future are segmented and isolated from each other, and in one manner or another this segmentation leads to either their physical or spiritual destruction. On the other hand, characters who experience time as a seamless flow in which past, present, and future merge and form an unsegmented whole can exist in the world because for Conrad such is a true representation of impressionist time and the way human beings experience it.

Standard time is mechanical time's other manifestation, and just as personal time and cyclical time intersect, so also do linear time and standard time. Their primary point of intersection is their segmentation of time. Westerners perceive time divided into essentially equal, regular, intervals – years, months, weeks, days, hours, minutes, seconds, and so on. Such a system of segmented time is, of course, a social convenience, and since human beings experience time at different rates from one another, synchronizing social interaction would be difficult without a mutually agreed upon outside reference point. A system that objectifies and segments time can overcome the vagaries of human time and aid in coordinating social interaction, but for Conrad the system is still arbitrary, and the fact that there are 24 hours in a day, 60 minutes in an hour, and 60 seconds in a minute is also arbitrary. One turn-of-the-century German reformer, for instance, advocated a day with 100 hours instead of 24.[33] Such a system would make it easier to calculate times, but is inherently no better than a 24-hour day. Both are arbitrary systems that are imposed upon the seamless flow of time and in no way represent actual human temporal experience. In fact, Conrad's characters experience difficulties precisely when they forget or fail to realize that mechanical time is merely a convenience, not an absolute measurement of time.

Besides the fact that human beings cannot experience mechanical time in any effectual way, linear time's segmentation itself reveals the system's shortcomings. Linear time is a construct imposed upon an essentially cyclical (actually elliptical) phenomenon – the rotation of the earth and the orbits of the earth around the sun and the moon around the earth. Again, the boundaries between time and space blur, but unlike the reinforcing effect this blurring has in cyclical time, the opposite effect occurs with linear time in that space undermines and reveals the system's underlying contradictions. Linear time unsuccessfully tries to combine elements of both chronology and cyclicality. In other words, weeks, hours, minutes, and seconds are essentially chronological representations of time, while days, months, and years are cyclical. Relatively speaking, the beginning of one day occurs at the same point in the earth's rotation as the beginning of any other day, as is true of months and years as well (although years are more problematic because they are roughly 364.25 days long), and this unevenness in the number of days in a year or a month points to inherent difficulties in the system of mechanical time. Even more problematic, though, is the attempt to make the cyclicality of years, months, and days into chronology. Linearity cannot accurately represent cyclicality, and so significant difficulties developed because, unlike human time, mechanical time did not adapt to the relationship between space and time. The time intervals of hours, minutes, and seconds were invented relatively long ago, and as long as travel and communication remained slow there was no difficulty with mechanical time (beyond its dislocation from human time). But as the perceived space of the earth began to shrink with the increased speed of transportation and communication, it became possible to travel and communicate faster than the rotation of the earth on its axis.[34] People soon discovered that the same instant was, for example, noon at the Greenwich Meridian and a different time of day in Boston. This effect of space on time was not something mechanical time had anticipated, and the difference of time based upon geographical difference could only lead to confusion for those communicating between two geographical areas or traveling from one area to another; therefore western civilization established standard time in the late nineteenth century in an attempt to universalize the world's temporal experience. The development of standard time would seem to solve the problem of noon occurring in the middle of the day in Greenwich and the middle of the night on the other side of the world – and to an extent it does. Stein, however, argues that the appearance of the Greenwich Observatory in *The Secret Agent* is "A Conradian jest with its own radical implications, the monument to a mathematical abstraction of time and space monitors the clock that super-intends all purposeful activity in the civilised world. The station exists only as a cerebral actuality, by a common agreement among nations to accept the reality of the imaginary line of zero meridian."[35] The decision to use the Greenwich Meridian Observatory as the starting point for standard time was arbitrary. As Stein suggests, the Greenwich Meridian is an "imaginary line" that is not inherently time's zero point but simply "a common agreement among nations"; any other spot on the globe would have served just as well. Even the time zones that the Greenwich Meridian makes possible are merely approximations, arbitrary segments in a seamless experience. In actuality, since the earth is in constant rotation, each individual point on the space of the earth exists in a different time zone, and so although standard time is a better approximation of time across large distances, it remains a system of convenience – not representation. Bender remarks of *The Secret Agent*, "As the Greenwich Observatory stands at the center of this affair, declaring that space and time are permanent, unchanging, univocal, measurable, the story teller renders his tale in remarkably fluid, cinematic time."[36] For Conrad the fact that standard time is universalized and imposed emphasizes its artificiality when compared to the relative and seamless flow of time itself. The Greenwich Observatory then becomes the most appropriate symbol of time in *The Secret Agent*. Its specter hovers over the action of the novel as the ultimate image of civilization and civilized progress. Located at the epicenter of western civilization, it is meant to represent the triumph of mechanical time over human time – to universalize the individual, civilize the primitive, and mechanize the human. Ironically, though, it fails in each of these endeavors, because the dominant and persistent movement of time in the novel (and throughout Conrad's works) is individual, primitive, and ultimately human, and that is the only form of time human beings can actually experience.

III

A major convergence of human time and mechanical time also occurs in Conrad's use of narrative time. In addition to comparing human time and mechanical time by juxtaposing incidents of each (i.e., Razumov experiencing time slowed as he waits for the clock's bell to toll [*UWE* 64–65]), Conrad's impressionist narrative techniques also investigate the relationship between human time and mechanical time. Conrad tries, as Marlow says, to interpret "into slow speech the instantaneous effects of visual impressions" (*LJ* 48), and it is particularly through his temporal narrative techniques that Conrad achieves these effects. Much has been written about Conrad's narrative time, and it is by far the most discussed aspect of time in his works. In fact, along with numerous articles, almost every lengthy study of Conrad's works at least touches upon this aspect of his fiction.[37] Various critics have effectively argued for a variety of purposes for Conrad's distinctive narrative technique. For example, Donald Davidson suggests that Conrad rearranges "events with regard to import rather than chronology";[38] Wendell Harris argues of *Nostromo*'s narration that it evokes "a sense of timelessness";[39] Hudspeth comments concerning *Chance*, "This intricate series of flashbacks deliberately destroys familiar linear chronology from past to present in order to make all of the events in Flora's life contemporaneous";[40] and Joseph Martin writes, "Conrad's boldness in violating the static and diffusive order of linear time enabled him to create a higher order, to build fictional structures in which the central moral experience shaped the plot."[41] These studies (and others) have added much to our understanding of Conrad's narrative technique. Of concern here, though, is the way narrative time interacts with human and mechanical time – and more particularly, how narrative time rejects mechanical time and reinforces human time.

The most discussed aspect of Conrad's narrative technique is its achronology. However, Conrad's impressionist narrative technique actually appears in three forms: achronological narration, multiple narrators, and *in medias res* narration. (These narrative techniques also sometimes combine for even greater effect.) Each technique relates in some way to the problem of time, and each sharply contrasts with traditional narrative methods, which create narrators who exist outside human time. Such narrators rehearse events chronologically and hence belong to the world of mechanical time, and as such they do not represent an actual human speaker but instead a mechanical construction meant to impose order and, in a sense, civilize the uncivilized phenomena of immediate human experience.

Achronological narration is the most distinctive feature of Conrad's narrative techniques. In contrast to traditional fiction, impressionist narrative is nonlinear and represents an individual observer's experience. Achronological narration then relates to human time in two ways: first, because the narrative is nonlinear, it approximates human time and rejects mechanical time, which is always linear in one form or

another; more important, though, achronological narration locates the
narrative at a single point of view and represents the way an individual
encounters phenomena. (Even with multiple narrators, each narrator is
an individual who encounters phenomena individually.) In other words,
human beings do not comprehend all facets of phenomena simultaneously (neither in time nor in space). Rather, as Ford argued, a person
learns certain aspects of a scene from one source and other aspects from
other sources, gathering information from one time and another.⁴² Only
then may the narrator have achieved a greater knowledge of the entire
scene (although Conrad's narrators' knowledge typically remains imperfect). Furthermore, the pieces of a scene are not gathered sequentially. The narrator may discover the conclusion of an event first and
then the beginning – or some other sequence may develop. However,
regardless of the situation, an immediate and simultaneous revelation of
the scene in its entirety never occurs.

Conrad's achronological narrative technique may appear as flashback, direct indirection, or radical dislocation. The flashback technique
he uses in *Almayer's Folly*, "Karain," and some of his early works in
particular is the most traditional (although innovative for its time) of his
achronological techniques. Naturally, Conrad uses this device for exposition, and it is certainly less sophisticated than some of his later techniques. However, Conrad's flashbacks are not as transparent as they
may at first appear; in the flashback, Conrad still works from the same
principle of achronology that shows his narrators gathering information
rather than dispensing knowledge, stumbling as it were through the
darkness of human existence rather than illuminating the way for
others. More than simply serving as a device for exposition, Stein
argues, "The flashback in *Almayer's Folly* intricately mingles the past,
present, and future of the protagonist over a span of five chapters. It
does not simply re-create the past; it gives concrete embodiment to
Almayer's experience *of* time *in* time – his reliving of the past in the
present with his thoughts on the future."⁴³ In this way, Conrad's flashback narratives have the ability to juxtapose past, present, and future, as
well as provide a sense of achronological narrative gathering, and these
aspects are much more important than the flashback's ability to provide
necessary exposition. In essence, Conrad's flashback is a precursor to his
later, more sophisticated narrative techniques of direct indirection and
radical dislocation.

Conrad's narratives of direct indirection are his most subtly achronological, with "Heart of Darkness" as a notable example. Initially,

this story appears to move essentially chronologically. Even though the narrative comes through Marlow and then through the frame narrator, it lacks the temporal dislocations of *Nostromo* or *Chance*, for instance. However, Stein argues, "The pattern of Marlow's recollections in 'The heart of darkness' [*sic*] completely inverts the primary narrator's conception of the stream of history."[44] As Stein suggests, Marlow does seem to reverse history and hence chronology in "Heart of Darkness," as he brings his listeners into a prehistoric world (*Y* 92). More important, though, even during the course of the narrative, as Marlow relates events he often digresses, as he thinks of something that reminds him of something else off the track of the main chronology. In some ways, Conrad's direct indirection anticipates stream-of-consciousness techniques in which narrative flow is determined epistemologically rather than chronologically. Often when looking back through the story for a particular piece of information, the reader has difficulty finding that information because it does not appear at the chronological point one expects. For example, much of Marlow's commentary on women occurs not when the women appear in the story, but rather when something else reminds him about them (i.e., *Y* 115). In this way, Conrad's direct indirection technique imitates an actual storyteller style; as people relate events, they often suddenly remember an important piece of information and then insert it out of sequence. In such a narration, the achronological effect occurs less through the actual shifting of events than through the shifting of the narrator's thoughts; this technique can also have the effect of fracturing the chronological sequencing of events similar to Conrad's more radical temporal dislocations in his later works.

Conrad's radical dislocation of sequence occurs most notably in such works as *Nostromo*, *Chance*, and *Lord Jim*. Jacobs argues that in *Lord Jim* Marlow's method demands that

the ordinary chronological units be rearranged – hence the strange order in which Marlow tells the story, moving backward and forward in time... The effect of such a technique upon a reader is a temporal dislocation akin to Jim's – by means of that awareness the reader is able to perceive the compelling significance of Jim's quite ordinary experience.[45]

Marlow's narrative then forces the reader into Jim's place and allows him or her to experience the time sequences much as Jim does. This association of reader with character is one of the primary goals of impressionist narrative; in effect, the reader enters a character's mind and becomes that character, and such a situation demonstrates the individual experience of objects of consciousness. Similarly, Gilliam notes the contrast between the language teacher's linear time and Razumov's impressionist time:

The language teacher believes he ought to compose a sequentially developed narrative; he even thinks of his relation as having a "straight course" [*UWE* 163]... [W]hatever order his narrative is to display, the language teacher thinks, will have to be "imposed" on it in violation of his espoused principle of sticking to the factually given.[46]

Gilliam then suggests that the language teacher's "repeated apologies [for narrative digressions] serve to signalize the conflict between the linear, future-oriented narrative and the disruptive but abidingly 'true' generalizations."[47] The language teacher tries to organize Razumov's impressionistic narrative, and in his attempt Conrad emphasizes the incongruity of applying mechanical time to human time. Gilliam goes on to argue that "any effort to assert a linear order appear[s] totally absurd... Instead of having a 'straight course' [*UWE* 163], the narrative actually has a circular one."[48] By placing the language teacher's narrative on top of Razumov's, Conrad reveals a significant disparity between traditional narrative and impressionist narrative, and the language teacher's inability to order and systematize Razumov's narrative dramatizes the shortcomings and artificiality of traditional chronological narration as well as traditional systems of mechanical time.

Along with *Lord Jim*, *Under Western Eyes*, *Chance*, and other works, Conrad also employs radical dislocation of narrative time in *The Secret Agent*. In the explosion's initial aftermath, the narrative shifts back and forth between various locations (the pub, police headquarters, Verloc's shop, etc.), as time first moves forward past the explosion and the subsequent discovery of Stevie's remains and then backtracks through the various events leading up to and just after the explosion. Conrad further underscores this temporal impressionism by depicting Winnie's perception of the events. In fact, Winnie's perception becomes a model for the reader's. As noted earlier, she pieces together the events from comments by Chief Inspector Heat and Verloc along with information she overhears from Verloc's conversations with the police. Only after she obtains information from various sources at different times and locations and then gathers this information together does she gradually come to know most of what has occurred. R. W. Stallman argues that *The Secret Agent*'s chronology is actually cyclical: "As the drama ends where it began, the final scene duplicating in setting and in method of presentation the scene in Chapter IV which initiates the entire action,

The Secret Agent is designed in circular form."[49] But whether cyclically disjointed or more randomly disjointed, the novel's narrative method is achronological, and Conrad's use of achronological narrative technique is particularly powerful in this novel because so much of *The Secret Agent* is taken up with the problem of time. The radical dislocation of narrative time in the novel is one more example of human time consistently asserting its priority over mechanical time, despite the shadow the Greenwich Meridian Observatory casts over the action of the novel.

Besides achronological narration, Conrad's use of multiple narrators also affects his representation of time. As discussed earlier, the technique of multiple narrators has more to do with Conrad's presenting of differing points of view (and thus demonstrating the individuality of objects of consciousness) than it does with the problem of time itself, but a side effect of differing points of view is that each narrator encounters an event at a different point in time and at a different point in the course of the event itself. For instance, in *Lord Jim*, Marlow encounters Jim's story before his listeners do. In addition, Gentleman Brown narrates only some of the later events of Jim's life, while Egström (one of Jim's employers after the *Patna* incident) can only narrate events earlier in Jim's life. As a result of Conrad's multiple narrators technique, chronological narration becomes all but impossible because of the limited knowledge each narrator brings to the narrative and the differing points at which the narrators enter the action of the narrative. Furthermore, this technique emphasizes individual point of view and thus reinforces human time and resists traditional narrative time sequences and hence mechanical time as well.

Finally, again as noted earlier, *in medias res* narrative is another form of impressionist narration, and like Conrad's other impressionist narrative techniques, *in medias res* narrative reinforces human time. Conrad's "The Brute" is the most striking example of impressionist *in medias res*, but he also employs this technique elsewhere effectively, for instance, in "Karain." The primary purpose of this technique is to force the reader into the place of the narrator and thereby discover information at the same moment the narrator does. This technique also takes parts of the two above methods; impressionist *in medias res* narrative emphasizes individual point of view, as does Conrad's multiple narrator technique, but it also emphasizes achronology because rather than experiencing an event at the beginning, both the narrator and the reader enter the scene in mid-flow. Like achronological narration, they must then gather together previous events and other pertinent information to make greater sense of the work's opening scene and its relationship to the rest of the action.

By employing impressionist narrative techniques, Conrad's fiction imitates the effects of human time on his narrators, characters, and readers. In this way, narrative form reinforces narrative content, and the result imitates actual human interaction with objects of consciousness. Then, not only do cyclical time and the subjective experience of personal time embody Conrad's impressionist theory, but the narrative method itself embraces temporal relativity and rejects temporal universality. Conrad sees chronological narration as an arbitrary system imposed upon the flow of phenomena just as chronological time is artificially imposed upon the achronological human temporal experience.

IV

Ultimately, Conrad's use of human time, mechanical time, and narrative time all point to a time that is individual and contextualized. At each point time is represented, it blurs with human consciousness and appears as subjective, irregular, and relative. Consequently, like Conrad's contextualized events, objects, and subjects, his contextualized time leads directly to concerns about the nature of western civilization and its relationship to time because western civilization established the system of mechanical time, a system that reflects the objective and absolute features of the western world of the nineteenth and early twentieth centuries. In "Heart of Darkness," Conrad uses the link between perception of objects and the novel's setting to reveal the relativity of western absolutes; in *Lord Jim*, he uses the tie between perception of subjects and the novel's characterization to show this same relativity. And, in *The Secret Agent*, Conrad uses the connection between the experience of time and the novel's plot to come to a similar conclusion. In addition to direct interaction between human and mechanical time, as well as an impressionist narrative technique that resembles human, nonlinear time, the novel's plot itself reinforces subjectivity and relativity and questions mechanical time and the system that produces it. As noted earlier, mechanical time is ordered, objective, segmented, and regular. Of these features, its ordered, regular nature is particularly important. Mechanical time's regularity demands that regardless of which particular hour, for instance, that one identifies, it will be of the same duration as every other hour. As such, mechanical time is objective and universal and cannot be influenced by human subjectivity, as evidenced by Winnie's surprise that only three minutes had elapsed during Verloc's murder scene (*SA* 197) and Sir Ethelred's surprise that as many as twenty-five minutes had passed during his interview with the Assistant Commissioner (*SA* 111). No matter which individual is involved, mechanical time's movement remains the same, and it is mechanical time's objective, ordered, and universal qualities that most resemble features of western society.

Throughout his works, Conrad often juxtaposes human and mechanical time to accentuate the contrasts between them. Similarly, he questions civilization by juxtaposing it against uncivilized phenomena. In "Heart of Darkness," and other works set in non-western locations, Conrad brings together western and non-western cultures in order to emphasize their differences. In *The Shadow Line, The Nigger of the "Narcissus," "Typhoon," "The Secret Sharer,"* and other sea tales, the microcosmic western world aboard ship contrasts with the open ocean such that the ship's orderly existence seems out of place or at best merely a social convenience. However, in *The Secret Agent, Under Western Eyes,* "The Anarchist," and "The Informer," for example, most of the important action takes place within western civilization itself, and the juxtaposition of western and non-western occurs because of the conflict between westerners and revolutionaries/anarchists so that the ordered western world directly confronts the chaotic anarchist world. In some ways, these latter assaults against western values are the most disturbing for Conrad's characters (and perhaps for his readers as well) because while other assaults come from without, these come from within. *The Secret Agent* exhibits the most dramatic of these internal assaults, and various causes bring about this effect. Not only does Conrad set the novel inside the geographical boundaries of the west, he places the action at the very heart of the western world. London, more than any other city, distinctly represented that world. It was the major city in Europe at the time, and it was the major city of England, the most powerful country in the world and the seat of the greatest empire on earth. Conrad uses the backdrop of the world of London's anarchists to investigate civilization. He sets up a world of chaos alongside a world of order. In fact, the chaos of anarchy occurs in the very heart of the ordered western world.

Throughout the novel, the ideas of order and chaos interact. Although both criminal and anarchist are outside the law, Conrad establishes a clear distinction between them, and the criminal actually has more in common with the police than with the anarchists. The narrator remarks that Chief Inspector Heat "could understand the mind of a burglar, because, as a matter of fact, the mind and the instincts of a burglar are of the same kind as the mind and the instincts of a police officer. Both recognise the same conventions, and have a working knowledge of each other's methods and of the routine of their respective trades" (*SA* 74). Although police and burglar are on opposite sides of the law, they hold to "the same conventions," but the anarchists reject those conventions altogether. The narrator of "The Informer" implies this view when he suggests, "Anarchists, I suppose, have no families – not, at any rate, as we understand that social relation. Organization into families . . . is based on law, and therefore must be something odious and impossible to an anarchist" (*SS* 75). Similarly, in *The Secret Agent*, during the anarchists' discussion at Verloc's shop, Ossipon says, "There is no law and no certainty" (*SA* 43–44); Michaelis comments, "[E]verything is changed by economic conditions – art, philosophy, love, virtue – truth itself!" (*SA* 43); and Ossipon asks the rhetorical question: "And what is crime?" (*SA* 41). The anarchists' views directly oppose the conventions the criminal and the police recognize because the anarchists reject all civilized conventions. The narrator of *The Secret Agent* further emphasizes this fact by noting that "[t]here were no rules for dealing with anarchists. And that was distasteful to the Chief Inspector" (*SA* 78). The inspector dislikes dealing with the anarchists precisely because they reject society's fundamental assumptions, in contrast to the criminals, who do not reject those assumptions but simply ignore them.

The narrator of "The Informer" echoes Chief Inspector Heat's sentiments when he says, "[A]narchists in general were simply inconceivable to me mentally, morally, logically, sentimentally, and even physically" (*SS* 97). Because the anarchists seek to blow up social conventions, the narrator tries to distance himself from them. Only by excluding anarchists from the social group – by making them the other-unlike-self – can the narrator contemplate them. However, he cannot dismiss them so easily once he meets Mr. X:

Some Chinese bronzes are monstrously precious . . . [H]ere I had before me a kind of rare monster. It is true that this monster was polished and in a sense even exquisite. His beautiful unruffled manner was that. But then he was not of bronze. He was not even Chinese, which would have enabled one to contemplate him calmly across the gulf of racial difference. He was alive and European; he had the manner of good society, wore a coat and hat like mine, and had pretty near the same taste in cooking. It was too frightful to think of. (*SS* 76)

Concerning himself and Mr. X, the narrator is disturbed as much by their similarities as their differences. The narrator finds it easy to reject anarchists as the other-unlike-self as long as he has never met one, but when he finds that Mr. X is not the other-*unlike*-self but rather the other-*like*-self, the narrator's ordered world and sense of right and wrong suddenly becomes hazy. The narrator imagined anarchists to be mad-men and social misfits, but he finds Mr. X to be urbane, cultured, and – most frightening – very much like the narrator himself. Outside the social group, the narrator could "contemplate him calmly," but within that group Mr. X is too terrifying altogether, as he represents in part the narrator himself, as well as the annihilation of their shared society from within.

Like the narrator of "The Informer," for most of Conrad's west-erners, the idea of living in political anarchy is terrifying because nothing can be expected or predicted. All social rules and regulations disappear. In "The Anarchist," Harry Gee sums up this concern when he says, "But that subversive sanguinary rot of doing away with all law and order in the world makes my blood boil. It's simply cutting the ground from under the feet of every decent, respectable, hard-working person" (*SS* 144). More than this, though, the westerners see the destruc-tion of their social values as a blow at truth. So for those such as Chief Inspector Heat, the narrator of "The Informer," and Harry Gee, anarchists appear to be madmen, and this is precisely the response Mr. Vladimir wishes to evoke from the public by blowing up the Greenwich Observatory. He says to Verloc, "But what is one to say to an act of destructive ferocity so absurd as to be incomprehensible, inexplicable, almost unthinkable; in fact, mad? Madness alone is truly terrifying, inasmuch as you cannot placate it either by threats, persuasion, or bribes" (*SA* 30–31). Mr. Vladimir knows that acts of madness are particularly frightening to those used to an orderly existence. Such acts do not proceed upon any logical basis. A bank robbery may happen because of greed, a murder may happen because of revenge – both perhaps somewhat understandable. But acts of madness are incompre-hensible precisely because they are irrational and chaotic (just as are the phenomena of dreams). And without rationality or order, acts of mad-ness can neither be solved nor prevented through conventional social restraints. Furthermore, Mr. Vladimir understands well the fear western society of that time has toward anything that would irrationally destroy order and the fundamental assumptions upon which it rests. The Greenwich Observatory then is the perfect target for such an act of madness, because it represents order and the culmination of science over the natural elements, a science that many saw as the direct product of their cultural development. The observatory symbolizes science imposed on human existence through the structuring of time. As suggested earlier, by the late nineteenth century, science had become a religion to many. Both Mr. Vladimir and Ossipon acknowledge its prominent position in European society (*SA* 29, 227). In this way, not only do the anarchists blow up social values in their disregard for property and lives (even their own), but they also blow up the definitive symbol of science and the progress of western civilization.

Along with its association with scientific progress, the Greenwich Observatory is most closely associated with western time, and since mechanical time so uniquely represents the society of that time, it also becomes symbolic of other values that organize human experience on the premise of universality. As discussed earlier, in Conrad's works, just as all civilized perception is a construct that mirrors the imposed construct of a western worldview, so also is mechanical time a construct imposed upon the flow of time. Western time is a convenient system for organizing time, and western worldview is a convenient system for organizing social behavior, but for Conrad neither is absolute nor transcendental. However, not only the similarities between western worldview and western time bring these two into question; the parallel between them in *The Secret Agent* becomes all encompassing when it extends even to the novel's plot, which culminates in the anarchist attack on the Greenwich Observatory. This assault is the centering event around which all others revolve, and, because it is directed against this particular monument to civilization's scientific progress, it becomes crucial to Conrad's notion of the experience of time and its relationship to human existence and western civilization. The observatory is the ultimate symbol of western time. Juxtaposed against the relativity of human time (with all its irregular qualities), the Greenwich Observatory represents an organized and absolute system imposed on an unorganized, relative phenomenon. The Greenwich Meridian Observatory becomes the final triumph of civilizing the primitive. In this edifice, society has civilized even the workings of time itself. The anarchist attack, then, strikes a blow at this system of time and at the values that stand behind it – an act of madness in effect directed against civilization itself.

In addition to attacking civilization and the scientific progress that the Greenwich Observatory represents, the anarchists also try to destroy the phenomenon of time that the observatory represents. Tyley writes of the Professor, "In the same way as he claims superiority of character, through his dependence on death, over those who depend upon life, conventional morality and the social order, so he aims to negate the traditional properties of time by manufacturing a perfect detonator, based on the principle of instantaneity."[50] Similarly, Miller argues that "[t]he imperfection of the Professor's detonator is a symptom of his inability to reconcile time and eternity."[51] But more important, developing an instantaneous detonator is an attempt to destroy the effects of western time. With a twenty-second detonator, the Professor is still subject to linear time, but if he can invent an instantaneous detonator, then he can both escape time and also destroy it by moving outside its scope. With such a detonator, the Professor can destroy western structures, people, values, and time all in the one blow. Besides the Professor's personal assault on time, anarchists in general assault time. Kertzer argues, "Anarchy is the constant disruption of time, a form of madness breaking all connection with the past and permitting no fruitful future development."[52] Because anarchists reject past and future, they would seem then to be securely fixed in the present, but in fact they are not. Instead, their entire view is focused on the future – once they have blown up the present society. But with "no fruitful future development," as Kertzer puts it, their focus on the future negates itself, and thus the anarchists seem to exist outside of time altogether, and consequently they do nothing during the entire novel. Hay argues that they "neither set the world on fire nor rise to sterile heroisms. Their conspiracies are worse than vain; they achieve disaster inadvertently."[53] To a man, their actions are futile. Verloc enlists Stevie to perform the botched bombing attempt on the Greenwich Observatory and is later helpless against Winnie's attack. Michaelis spends his days in self exile writing voluminous, incoherent memoirs. Ossipon occupies himself more with women than politics. Karl Yundt is equally ineffectual and pathetic. And the Professor waits for an opportunity to blow himself up. Stevie is the only one who actually accomplishes something – accidentally blowing himself to pieces – and he is unaware that he is even involved in anarchist activities. By destroying the past and at the same time negating the present and future, the anarchists in a sense destroy time itself, but this endeavor is just as futile as western civilization's attempt to impose order on time through establishing mechanical time because it is impossible to exist outside of time. Kertzer remarks:

Conrad's anarchists seek an explosive break with the past through revolution but, ironically, they become obsessed with the very thing they wish to destroy, and dependent on it. They are grotesque men because they live on hatred of the past. A man can neither escape nor destroy his past because experience is cumulative: he carries the past within himself. To destroy it is suicidal.[54]

However, not only do human beings carry the past within themselves, but also time filters through human consciousness such that the boundaries between the two blur as they modify each other. Time is altered by the consciousness through which it filters, and human consciousness is altered by its experience with time; therefore an attempt to destroy time is also an attempt to destroy one's self.

Conrad rejects the idea that either the western world or the anarchist world is founded upon absolutes, and he sides with neither the authorities nor with the anarchists. Conrad portrays the authorities at times as fools, as with Sir Ethelred, at times as incompetent, as with those who bring about Michaelis' release from prison, and at times as corrupt, as with the police who cover up Verloc's murder. In fact, much evidence exists in the novel suggesting that the distinctions between the authorities and the anarchists are not so clear as Conrad's readers may wish to believe. Daleski argues that "in breaking established forms . . . the Home Secretary is startlingly aligned with the anarchists – and his doing so proves to have a subtly disintegrative effect on the Assistant Commissioner's department: it leads Heat to believe, as the Commissioner has already discovered, that he can act as a law unto himself in the department."[55] Daleski goes on to suggest that Chief Inspector Heat "clearly believes with some confidence that the end justifies the means; but that this in effect signifies his acceptance of a moral nihilism as radical as that of the Professor's is revealed in his expressed readiness to 'deal with the devil himself'" [*SA* 103].[56] Miller goes even further, arguing that "Conrad sees all society as rotten at the core, as a vast half-deliberate conspiracy of police, thieves, anarchists, tradesmen, aristocratic bluestockings, ministers of state, and ambassadors of foreign powers."[57] Whether Conrad's view is as extreme as Miller suggests is debatable, but he clearly questions the morality of the established society and authorities – as he does that of the anarchists. At the same time, he introduces some uncomfortable similarities between the authorities and the anarchists. For Conrad, such a society and its representatives do not have absolute truth at their backs.

Conrad similarly rejects the anarchists, in part because he rejects politics in general.[58] Guerard argues that it seems Conrad's "skepticism concerning historical and political process is ... at times, total. There is ... a total distrust of political discourse, spoken or written."[59] Hay agrees, suggesting that "[i]deologies are often villainous in Conrad's political *Weltanschauung*."[60] In yet stronger terms, Daniel Schwarz argues that Conrad's "political novels *enact* a pox on politics"[61] and that "Conrad indicts political activity as both suspect in its causes and pernicious in its effects."[62] The narrator of *Under Western Eyes* confirms this view: "It seems that the savage autocracy, no more than the divine democracy, does not limit its diet exclusively to the bodies of its enemies. It devours its friends and servants as well" (*UWE* 306). Not only does Conrad see politics destroying its enemies, he sees it as destroying its allies also. And although he rejects politics in general, Conrad particularly rejects the ideas of anarchy and revolution. In the "Author's Note" to *Under Western Eyes*, he argues,

The ferocity and imbecility of an autocratic rule rejecting all legality and in fact basing itself upon complete moral anarchism provokes the no less imbecile and atrocious answer of a purely Utopian revolutionism encompassing destruction by the first means to hand, in the strange conviction that a fundamental change of hearts must follow the downfall of any given human institutions. These people are unable to see that all they can effect is merely a change of names. (*UWE* x)

Hauntingly prophetic in his assessment of Russia, Conrad's comments encompass other idealistic revolutions as well (as in for instance *Nostromo* and *The Secret Agent*). Ford confirms Conrad's views on revolution when he states, "Revolutions were to him always anathema since, he was accustomed to declare, *all* revolutions always have been, always must be, nothing more in the end than palace intrigues – intrigues either for power within, or for the occupancy of, a palace."[63] And Conrad himself said, "The revolutionary spirit is mighty convenient in this, that it frees one from all scruples as regards ideas" (*PR* xxi). For Conrad, in revolutions based on conviction, the revolutionists assume that change is possible because the present political rulers – not the convictions – are faulty. In "Autocracy and War," however, Conrad writes, "[I]t is the bitter fate of any idea to lose its royal form and power, to lose its 'virtue' the moment it descends from its solitary throne to work its will among the people" (*NLL* 86). This phenomenon occurs in *Nostromo*, and in commenting on the actions of Sotillo and the Monteros, Guerard remarks, "Such are the men who initiate revolutions and profit from them, or who take over the revolutions begun on idealistic grounds."[64] When the revolution obtains power, without external restraints, convictions rarely curb political abuses because there are no absolute foundations for their convictions. The narrator of "The Anarchist" seems to speak for Conrad when he remarks that the engineer "was very much like many other anarchists. Warm heart and weak head" (*SS* 161). In particular, Conrad sees two problems with the anarchist creed, which Mr. X summarizes in his description of the anarchist professor: "Explosives were his faith, his hope, his weapon, and his shield" (*SS* 88). First, Conrad scorns anarchists not so much because they attack social values but because they want to blow it all up and start again.[65] Mr. Vladimir states, "You anarchists should make it clear that you are perfectly determined to make a clean sweep of the whole social creation" (*SA* 30). The anarchists looked at the injustice of society and decided it went wrong somewhere. The Professor tells Ossipon, "You plan the future, you lose yourselves in reveries of economical systems derived from what is; whereas what's wanted is a clean sweep and a clear start for a new conception of life" (*SA* 60–61).[66] But in a sense, the anarchists' views (even those of the Professor) are simply the flip side of society's coin; their views are just as much based upon absolutes as those they wish to destroy. In "The Anarchist," the narrator notes that the anarchists "applaud his [the engineer's] humane indignation. Yes. The amount of injustice in the world was indeed scandalous. There was only one way of dealing with the rotten state of society. Demolish the whole *sacrée boutique*. Blow up the whole iniquitous show" (*SS* 147). Since Conrad rejects transcendental absolutes, he rejects anarchist absolutes as he does society's absolutes. For him, little difference exists between the present circumstances and those that would exist after the anarchists have blown it all up and begun again. The anarchists' new world would still be one based upon absolutes.

Nevertheless, although Conrad rejects an absolute foundation for a western worldview, as should become clear shortly, he still accepts its values in general as a convenient vehicle for responsible social interaction. As western time conveniently orders time, cultural norms conveniently order social existence. If individuals responded to time as they experienced it, for one a moment might be compressed while for another it might be extended. Social interaction could not be synchronized, and social experience would become chaotic. Similarly, the anarchist destruction of society would remove the artificial restraints on social behavior, and chaos would reign in the absence of either absolute or conventional restraints. Social chaos is unacceptable to Conrad, thus even though the present system may be flawed and merely a convenience, it is still more desirable than the chaos of anarchy.

Throughout *The Secret Agent*, Conrad deftly weaves the strands of time, western civilization, and anarchy. Each strand leads to the same end: the individuality of human experience and its resistance to artificially imposed systems meant to civilize the primitive – to order human time, to order human existence, and to order human social interaction. These strands come together in an anarchist attack that occurs not in the jungles of Africa nor on the open ocean but within the heart of western civilization itself. Conrad's graphic representation of this incident emphasizes its significance. Stevie is so blown apart that he has to be gathered with a shovel. Both Chief Inspector Heat and Winnie are horrified at the complete annihilation of this human body, but Conrad is equally concerned with the annihilation of that which makes us human, whether it be through an arbitrarily imposed system that obscures human experience or the meaningless destruction of an anarchist bomb.

CHAPTER 5

Radical relativism, epistemological certainty, and ethical absolutes: Conrad's impressionist response to solipsism and anarchy

"And without you I would think myself alone in an empty universe."

"Letter to Edward Garnett"

I

As I have shown, throughout his works, Conrad investigates a variety of objects of consciousness: physical objects, human subjects, events, ideas, space, and time. With each object of consciousness, he employs impressionist techniques to show that the epistemological process is individual, and his impressionism consistently leads to human subjectivity as the common element in the appearance of these objects. This common element demonstrates a kind of unity in Conrad's works that may not initially be apparent. Not only is the epistemological experience individual, but it also forms the building block for knowledge of the nature of human existence and the external world, and since objects of consciousness are individual, knowledge is individual as well. Furthermore, the individual nature of the epistemological process also points to questions concerning western civilization of that time, and these questions lead to an uncertainty about what human beings can know.

Conrad specifically emphasizes the uncertainty of knowledge in several instances. The clearest demonstration of this fact occurs when Jim claims that Marlow cannot know what he would have done had he been in Jim's place on the *Patna*: "You can't tell – nobody can tell" (*LJ* 92). The uniqueness of the context (physical circumstances and human subjectivity) makes it impossible for others to know how they would respond to a given situation. This uncertainty of knowledge also appears in *Under Western Eyes*, when Peter Ivanovitch asks rhetorically, "But what is knowledge?" (*UWE* 119). Some debate exists, however, concerning the nature or degree of skepticism that Conrad's works exhibit. Some critics see Conrad's skepticism as a form of nihilism; perhaps the first to fully articulate this view was Miller: "The special place of Joseph Conrad in English Literature lies in the fact that in him the nihilism covertly dominant in modern culture is brought to the surface and shown for what it is."[1] Others, such as Warren, Guerard, Watt, and Wollaeger are more circumspect in assessing Conrad's skepticism. Conrad's skepticism is undeniable, but for them it does not reach as far as nihilism. Watt remarks, "Nor can Conrad's social and moral purport be regarded as ultimately nihilist."[2] Warren suggests, "Conrad's skepticism is ultimately but a 'reasonable' recognition of the fact that man is a natural creature who can rest on no revealed values and can look forward to neither individual immortality nor racial survival."[3] And Wollaeger argues, "In Conrad visionary experience would seem to catalyze world-consuming skepticism, yet a nostalgic investment in the recovery of lost immanence prevents skepticism from becoming nihilism."[4] I tend to agree with these latter critics, particularly Warren and Wollaeger, who see Conrad moving between a radical skepticism and a desire to find some point of belief. Warren sees this as an "apparent discrepancy" in Conrad's works "between his professions of scepticism and his professions of faith."[5] Wollaeger, on the other hand, seems to see less of a contradiction. Although he notes that in Conrad "[t]he hunger for the absolute always returns, as does the vision of the abyss opened by total skepticism,"[6] this duality is not so much a contradiction as it is a movement toward a realization of the relationship between skepticism and transcendence: "In Schopenhauer and Conrad alike, as in the emerging modernist sensibility that sustained them, the claims of skepticism are contested by the consolations of transcendence."[7] Ultimately, as Wollaeger notes, Conrad believes "that a vision of total skepticism cannot be sustained."[8] Conrad is unwilling to accept total skepticism and instead looks for a way to identify meaning for human existence. For instance, although, as Guerard argues, "[t]he degree to which he echoes Decoud suggests that Conrad shared no little of this skepticism,"[9] Conrad also clearly criticizes his most famous fictional skeptic. In the end, it is Decoud's skepticism that destroys him (N 497–98); he has nothing to sustain him because he believes nothing (N 500). Skepticism, when tempered however, can even lead to truth. In a letter to John Galsworthy, Conrad writes, "The fact is you want more scepticism at the very foundation of your work. Scepticism the tonic of minds, the tonic of life, the agent of truth – the way of art and salvation."[10] But if skepticism is the way of "salvation," it is also the way of damnation – as is clear in Decoud's case. Therefore, Conrad must walk a thin line between the two: on the one hand, skepticism can lead to some knowledge of the truth, but on the other, it can also lead to the abyss of despair. Conrad's balancing act between the two is the ability to recognize the nature of human existence but at the same time possess a means to shelter one's self from such potentially withering knowledge. Wollaeger argues that for Conrad "[a]n investment in tradition, for instance, represents a logical bulwark against skepticism, for if informed judgments are impossible and all knowledge a chimera, one might as well adhere to a tradition or an arbitrary code of conduct."[11] However, although Wollaeger in part accurately summarizes Conrad's view, one does not "adhere to a tradition or an arbitrary code of conduct" simply because it is familiar or because it provides structure or because it is just as good as any other way of life. On the contrary, Conrad carefully selects the values and systems that his novels advocate in order to access whatever small truths may be available to humanity. Therefore, his primary interest in the problems of skepticism has to do with the uncertainty of truth itself. In a letter to R. B. Cunninghame Graham, Conrad wrote, "And suppose Truth is just around the corner like the elusive and useless loafer it is? I can't tell. No one can tell. It is impossible to know. It is impossible to know anything."[12] This is the key to Conrad's concern about the uncertainty of knowledge, because not only can we know nothing with absolute certainty, we cannot know truth – particularly ethical truth – with certainty. Conrad touches on this issue when Jim says of the *Patna* incident, "There was not the thickness of a sheet of paper between the right and wrong of this affair" (*LJ* 130). The right and wrong of the incident is difficult to know for certain because the context is relative and individual. Nevertheless, as should become clear, Conrad was not a moral relativist who advocated situational ethics, far from it since such a course can only lead to a kind of ethical anarchy; instead, although context influences ethics and makes certainty difficult, Conrad's goal is to find a response to the possibility of ethical anarchy.

Precisely this problem of ethical certainty also appears in "The Return." When Hervey talks to his wife about "adherence to what is right," she responds, "What is right?" Horrified, Hervey replies, "Your mind is diseased! Such a question is rot – utter rot. Look round you – there's your answer, if you only care to see. Nothing that outrages the received beliefs can be right. Your conscience tells you that. They are the received beliefs because they are the best, the noblest, the only possible. They survive" (*TU* 157). Hervey's reasoning, however, is circular: values are right because they are received by society, and society receives these values because they are right. Hervey admonishes his wife to look around her for confirmation of the absolute nature of these values, but such a look provides no confirmation. Rather, the truth of these values is uncertain. The world is not what it appears and is ultimately unknowable. Hervey himself experiences this uncertainty when he looks at his wife and perceives she is not what she seems. She has been unfaithful to him (after a fashion), and yet she appears the same as when she was faithful (*TU* 171). When he tries to obtain a clear knowledge of her, he concludes that it is "impossible to know [her]" (*TU* 172; see also 173, 174). The views of ethical conduct that "survive" do not "survive" because they are absolute but because they are "received" by society. People adhere to "the received beliefs" out of habit, convenience, or convention. Throughout Conrad's works, the relativity he demonstrates regarding the knowledge of objects of consciousness and of the foundations of western civilization leads to a relative universe, and this relative universe is Conrad's ultimate concern.

Conrad's relative universe is both irrational and indifferent. In a well-known letter to Cunninghame Graham, Conrad elaborates on his views:

There is a – let us say – a machine. It evolved itself . . . out of a chaos of scraps of iron and behold! – it knits. I am horrified at the horrible work and stand appalled. I feel it ought to embroider – but it goes on knitting . . . And the most withering thought is that the infamous thing has made itself; made itself without thought, without conscience, without foresight, without eyes, without heart. It is a tragic accident, – and it has happened. You can't interfere with it. The last drop of bitterness is in the suspicion that you can't even smash it. In virtue of that truth one and immortal which lurks in the force that made it spring into existence it is what it is, – and it is indestructible! It knits us in and it knits us out. It has knitted time space, pain, death, corruption, despair and all the illusions – and nothing matters.[13]

This indifferent universe, which "knits us in and knits us out," is where we must exist, and in "Heart of Darkness" Marlow recognizes such a universe and thus refers to life as "that mysterious arrangement of merciless logic for a futile purpose" (*Y* 150).

Throughout Conrad's works, examples of an irrational universe abound. In *Under Western Eyes*, Razumov's life is progressing on what appears to him to be a predictable and controllable course when suddenly everything changes: he "experienced that sensation of his conduct being taken out of his hands by Haldin's revolutionary tyranny" (*UWE* 82). Razumov thinks, "[T]hree years of good work gone, the course of forty more perhaps jeopardized – turned from hope to terror, because events started by human folly link themselves into a sequence which no sagacity can foresee and no courage can break through" (*UWE* 83). As discussed earlier, when Haldin arrives uninvited to Razumov's apartment, he alters Razumov's entire existence. The narrator of "Falk" finds himself in an equally absurd situation – again one wholly out of his control. Unbeknownst to him, Falk wishes to marry one of Hermann's daughters and mistakenly assumes the narrator is courting the same woman. As a result, Falk refuses to tow the narrator's ship (*T* 186). Since Falk has the only towing service, the narrator can do nothing. The narrator actually has no interest in Hermann's daughter, and the whole incident becomes "an absurd episode" (*T* 147). Eventually, the narrator clears up the misunderstanding, but not until he has come to an important conclusion: "I know that there are often in men's affairs unexpectedly – even irrationally – illuminating moments when an otherwise insignificant sound, perhaps only some perfectly commonplace gesture, suffices to reveal to us all the unreason, all the fatuous unreason, of our complacency" (*T* 169). For D'Hubert, the absurdity of the duel constantly impresses itself upon him. It begins from an inconsequential incident, and D'Hubert initially responds to Feraud's challenge by saying, "This is perfectly absurd" (*SS* 177). Nevertheless, Feraud forces him to fight a series of duels over a number of years, and D'Hubert has no control over his own existence: "For years General D'Hubert had been exasperated and humiliated by an atrocious absurdity imposed upon him by this man's [Feraud's] savage caprice" (*SS* 256; see also 182, 206, 208). And in "The Anarchist," an almost Kafka-like sequence of events condemns the "anarchist" on the basis of a single, drunken statement. Once the chain of events begins, all sense and control over his existence cease.[14]

In each instance, events cannot be predicted, understood, or controlled. Often this situation leads to tragic consequences that are tied to the indifference of Conrad's universe, for not only is there no rational justification at its foundations, there is also no moral justification. In "Youth," when the *Judea* blows up from under Marlow, he notes,

I did not know that I had no hair, no eyebrows, no eyelashes, that my young moustache was burnt off, that my face was black, one cheek laid open, my nose cut, and my chin bleeding... I was amazed to see the ship still afloat, the poop-deck whole – and, most of all, to see anybody alive. Also the peace of the

sky and the serenity of the sea were distinctly surprising. I suppose I expected to
see them convulsed with horror. (*Y* 23–24)

Marlow's humorous tone deflates the horror of this incident, but behind
his tone is the realization that "the peace of the sky and the serenity of
the sea" are indifferent to human suffering. On a more serious note, the
narrator of "The Warrior's Soul" comments, "I had the intimate
sensation of the earth in all its enormous expanse wrapped in snow, with
nothing showing on it but trees with their straight stalk-like trunks and
their funeral verdure; and in this aspect of general mourning I seemed to
hear the sighs of mankind falling to die in the midst of a nature without
life" (*TH* 20). Set during Napoleon's Russian campaign, the story
graphically describes the French army's retreat. In the midst of a
dispassionate universe, soldiers die of cold, starvation, and battle
wounds. Perhaps most representative of an indifferent universe, however, is Decoud's fate in *Nostromo*:

After a clear daybreak the sun appeared splendidly above the peaks of the
range. The great gulf burst into a glitter all around the boat . . . The stiffness of
the fingers relaxed, and the lover of Antonia Avellanos rolled overboard
without having heard the cord of silence snap in the solitude of the Placid Gulf,
whose glittering surface remained untroubled by the fall of his body . . . [T]he
brilliant Don Martin Decoud, weighted by the bars of San Tomé silver,
disappeared without a trace, swallowed up in the immense indifference of
things. (*N* 500–1)

Conrad represents the beauty and brilliance of nature as wholly divorced from the human tragedy occurring in its midst.[15]

This overt knowledge of an irrational and indifferent universe is
usually submerged, but periodically it emerges, sometimes with disastrous consequences. In various instances, characters experience a revelation concerning the nature of the universe. The extent of this glimpse
varies from character to character. Some suddenly realize in an almost
tangible way simply that they are mortal and will die. The narrator of
"Typhoon" suggests that Captain MacWhirr momentarily has such an
experience just before he faces the storm. As MacWhirr replaced a
matchbox in his cabin, "it occurred to him that perhaps he would never
have occasion to use that box any more. The vividness of the thought
checked him and for an infinitesimal fraction of a second his fingers
closed again on the small object as though it had been the symbol of all
these little habits that chain us to the weary round of life" (*T* 85).
MacWhirr then goes back to his normal, somnolent existence of immediacy, "[h]aving just enough imagination to carry him through each

successive day, and no more" (*T* 4). But for an instant, he glimpses the actuality of his mortality. Similarly, in *The Nigger of the "Narcissus,"* as a result of Singleton's experience during the storm, he also glimpses his mortality:

He had never given a thought to his mortal self. He lived unscathed, as though he had been indestructible, surrendering to all the temptations, weathering many gales... It seemed to him he was broken at last. And like a man bound treacherously while he sleeps, he woke up fettered by the long chain of disregarded years. He had to take up at once the burden of all his existence. (*NN* 99)

Despite Conrad's admiring MacWhirr and Singleton, he also presents them as two of several characters who go through life almost completely oblivious to larger issues and who focus solely on the immediate. Conrad remarks of Singleton, "Would you seriously ... cultivate in that unconscious man the power to think. Then he would become conscious – and much smaller – and very unhappy. Now he is simple and great like an elemental force."[16] For that brief moment, however, Singleton, like MacWhirr, does become "conscious." The fact that even these two characters experience such revelations underscores the pervasiveness of these events and the degree of disillusionment such enlightenment brings. And although Singleton and MacWhirr only realize they are mortal, the extent of their revelation is, nevertheless, significant to Conrad. In a letter to Cunninghame Graham, Conrad writes, "What makes mankind tragic is not that they are the victims of nature, it is that they are conscious of it." The consciousness of mortality sets human beings apart from animals, and many people wish to suppress this knowledge. Conrad continues, "Our refuge is in stupidity, in drunkenness of all kinds, in lies, in beliefs, in murder, thieving, reforming – in negation, in contempt – each man according to the promptings of his particular devil."[17] This same pattern of revelation and need of shelter from that revelation appears in Conrad's fiction as well. Of the *Narcissus'* crew, the narrator remarks, "Men stood around very still and with exasperated eyes. It was just what they had expected, and hated to hear, that idea of a stalking death, thrust at them many times a day like a boast and like a menace" (*NN* 35–36). In James Wait's consumptive cough and constant insistence on his imminent death, the crew faces daily the knowledge of their own mortality, a knowledge they would rather repress. Later in the novel, Wait himself tries to deny precisely this knowledge when it becomes clear that he is in fact dying: "Jimmy's steadfastness to his untruthful attitude in the face of the inevitable truth had the proportions of a colossal enigma – of a manifestation grand and incomprehensible that at times inspired a wondering awe" (*NN* 138). This "colossal enigma" is Wait's wish to repress the knowledge of mortality. Even for such somnolents as Singleton and MacWhirr, the glimpse of their own mortality shocks them (even if only temporarily) out of their oblivious existence of immediacy and into a knowledge of human mortality.

More than this, though, in many instances characters not only become aware of their mortality but also of the nature of Conrad's universe as a whole. Stein says, "And because you not always can keep your eyes shut there comes the real trouble – the heart pain – the world pain. I tell you, my friend, it is not good for you to find you cannot make your dream come true" (*LJ* 213). With "eyes shut," Conrad's characters can believe the world is at their feet and that they are at the center of the universe, but if they open their eyes they find instead a universe indifferent to them. In *Lord Jim*, Marlow contrasts the immediacy of facts with the revelatory quality of ideas: "Hang ideas! They are tramps, vagabonds, knocking at the back-door of your mind, each taking a little of your substance, each carrying away some crumb of that belief in a few simple notions you must cling to if you want to live decently and would like to die easy!" (*LJ* 43). Ideas, particularly those that point to an indifferent universe, forever alter a person's perception of existence. As Stein says, "[T]hat is the trouble – the great trouble" (*LJ* 217). Winnie Verloc illustrates this same sentiment when she decides that "things don't bear looking into very much" (*SA* 138; see also 130, 136, 182). And the narrator of "The Warrior's Soul" is even more explicit when he says, "I had become awake with an exaggerated mental consciousness of existence extending beyond my immediate surroundings. Those are but exceptional moments with mankind, I am glad to say" (*TH* 20).

Most characters are able to shelter themselves at least partially from the knowledge of an indifferent universe: as the narrator of *Victory* remarks, "For every age is fed on illusions, lest men should renounce life early and the human race come to an end" (*V* 94). Marlow's experience in *Lord Jim* is the clearest and most compelling example of a character's revelation and return to shelter. He says that Jewel's description of her mother's death scene

had the power to drive me out of my conception of existence, out of that shelter each of us makes for himself to creep under in moments of danger, as a tortoise withdraws within its shell. For a moment I had a view of a world that seemed to wear a vast and dismal aspect of disorder, while, in truth, thanks to our unwearied efforts, it is as sunny an arrangement of small conveniences as the mind of man can conceive. But still – it was only a moment: I went back into my shell directly. One *must* – don't you know? – though I seemed to have lost all my words in the chaos of dark thoughts I had contemplated for a second or two beyond the pale. These came back, too, very soon, for words also belong to the sheltering conception of light and order which is our refuge. (*LJ* 313; emphasis is Conrad's; see also 225)

Marlow encounters an unobstructed view of an indifferent universe, but the thought of such a scene occurring undisturbed is so unsettling that he must retreat into his shelter and make the universe tidy once again. The French Lieutenant says, "One truth the more ought not to make life impossible" (*LJ* 148), but for Marlow the truth of an indifferent universe is one that can make life impossible, and so he shelters himself from that knowledge.

In "The Return," Hervey experiences a revelation similar to Marlow's, along with the consequences of his inability to shelter himself from the knowledge it reveals. After his wife's abortive attempt to leave him for another man, Hervey thinks,

[T]hose two had been engaged in a conspiracy against his peace – in a criminal enterprise for which there could be no sanction of belief within themselves. There could not be! There could not be! And yet how near to ... With a short thrill he saw himself an exiled forlorn figure in a realm of ungovernable, of unrestrained folly. Nothing could be foreseen, foretold – guarded against. And the sensation was intolerable, had something of the withering horror that may be conceived as following upon the utter extinction of all hope. In the flash of thought the dishonouring episode seemed to disengage itself from everything actual, from earthly conditions, and even from earthly suffering; it became purely a terrifying knowledge, an annihilating knowledge of a blind and infernal force. (*TU* 159–60; ellipsis is Conrad's)

For a moment, Hervey glimpses the uncertainty of all things and together with it a universe indifferent to ethical, legal, and social codes, a universe in which nothing can be prevented or predicted. After such a terrifying revelation, he must repress that knowledge: "[T]hen came the idea, the persuasion, the certitude, that the evil must be forgotten – must be resolutely ignored to make life possible; that the knowledge must be kept out of mind, out of sight, like the knowledge of certain death is kept out of the daily existence of men" (*TU* 160; see also 175). Despite Hervey's attempt to repress this knowledge, however, he cannot retreat back into oblivion. His perception of existence is forever altered, and he ends by leaving home, never to return. Life exposed to such a universe becomes intolerable.

There are numerous examples of characters who shelter themselves from the awareness of an indifferent universe. Warren argues that Conrad "admires the men of natural virtue, their simplicity, their dogged extroverted sense of obligation and self-respect. But his attitude toward them is ambivalent... They live in a moral limbo of unaware-ness."[18] Conrad seems to both envy and scorn this need for shelter, while at the same time grudgingly acknowledging its necessity. He vacillates between regarding it as self-delusion and self-preservation. Concerning the inhabitants of the "sepulchral city," who are oblivious to the nature of Conrad's universe, Marlow says,

They were intruders whose knowledge of life was to me an irritating pretence, because I felt so sure they could not possibly know the things I knew. Their bearing, which was simply the bearing of commonplace individuals going about their business in the assurance of perfect safety, was offensive to me like the outrageous flauntings of folly in the face of a danger it is unable to comprehend. (*Y* 152)

Marlow scorns these people because they feel safe and contented within a seemingly moral and rational universe. To Marlow, such people are deluded, and their self-importance is a sham. Conrad made a similar assessment of himself. He remarked to Garnett, "Before the Congo I was just a mere animal."[19] Only after such an experience did Conrad's conception of the universe become clear.

In other instances, though, Conrad genuinely seems to envy such obliviousness: "I suffer now from an acute attack of faithlessness in the sense that I do not seem to believe in anything, but I trust that by the time we meet I shall be more like a human being and consequently ready to believe any absurdity – and not only ready but eager."[20] His eagerness results from a desire to forget an indifferent universe. This same desire also appears in Conrad's works. In "Typhoon," the nar-rator remarks that "some men go skimming over the years of existence to sink gently into a placid grave, ignorant of life to the last, without ever having been made to see all it may contain of perfidy, of violence, and of terror. There are on sea and land such men thus fortunate" (*T* 19). In this instance, the narrator suggests that those who can focus on the immediate and remain oblivious to all else may be "fortunate." Similarly, in *Lord Jim*, Marlow notes that "there are men here and there to whom the whole of life is like an after-dinner hour with a cigar; easy, pleasant, empty, perhaps enlivened by some fable of strife to be forgotten before the end is told" (*LJ* 35; see also 225).[21] Conrad's dilemma is the dual nature of their lives – "easy" and "pleasant" but also "empty." In "Heart of Darkness," Marlow sums up this attitude when he says that "no fool ever made a bargain for his soul with the devil" (*Y* 117). In other words, fools do not sell their souls to the devil because they are oblivious to the possibility, just as an animal would be. Marlow scorns such individuals because they are deluded, but being oblivious to the nature of the universe can also can make life tolerable. The narrator of *Victory* remarks, "Great achievements are accomplished in a blessed, warm mental fog" (*V* 92). Marlow suggests that through mundane daily tasks "the inner truth [concerning the nature of the universe] is hidden – luckily, luckily" (*Y* 93; see also 85, 97, 98, 99–100, and *TU* 40). But, as he also suggests in *Lord Jim*, the individuals who can go through life completely oblivious of the nature of the universe are few:

It's extraordinary how we go through life with eyes half shut, with dull ears, with dormant thoughts. Perhaps it's just as well; and it may be that it is this very dullness that makes life to the incalculable majority so supportable and so welcome. Nevertheless, there can be but few of us who had never known one of these rare moments of awakening when we see, hear, understand ever so much – everything – in a flash – before we fall back again into our agreeable somnolence. (*LJ* 143)

Since we cannot always remain oblivious to the nature of the universe, and since oblivion, though "easy" and "pleasant," is also "empty," the question in Conrad's works is how to exist with meaning in such a universe.

This question of how to exist in a universe irrational and indifferent to human beings, knowing that no absolutes exist, is ultimately Conrad's fundamental concern. In a famous passage from *Lord Jim*, Stein suggests: "The way is to the destructive element submit yourself, and with the exertions of your hands and feet in the water make the deep, deep sea keep you up" (*LJ* 214). Although Stein's universe is a "perfect equilibrium" (*LJ* 208), human beings do not hold a privileged position in it, as they do in the traditional western universe, and these "exertions of your hands and feet" are those things human beings do to create meaning for their existence. Marlow says, "[T]he question is not how to get cured, but how to live" (*LJ* 212). In other words, Conrad's characters cannot alter a relative universe, and so the question then is how to live in such circumstances, how to "breathe dead hippo, so to speak, and not be contaminated" (*Y* 117).

The answer to this question is possible only through Conrad's belief in the certainty of human existence. In the end, Conrad's impressionism is based upon the relativity of human epistemology. All knowledge filters through a human subject, and so the human being is the building block from which Conrad then constructs his world. In his essay on Henry James, Conrad suggests that "everything is relative, and the light of consciousness is only enduring, merely the most enduring of the things of this earth, imperishable only as against the short-lived work of our industrious hands" (*NLL* 13). In *Lord Jim*, Marlow echoes this remark: "The human heart is vast enough to contain all the world" (*LJ* 323; see also 342). And in "Heart of Darkness," Marlow comments, "The mind of man is capable of anything – because everything is in it, all the past as well as all the future" (*Y* 96). The common element therefore in objects of consciousness, the ultimate source of knowledge and the very foundation of our existence, is human existence itself – not because Conrad was necessarily a humanist who believed in the perfectibility of humanity nor that human beings hold a privileged place in the universe,[22] but because the fact of human existence is the only certainty for him. Although I would not argue that Conrad is a Cartesian, I would argue that, like Descartes, he starts from this single kernel of certainty to build his world. Unlike Descartes, however, Conrad's world is neither systematic nor certain – but it is the best Conrad can do to provide some meaning for human existence. In a letter to Cunninghame Graham, Conrad remarks, "There is no morality, no knowledge and no hope; there is only the consciousness of ourselves which drives us about a world that whether seen in a convex or a concave mirror is always but a vain and floating appearance."[23] For Conrad, all else, the whole world around us, is relative and uncertain, but our own existence is certain, and only from that small yet crucial certainty does the possibility for meaning exist.

II

To create meaning in a relative and uncertain universe, Conrad must first come to terms with the logical conclusions of such a universe: epistemological solipsism and ethical anarchy. If knowledge is relative and dependent upon context, then how can one be sure that what one knows is the same as what others know, and more important how does one know it is certain? Similarly, if western civilization's ethical values are based upon a relative rather than an absolute foundation, how can society justify its values over others that are different, opposing, or even absent altogether? The solution – or rather Conrad's tentative response – to these problems is similar and is a direct result of his emphasis on human subjectivity: Conrad looks to humanity to avoid both solipsism and ethical anarchy. In a sense, this is ironic because their logical possibility directly results from human subjectivity in the first place – the fact that all phenomena filter through human consciousness. Nevertheless, for Conrad, consensus among human subjects concerning phenomena and consensus among members of society concerning moral values avoid the abyss of ethical anarchy and epistemological solipsism.

Solipsism is one of the primary risks of impressionism. De Lange suggests, "The isolation of the individual is furthermore one of the logical consequences of impressionism."[24] Bender goes even further, arguing that "if there is no direct correspondence between impressions and the world exterior to the mind, there can be no proof that the impressions of one mind correspond to those of any other when faced with the same stimuli. Indeed, the assumption must be to the contrary, that no two minds receive the same impressions."[25] Although he would probably not go as far as either de Lange or Bender, Conrad was not unaware of the problems associated with solipsism. Wollaeger comments that Conrad and Pater "clearly share a concern with solipsism."[26] When Marlow asserts that phenomena always filter through an individual human consciousness, that the self cannot easily know the other (i.e., *LJ* 180) nor the other easily know the self (i.e., *Y* 85),[27] and that trying to convey the sense of one's own experience to another is "a vain attempt" (*Y* 82),[28] he in effect asks whether solipsism is not the final result of human knowledge. Nevertheless, Conrad was unwilling simply to accept solipsism as the final consequence of his epistemological investigations. His concern and response to this problem runs at the back of all these investigations and hence at the back of all his major works (and many of his minor works as well), and his response to solipsism has its origin in human subjectivity.

As the boundaries between self and other-like-self blur, the danger of solipsism diminishes. One way this blurring occurs is by acknowledging the reality of the other. In *A Personal Record*, Conrad writes, "And what is a novel if not a conviction of our fellow-men's existence strong enough to take upon itself a form of imagined life clearer than reality" (*PR* 15). By looking to the other – by acknowledging the other's existence and experience – Conrad's characters can, in part, escape solipsism. Wollaeger remarks,

Marlow's sense of Jim's sudden effacement and of Stein's self-regarding nostalgia brings him to the threshold of a solipsistic vision that follows inevitably from the assumption that only our own impressions are real: another's pain becomes our bundle of sensory experience. But Marlow recoils from the eerie spectacle of "a crystalline void" [*LJ* 216]. We escape the solipsism of total skepticism with respect to others by acknowledging the reality of another's pain.[29]

As the self experiences what the other (that is the other-like-self) experiences, the self may be able to escape the sealed cloister of its own consciousness. In this way, reality is not simply a reflection of one's self. "Dispelling the potential for solipsism in Marlow's narration, it [Marlow's epiphany at Stein's] replaces Marlow's reflection in the mirror with the 'imperishable reality' [*LJ* 216] of someone whose otherness is now acknowledged."[30] Furthermore, as one acknowledges the existence of the other, one also acknowledges the existence of the self. The other's experience then becomes in part the self's experience, and the existence of each becomes more real, and hence each may avoid solipsism.

However, not only the self's ability to experience what the other experiences diminishes the possibility of solipsism. The process also works in reverse. In fact, Conrad seems even more interested in investigating the possibility of the self projected on to the other than of the other projected on to the self. The epigraph to *Lord Jim* best encapsulates Jim's (and certainly Marlow's as well) response to solipsism: "It is certain my Conviction gains infinitely, the moment another soul will believe in it" (Novalis). Guerard notes that Jim "wants the confirmation of other men's admiration and love and at the least needs one man (Marlow) who will believe in him."[31] Jim himself echoes this view when he says to Marlow, "You don't know what it is for a fellow in my position to be believed" (*LJ* 128). He later reiterates this sentiment when he tells Marlow, "I must stick to their [Doramin's people's] belief in me to feel safe" (*LJ* 334). Jim "cannot believe in himself unless he has found another to do so. And he needs a judge, witness, and advocate in the solitude of his battle with himself."[32] Jim's confidence in his knowledge is directly proportional to the degree others concur with his experience. During the trial, when no one perceives the *Patna* incident as he does, his confidence drops to its low point. It begins to rally only after Jim believes that Marlow perceives things as Jim does, when Marlow tells us that he "was moved to make a solemn declaration of [his] readiness to believe implicitly anything he [Jim] thought fit to tell [him]" (*LJ* 127).[33] Both Jim and Marlow need others to concur with their experience; for Jim it is his jump from the *Patna*, and for Marlow it is his view of an indifferent universe and his perception of Jim.

In all of his narratives, Marlow tries to obtain consensus concerning his knowledge of phenomena. As discussed earlier, one of the goals of all impressionist techniques is identification between reader and writer. Therefore, Marlow forces his listeners to experience phenomena from his own particular point of view. He locates his listeners at his vantage point and hopes they will experience phenomena as he does.[34] *Lord Jim*, *Chance*, "Heart of Darkness," and "Youth" all have at heart the same desire for confirmation. Periodically, Marlow interrupts his narratives to seek his listeners' consensus. In *Lord Jim*, he says, "Yet you, too, in your time must have known the intensity of life" (*LJ* 225). In "Heart of Darkness," he asks, "Do you see him [Kurtz]? Do you see the story? Do you see anything?" (*Y* 82). In *Chance*, Marlow says, "And you are startled! I am giving you the naked truth. It's true too that nothing lays itself open to the charge of exaggeration more than the language of naked truth" (*C* 80). And in "Youth," he asks, "[A]nd, tell me, wasn't that the best time, that time when we were young at sea?" (*Y* 42). At each narrative interruption, Marlow presents his listeners with his experience and solicits their agreement concerning their experiences. He wants to know whether they perceive what he perceives, whether they experience what he experiences – whether they know what he knows. If they concur, his knowledge becomes for him more real, and this is important because often Marlow himself is uncertain of the certainty of his knowledge. In *Lord Jim*, as occurs throughout (*LJ* 177, 221, 223, 241, 306, 330–31, 339), the novel closes with Marlow's asserting his uncertainty concerning his experience (*LJ* 416), and in "Heart of Darkness," he comments on the haziness and dreamlike quality of his experience in Africa (i.e., *Y* 82, 93). In fact, "Heart of Darkness" actually presents perhaps the best example of his audience's confirmation of his narration. Early in the story, the frame narrator exhibits some resistance to listening to Marlow when he says, "[W]e knew we were fated, before the ebb began to run, to hear about one of Marlow's inconclusive experiences" (*Y* 51). While they wait for the ebb to run so they can proceed, they listen to Marlow's tale. But at the close of the story, the listeners have been so drawn into Marlow's experience that they miss their opportunity to catch the ebb (*Y* 162). Marlow has "changed the way that the primary narrator, at least, sees the Thames; for when he raises his head, the narrator's vision, now coloured by the expensive power of Marlow's primary symbol, discovers that 'the tranquil waterway ... seemed to lead into the heart of an immense darkness.'"[35] The story ends with the frame narrator's language and imagery indistinguishable from Marlow's own (*Y* 162). In fact, Marlow's listeners perceive what Marlow perceives and experience what Marlow experiences; in effect, they have come to know what Marlow knows.

Conrad himself longed for the confirmation of the other concerning the self's experience; in a letter to Galsworthy, he wrote, "I was more concerned than uneasy at your seediness which I seemed to know so well. It was like beholding ones own weird acquaintance in a looking glass; my own well known mysterious, disturbing sensations reflected in Your personality which is as near the inner *me* as anything not absolutely myself can be."[36] By witnessing his reflection in Galsworthy's experience, Conrad's own experience becomes more real and helps him to escape the solipsism of his own consciousness. In this same way, Conrad, as final author of phenomena in his works, also wants his readers to agree with his assessments and experiences. The preface to *The Nigger of the "Narcissus"* clearly represents this desire. Although, as is generally assumed, Conrad is interested in making his readers "see" the truths he presents in his works,[37] he also wants his readers to concur with his experience of phenomena. Wollaeger suggests that "if author and reader can, in every sense of the word, 'see' together, they join in a community of understanding."[38] If Conrad can make his readers hear, feel, and see what he hears, feels, and sees, then his own experience of the world takes on an actuality unavailable in isolation, and Conrad feels generally successful in his attempt: "I have been understood as completely as it is possible to be understood in this, our world, which seems to be mostly composed of riddles" (*MS* ix). In order for Conrad himself to escape solipsism, his readers must confirm his epistemological experience. As a result, he, like Marlow, consistently looks for his readers to reflect back his own experience.

In a relative world, Conrad and his characters long for a closure and certainty that is impossible; they can never be sure their knowledge is certain. The society of that time asserted that western civilization rests upon solid, absolute foundations and that such foundations are necessary or all meaning and certainty departs from human existence. But for Conrad, with knowledge founded on a limited and relative point of view, neither empirical nor rational evidence is certain. Human beings can never be sure that what they experience is what others do. Nevertheless, the concurrence of others makes one's knowledge seem more certain. Ultimately, such confirmation is not proof, but it is the only assurance available, and so Conrad's characters consistently embrace consensus concerning their own epistemological experience. To simply accept solipsism would make life impossible; all would be unknowable, unpredictable, and uncontrollable. In such a world, only isolation and despair could exist.

Just as Conrad looked to the certainty of human existence for a solution to solipsism, so also does he look to that certainty for a solution to ethical anarchy. As discussed earlier, throughout his works, Conrad clearly rejects any absolute foundation for western civilization and its system of values. He often removes his characters from Europe's familiar surroundings and forces them to exist without such external restraints as police and public opinion. In "Heart of Darkness," for instance, Marlow says to his listeners,

[W]ith solid pavement under your feet, surrounded by kind neighbours ready to cheer you or to fall on you, stepping delicately between the butcher and the policeman, in the holy terror of scandal and gallows and lunatic asylums – how can you imagine what particular region of the first ages of a man's untrammelled feet may take him into by the way of solitude – utter solitude without a policeman – by the way of silence – utter silence, where no warning voice of a kind neighbour can be heard whispering of public opinion? These little things make all the great difference. (Y 116)

Invariably, these characters then learn that the system of values they have accepted as absolute is not absolute at all but simply a convenience, a social contract between the members of a society. If the value system is without an absolute foundation, however, then what compels one to adhere to it? This is why the restraints of law and public opinion are so important to Marlow.

In "Heart of Darkness," Conrad shows how this lack of external restraints affects various characters. For the Central Station Manager, it results in his total amorality, in which Kurtz's pillaging is "vigorous action" (Y 137) and is not morally reprehensible but simply an "unsound method" (Y 137). Kurtz, without restraints, becomes completely immoral, giving himself up to "unspeakable rites, which . . . were offered up to him" (Y 118). This is particularly ironic, since he goes into the wilderness with the idea of propagating European values (Y 79, 88, 91). Once there, Kurtz expects civilization's absolute values to be self-evident, but they are not. This loss of an absolute foundation apparently brings him to a crisis of faith, and with his value system overturned and with no external enforcement, his existence becomes one of ethical anarchy. Watt argues that "the individual colonist's power, combined with the lack of any effective control, was an open invitation to every kind of cruelty and abuse."[39] The Russian makes this clear when he says that Kurtz "declared he would shoot me unless I gave him the ivory and then cleared out of the country, because he could do so, and had a fancy for it, and there was nothing on earth to prevent him killing whom he jolly well pleased. And it was true, too" (Υ 128). In this state, Kurtz "had kicked himself loose of the earth" (Υ 144). Since he no longer had confidence in his cultural values, he had nothing on which to rely. His whole existence had been based on that foundation. In his essay on the suppression of savage customs, Kurtz's confidence in the correctness of his mission is possible only within an absolute system. The scrawled postscript, "Exterminate all the brutes!" (Υ 118), is his disillusioned response. Kurtz's dealings with the Africans have exposed him to another society that exists outside the views of his European society, and as a result he comes to believe that his system of values is not the only way to order one's existence and hence cannot be based upon an absolute foundation. Furthermore, when Kurtz discovers that he can kill "whom he jolly well pleased" without consequences, he also reveals his disillusionment concerning the certainty of western values and society and, consequently, can find no real shelter from such knowledge. He blames the Africans for his disillusionment and hates them for it, just as the chief accountant remarks, "When one has got to make correct entries, one comes to hate those savages – hate them to the death" (Υ 70). The Africans intrude upon the constructs of western civilization, reminding the Europeans that their system is not absolute.[40]

Despite his rejection of absolutes, Conrad affirms adherence to western values in general, as evidenced by his critical attitude toward both the amoral Station Manager and the immoral Kurtz. Adhering to western values because they provide for orderly social interaction, however, is very different from adhering to them because they are based upon absolutes. In fact, in "Heart of Darkness" the belief that western values are grounded in absolutes hinders adhering to those principles because the Europeans assume that such principles will be self-evident, but they are not. Instead, Marlow says that a man "must meet that truth with his own true stuff – with his own inborn strength. Principles won't do. Acquisitions, clothes, pretty rags – rags that would fly off at the first good shake. No; you want a deliberate belief" (*Y* 97).[41] All else but inner strength will not bear out upon trial, as Daleski argues, "The resolution for such control stems from a man's 'own true stuff,' from his 'own inborn strength,' stems, in short, from an innate capacity to hold himself together, from an innate self-possession."[42] In "Heart of Darkness," society dictates principles based upon false absolutes, whereas "a deliberate belief" is a conscious decision to act in a particular manner, not necessarily because it is inherently right but because it is the best course of action for establishing meaning for human existence. As is true of Kurtz, Fresleven, the Station Manager, the manager's uncle, the pilgrims, and others, once removed from civilized restraints, they discover that their values are not self-evidently absolute and that nothing prevents them from doing whatever they want. Kurtz says this when he threatens to shoot the Russian (*Y* 128). The Station Manager's uncle says of the Russian, "Certainly, get him hanged! Why not? Anything – anything can be done in this country" (*Y* 91). Marlow says, "[O]ut there there were no external checks" (*Y* 74). And the Russian clears out before the Station Manager can hang him saying, "[T]hey would soon find some excuse. What's to stop them?" (*Y* 139).

Elsewhere in Conrad's works, Jim tells Marlow, "After the ship's lights had gone, anything might have happened in that boat – anything in the world – and the world no wiser" (*LJ* 120). In "Because of the Dollars," Hollis remarks that "nothing prevented the old fellow [the Rajah of Dongala] having Bamtz's throat cut and the carcase thrown into deep water outside the reefs" (*WT* 178). In the same story, the Frenchman suggests, "We can do with him [Bamtz] what we like" (*WT* 188). In *Victory*, Ricardo says that Pedro and his brother "must have been saying to each other: 'No one's ever likely to come looking for these two fellows [Ricardo and Mr. Jones] ... Let's cut their throats'" (*V* 138). In "The Secret Sharer," the narrator notes they are "far from all human eyes, with only sky and sea for spectators and for judges" (*TLS* 92). And Conrad himself touches upon another place of absent restraints when he writes of the author's task: "In that interior world where his thought and his emotions go seeking for the experience of imagined adventures, there are no policemen, no law, no pressure of circumstance or dread of opinion to keep him within bounds. Who then is going to say Nay to his temptations if not his conscience?" (*PR* xx). Whether in the heart of Africa, the open ocean, or the interiority of the mind, nothing can force Conrad or his characters to adhere to their values. Instead, they must make a conscious decision to practice restraint because although knowledge may be uncertain, "it is possible to believe a thing or two."[43] Unable to wholly escape their cultural experience, they also cannot escape the necessity of cultural values in their existence; such values create a safe social interaction and a meaning for human existence, not one that is universal nor even one that is necessarily superior to other systems but one that is faithful to the only certainty in Conrad – the certainty of human existence itself.

An existence that cultivates restraint based upon a conscious decision is not founded upon anything outside itself and depends solely upon inner strength. Marlow emphasizes this effect when he tries to puzzle out the seeming paradox of the cannibals practicing restraint but the Europeans lacking restraint. The cannibals appear to have no food with them, and yet they offer no threat to the Europeans. Marlow remarks, "Restraint! I would just as soon have expected restraint from a hyena prowling amongst the corpses of a battlefield. But there was the fact facing me – the fact dazzling, to be seen, like the foam on the depths of the sea, like a ripple on an unfathomable enigma" (Y 105). As Daleski suggests, "The cannibal crew thus posit a capacity for the ultimate abandon of utter savagery at the same time as they exemplify the innate restraint that Marlow considers the only effective safeguard of civilized behaviour."[44] According to Marlow, this restraint is not a result of externals:

Restraint! What possible restraint? Was it superstition, disgust, patience, fear – or some kind of primitive honour? No fear can stand up to hunger, no patience can wear it out, disgust simply does not exist where hunger is; and as to superstition, beliefs, and what you may call principles, they are less than chaff in a breeze . . . It takes a man all his inborn strength to fight hunger properly . . . And these chaps, too, had no earthly reason for any kind of scruple. (Y 105)

In other words, Marlow believes the cannibals neither adhere to some absolute principle nor fear reprisal (since they outnumber the Europeans thirty to five). Instead, he sees an internal restraint, not necessarily "true" but nevertheless one the cannibals accept individually and collectively. This is precisely what Kurtz, the Station Manager, and the pilgrims lack, as does almost every other European whom Marlow encounters in Africa. For them, adherence to a value system is based solely on either external absolutes or external enforcement (more often the latter).[45] Consequently, when removed from those externals, all restraint disappears, and ethical anarchy reigns.

For Conrad, human beings cannot rely on externals to keep them from ethical anarchy: ethical actions instead must come from an inner strength. But the problem becomes knowing what is ethical if neither absolutes nor social mandates reveal such information. In Conrad's world, since all knowledge but the actuality of human existence is uncertain, ethical knowledge is not immune from such uncertainty. As was true of his response to solipsism, Conrad can rely only on his belief in the certainty of human existence to avoid ethical anarchy. Therefore, those things that affirm the existence of self and other-like-self create meaning for our lives. Conrad affirms such qualities as kindness, love, friendship, compassion, companionship, and community because they protect and maintain human existence – not because they are necessarily true in an absolute sense, but because they affirm humanity. By the same token, he condemns cruelty, selfishness, and betrayal; again, not because they are inherently false, but because they deny humanity. Such acts negate Conrad's only certainty, leaving only annihilation and oblivion in their wake. As a result, affirming humanity becomes the only possible alternative to ethical anarchy.

In Conrad's writings, both work and community affirm humanity. Each is important because each affirms self and other as human beings; work relates primarily to the self while community relates primarily to others (although the two are not mutually exclusive). Work creates meaning for human beings in three ways. First, it provides shelter from the actuality of an indifferent universe; second, it allows the self to circumscribe an area wholly its own; third, it emphasizes the relationship between self and other through mutual reliance.

In "Heart of Darkness," Marlow argues for the significance of work as a means to shelter us from the actuality of the nature of the universe. He comments that the wilderness had "the stillness of an implacable force brooding over an inscrutable intention" (*Y* 93); after a time, Marlow gets used to this sensation but not because he grows accustomed to the idea of an indifferent universe. Instead, he says,

I had no time. I had to keep guessing at the channel; I had to discern, mostly by inspiration, the signs of hidden banks; I watched for sunken stones . . . I had to keep a look-out for the signs of dead wood we could cut up in the night for next day's steaming. When you have to attend to things of that sort, to the mere incidents of the surface, the reality – the reality, I tell you – fades. The inner truth is hidden. (*Y* 93; see also 97, 98)[46]

Here Marlow provides a concrete way to retreat from the knowledge of an indifferent universe, "as a tortoise withdraws within its shell" (*LJ* 313). As long as Marlow must attend to the surface details of his work, he keeps himself from facing the knowledge of an indifferent universe, and because "the inner truth is hidden," life is tolerable. As suggested earlier, Marlow also emphasizes how work creates meaning for human existence by allowing the individual to carve out an entity that is uniquely that individual's, and through that individuality to create a meaning for the self (i.e., *Y* 85). Finally, by emphasizing the necessity of others, work creates meaning for human existence through cooperation and community. All work is intertwined with and responds to the work of others. As a result, a chain of interconnected links of labor forms a working whole. By the same token, removing links from the chain can threaten the existence of the whole. The importance of mutual labor is most apparent in Conrad's sea tales, particularly in *The Nigger of the "Narcissus"* and "Typhoon." In both works, the crews encounter storms, so powerful that the men doubt they will survive, and to survive they must work together for their mutual safety. In "Typhoon," the narrator comments that Jukes

felt ready to wring all their necks at the slightest sign of hanging back. The very thought of it exasperated him . . . The impetuosity with which he came amongst them carried them along . . . [H]e appeared formidable – busied with matters of life and death that brooked no delay. At his first word he heard them drop into the bunker one after another obediently. (*T* 76)

Jukes knows the severity of their situation: he knows that if the crew "hang back" their chances of surviving are slim.[47] The work of each individual crew member is necessary for the survival of the others, and the work of the other crew members is necessary for the survival of each individual. In other words, the work of others demonstrates the necessity of their existence for our existence, and our work demonstrates the necessity of our existence for theirs. Work thereby creates meaning both individually and collectively.

Collective work is simply one form of Conrad's emphasis on community that is so important throughout his works. In *Lord Jim*, Marlow remarks, "Woe to the stragglers! We exist only in so far as we hang together" (*LJ* 223). For Conrad, our primary means for existence depends upon communion with others. Conrad himself experienced this phenomenon; Watt suggests that "the first half of his life had forced Conrad to see that his problematic dependence on others was a necessary condition for the very existence of the individual self."[48] Such dependence comes in the form of community. In Conrad's works, community usually takes two forms: the communion between two individuals and the community of the group. Both are important to Conrad, and both hold a privileged position in his works because they affirm human existence. Conrad affirms community and rejects its betrayal,[49] particularly when characters choose material interests or an absolute idea over human communion.

Communion between individuals takes the form of friends, lovers, or family members, and Conrad often presents these relationships juxtaposed against fixed ideas. The narrator of *The Rover* notes, "The motive force of a fixed idea is very great" (*Ro* 193). Such ideas may take the form of either material interests or absolute ideas, and often the two are linked, as with Gould's perception of the San Tomé mine.[50] The narrator of *Nostromo* notes that fixed ideas are dangerous: "A man haunted by a fixed idea is insane. He is dangerous even if that idea is an idea of justice; for may he not bring the heaven down pitilessly upon a loved head?" (*N* 379). Conrad rejects fixed ideas because they always de-emphasize humanity. They prioritize something other than humanity and hence something less certain. Examples abound in Conrad's works contrasting human communion with either absolute ideas or material interests. The most obvious example of tension between the two occurs in *Nostromo*. Both Charles Gould and Nostromo choose material interests over communion with others. "Just as Gould is consumed by the mine that takes possession of him and reduces him to a fortified hollowness, so Nostromo is eaten up by the criminality that takes hold of him."[51] In a letter to his sister, Decoud writes of Mrs. Gould: "The little woman has discovered that he [Gould] lives for the mine rather than for her" (*N* 245). Although the Goulds' relationship begins with love, Charles' attachment to the mine soon overshadows all else. Not only does Gould lose possession of his self through his obsession, he also loses the communion that existed between him and his wife. The narrator suggests that Mrs. Gould "would never have him [Gould] to herself. Never; not for one short hour altogether to herself" (*N* 521–22). Nostromo's situation is similar. He chooses the silver over humanity. Once he steals the silver, he ceases to be the man he was. His communion with others diminishes, but more important he is ultimately unfaithful even to Giselle – not with another woman but with the silver. Speaking from experience, Mrs. Gould says to Giselle when Nostromo dies, "Console yourself, child. Very soon he would have forgotten you for his treasure" (*N* 561). Mrs. Gould, however, does not know that Nostromo had already begun to forget Giselle.[52]

Many instances also exist of the tension between human communion

and absolute ideas in Conrad's works. In "The Return," Hervey initially places his confidence in absolutes. He says to his wife, "The world
is right – in the main – or else it couldn't be – couldn't be – what it is"
(*TU* 161). In other words, civilization is based upon absolutes and
therefore must be true. As a result of his revelation, though, Hervey
discovers not that the "world is right" but rather that "it couldn't be."
And when he cannot repress this knowledge, he tries to connect with
another human being, the only certainty left to him in a relative
universe. Hervey thinks, "There can be no life without faith and love –
faith in a human heart, love of a human being!" (*TU* 177). He turns to his
wife for this certitude; as Hervey looks at her,

> it occurred to him that the woman there had in her hands an indispensable gift
> which nothing else on earth could give; and when he stood up he was
> penetrated by an irresistible belief in an enigma, by the conviction that within
> his reach and passing away from him was the very secret of existence – its
> certitude, immaterial and precious! (*TU* 176)

This certitude is the communion between two people that confirms their
mutual existence and becomes the basis for moral action; in other
words, taking their mutual existence as the only certainty, they form a
bond that is meant to support and protect their existences. But this
possibility fails him too when he realizes that his wife has only returned
to him out of conformity to convention – not out of love or support for
their relationship. Like his revelation concerning the nature of the
universe, Hervey cannot repress the knowledge that nothing exists
between him and his wife. He thinks of all his material possessions, "All
– all the blessings of life. All – but the certitude immaterial and precious
– the certitude of love and faith" (*TU* 180). He lacks, however, the one
certitude he has identified. He must confront an existence of mutual
solitude with his wife, but he cannot live under those conditions, and so
he despairs and flees.[53]

Lord Jim represents equally strongly the importance of human communion. The relationship between Jim and Jewel is powerful; Jewel
saves Jim's life by warning him of the assassins (*LJ* 296–302). More
important, though, in this incident, Conrad impresses upon the reader
the fundamental importance of human communion. In the midst of
the attack, Jim "realised that for him there was no refuge from that
loneliness which centupled all his dangers except – in her [Jewel]"
(*LJ* 300). Despite his immediate danger, Jim realizes that communion
with another person is all that matters. Later, he expresses the significance of this feeling in confirming the certitude of his existence: "I love

her [Jewel] dearly. More than I could tell ... You take a different view of your actions when you come to understand, when you are *made* to understand every day that your existence is necessary – you see, absolutely necessary – to another person" (*LJ* 304; emphasis is Conrad's). In communing with Jewel, Jim finds the certitude he has sought since the *Patna* incident. Unfortunately, the novel's tragedy is that Jim is not "equal to" the trust Jewel places in him. At the novel's close, Marlow comments that Jim "goes away from a living woman to celebrate his pitiless wedding with a shadowy ideal of conduct" (*LJ* 416). When Dain Waris dies, Jim has three alternatives: he can stay and fight; he can flee from Patusan; or he can give himself up to Doramin. These options come down to a choice between remaining faithful to Jewel or to an ideal of conduct. When Jewel calls Jim "false" and Stein calls him "true" (*LJ* 350), the dichotomy becomes clear. Jewel sees Jim as false to the communion between them, while Stein sees Jim as true to the ideal of conduct. But for Marlow giving up the real – the human – for an indefensible ideal is highly questionable. The woman is "living," but the ideal is "shadowy." The existence of Jewel is real; the existence of the ideal is not.

Unlike Jim, who holds to an absolute idea over human communion, in *Under Western Eyes*, both Tekla and Razumov ultimately choose humanity over absolute ideas. For many years, Tekla has been part of the revolutionary movement, but she finally finds meaning for her existence not in the absolute ideas of the revolution but rather in human communion. Initially, she finds this feeling with her young revolutionary lover. She also finds it with Razumov:

I have been starving for, I won't say kindness, but just for a little civility, for I don't know how long ... Yes, if you were to get ill, or meet some bitter trouble, you would find I am not a useless fool. You have only to let me know. I will come to you. I will indeed. And I will stick to you. Misery and I are old acquaintances – but this life here is worse than starving. (*UWE* 233)

Life in the revolutionary house of Madame de S__ is worse than starving because although Tekla does not starve physically, she does starve spiritually. Peter Ivanovitch's actions toward Tekla best evidence this situation. Ironically, while dictating to Tekla his revolutionary works for improving the human condition, Peter treats her like a slave – not only without kindness but without even civility. The revolutionary ideals do nothing toward creating meaning for Tekla's existence, but communion with Razumov (and earlier with her revolutionary lover) does. Similarly, Razumov first looks for meaning for his existence in loyalty to his country and his scholarly life. But to remain loyal to these, he must betray Haldin. He then compounds the problem by trying to exact yet further vengeance on Haldin by determining to "steal his sister's soul from her" (*UWE* 359). Razumov, however, discovers that loyalty to an idea holds no value because "there *is* 'a moral bond' [*UWE* 37] between Haldin and himself, the bond of fellowship or brotherhood which Haldin asserts in turning to him for help (and indirectly affirms when he constantly refers to Razumov as 'brother'), the bond of their common humanity whose obligations are as strong as those of a 'common faith' [*UWE* 37–38] or 'common conviction.' [*UWE* 38]."[54] Razumov tries to ignore his bond with Haldin, or with anyone else for that matter, but he cannot ignore these bonds and ultimately remarks that "[i]n giving Victor Haldin up, it was myself, after all, whom I have betrayed most basely" (*UWE* 361). When confronted with Natalia's humanness, as she opens her heart to him, he can no longer find meaning for his existence in such ideas as patriotism and vengeance and instead writes to Natalia, "I had ended by loving you" (*UWE* 361). For Razumov, this discovery is particularly important because as he tells Natalia, "I've never known any kind of love" (*UWE* 360; see also 353–54). Like Jim, Razumov finds meaning for his existence only through being necessary to another. Razumov learns, "A man's real life is that accorded to him in the thoughts of other men by reason of respect or natural love" (*UWE* 14). When Natalia asks for Razumov's help in comforting her mother, he says, "No one has ever expected such a thing from me before. No one whom my tenderness would have been of any use to" (*UWE* 344). Later, Sophia Antonovna illustrates how human communion finally gives meaning to Razumov's existence:

It was just when he [Razumov] believed himself safe and more – infinitely more – when the possibility of being loved by that admirable girl first dawned upon him, that he discovered that his bitterest railings, the worst wickedness, the devil work of his hate and pride, could never cover up the ignominy of the existence before him. There's character in such a discovery. (*UWE* 380)

Before Razumov makes this discovery – before he loves Natalia – he was physically whole but spiritually crippled. But at the close of the novel, though physically crippled, he is spiritually whole through his communion with Natalia and Tekla.

The relationship between human communion and political ideal takes an unusual turn in *Nostromo*. The narrator refers to Decoud as "the young apostle of Separation" (*N* 496). He is a strong proponent of separation, but he says himself, "Yes; separation of the whole Occidental Province from the rest of the unquiet body. But my true idea, the only one I care for, is not to be separated from Antonia" (*N* 215). Decoud holds to the ideal not because of powerful political convictions but because through political change he can establish a more permanent relationship with Antonia. Later, in trying to convince the provincial leaders to choose separation, he says, "I poured out an impassioned appeal to their courage and manliness, with all the passion of my love for Antonia" (*N* 236). To his listeners, Decoud's "impassioned appeal" is an appeal for political stability, but to Decoud it is simply an appeal for communion with Antonia.

In some instances, though, maintaining communion is not so clear cut. In "Karain," Matara's sister dishonors her family and people when she goes to live with a Dutch trader despite having been promised in marriage to another man. When the woman and the Dutch trader flee the country, Matara and Karain pursue them to avenge the dishonor. During a pursuit that lasts many years, their sole *raison d'être* is to find and kill the couple. The idea of finding the woman was the only thing that carried Karain through the extremities they suffered in her pursuit; she was the goal of their tribulations. After a time, however, a curious transformation occurs. The woman becomes the reward for enduring their trials – not a reward to destroy but rather one to cherish. Karain develops an obsessive attachment to her, and instead of an object of vengeance she becomes an object of love. He says, "She never left me ... She was beautiful, she was faithful ... In daylight she moved with a swaying walk before me upon the weary paths ... At night she looked into my face ... She gave me the courage to bear weariness and hardships. Those were times of pain, and she soothed me" (*TU* 34–35). The woman becomes the sole reality that makes Karain's existence tolerable – or even possible. Consequently, when Matara and Karain finally find the couple, Karain cannot allow Matara to kill the woman and shoots him as Matara tries to kill the couple. Matara is Karain's friend (cf. *TU* 23, 34), and killing Matara breaches the communion between them, but to allow Matara to kill the woman is to follow an absolute: the necessity of avenging dishonor. Karain affirms the human, where Matara affirms the absolute. The tragedy of the story is the necessity of breaching one relationship to protect another, and although Karain ultimately chooses humanity over an absolute, he still suffers for the choice, as he would have had he chosen otherwise.

A similar dilemma occurs in "The Lagoon." Arsat is in love with Diamelen, and he and his brother steal her from their ruler's home.

During their escape, Arsat's brother offers to hold off the pursuers as long as he can while Arsat takes Diamelen ahead to a canoe waiting to bear them away to freedom. Arsat is to wait for his brother to join them at the canoe, but while Arsat waits he grows afraid that his brother may not arrive soon enough ahead of their pursuers for them to escape, and so he pushes off the canoe, leaving his brother behind to die. Arsat affirms his love for his brother (*TU* 195, 202), and yet he leaves him to die. This incident differs, though, from that in "Karain." In this case, Arsat's action is selfish at heart. His concern is not to save a human life from the demands of an ideal. Instead, he sacrifices his brother's life in order to satisfy his own desires. A tie exists between Arsat and Diamelen, and by sacrificing his brother Arsat maintains that relationship (although it is unlikely that his brother had to be sacrificed at all), but his relationship with Diamelen is at the cost of his relationship with his brother. Although curiously misguided, Karain's concern is for another, whereas Arsat's is for himself. Selfishness is always at odds with communion because it focuses on the individual rather than the relationship. Arsat sacrifices a communion built upon the unselfishness of his brother, who says, "We are two who are like one" (*TU* 196). The brothers establish their very existence based upon mutual communion, but Arsat's selfishness destroys that relationship.[55]

As is true of communion between two individuals, communion among individuals in a group – that is community – is equally important in Conrad's works. Community can be as small as two individuals or as large as all of humanity, but in either case, it requires the mutual consent and mutual affirmation of humanity for its existence. Two facets of community are particularly important because they privilege human existence. First, community embodies the same human-affirming characteristics that occur in communion between two individuals; second, community relies on consensus to establish its foundation. And just as communal affirmation helps confirm one's epistemological and ethical convictions, so also does its rejection condemn one in Conrad's works. Because community is so fragile and because its foundation is only common consent, breach of community produces extreme reactions. In fact, Marlow remarks, "The real significance of crime is in its being a breach of faith with the community of mankind" (*LJ* 157). But whether affirming or rejecting community, its significance in Conrad's works does not vary because it always focuses on humanity.

Early in *The Nigger of the "Narcissus,"* the exchange between James Wait and Singleton exemplifies the role of community: Wait "asked without emphasis: – 'What kind of ship is this? Pretty fair? Eh?' Singleton didn't stir. A long while after he said, with unmoved face: – 'Ship! . . . Ships are all right. It is the men in them!'" (*NN* 24; ellipsis is Conrad's; cf. *MS* 129). The people make the situation – not the physical circumstances. On the ship, men must work together to protect and maintain their lives and their social group. Their mutual cooperation protects both their physical existence and their spiritual existence. The narrator closes the novel with a tribute to community when he says, "They pass and make a sign, in a shadowy hail. Haven't we, together and upon the immortal sea, wrung out a meaning from our sinful lives? Good-bye, brothers! You were a good crowd" (*NN* 173). The individuals may pass away, but the group remains. In an indifferent universe, community provides strength, protection, certainty, and, most important, meaning for their existence. This is why Donkin's actions so threaten the crew. He solicits the benefits of community and claims to act on its behalf, but in reality he is simply selfish:

He was the man that cannot steer, that cannot splice, that dodges the work on dark nights; that, aloft, holds on frantically with both arms and legs, and swears at the wind, the sleet, the darkness; the man who curses the sea while others work. The man who is the last out and the first in when all hands are called. The man who can't do most things and won't do the rest . . . The sympathetic and deserving creature that knows all about his rights, but knows nothing of courage, of endurance, and of the unexpressed faith, of the unspoken loyalty that knits together a ship's company. (*NN* 10–11)

Later in the novel, Donkin betrays his selfishness; he steals from Wait just before he dies (*NN* 154), and during the storm, when the crew realize Wait is trapped in his cabin, one man says, "Let's go and see," to which Donkin replies, "Damn him, who could go?" The response to Donkin is significant: "'Nobody expects you to,' growled the man next to him: 'you're only a thing'" (*NN* 64). This remark transforms Donkin into the other-unlike-self. Donkin's selfishness threatens the whole because community depends upon mutual reliance and contribution. Donkin relies on the group, but he contributes nothing.

Donkin's threat is not just spiritual, in that he threatens the universality of consensus and reveals the fragility of community; his selfishness also represents a genuine physical threat. On the high seas, divorced from the relative safety of land, the crew are in constant physical danger. In this particular instance, they are in the midst of a terrible storm, one that could easily drown them all. What saves them is the communal work that keeps the ship afloat; without that cooperation, they would probably all die. This danger is a metonym for the role of community in the novel and throughout Conrad's works. Once cooperation disappears, human beings are prey to the unsheltered truth of an indifferent universe. Donkin's danger to the crew does not end, though, with his selfishness during the storm. He also tries to incite the men to mutiny, not because he is concerned with their rights, as he suggests, but rather he hopes the blame will be spread out over the entire crew if something goes wrong. He also hopes to hide his guilt among the anonymity of the crowd. He throws a belaying pin from the cover of darkness and from the anonymity of the group, and when the time comes to account for his action, he tries to melt back into the crowd. His attempt to incite the crew threatens them with a disciplinary action that could ruin their lives, but Donkin is unconcerned with what happens to them.

The most complete assessment of Donkin comes from Singleton, when he simply says, "Damn you!" (*NN* 130) in response to Donkin's attempt to drive a wedge between the crew and the officers. The narrator sets up Singleton as the consummate community member, the embodiment of its attributes (*NN* 24–25). Singleton's damnation of Donkin has the effect of a kind of final judgment, and before the narrator's closing affirmation of the ship's community, he is careful to represent Donkin outside that group. He does so by aligning him with the company clerk, who is blind to Singleton's virtues and dismisses him as "a disgusting old brute" (*NN* 169). The clerk's assessment of Singleton shows he is outside the community of the sea. The clerk is a man of the land and the fact that he thinks Donkin "an intelligent man" (*NN* 169) and that they were "dropping h's against one another as if for a wager – very friendly" (*NN* 169) emphasizes that neither belongs to the community of the sea. It is no mistake that Donkin then rejects a sea job for a land job. His rejection, however, is superfluous; he had already forfeited his membership in the community when his selfishness endangered the group.[56]

Community is equally important in *The Shadow Line*. Again, a ship's crew is isolated from human contact. And although they do not encounter a storm, their predicament is no less precarious. Once out of port, they experience a dead calm, and to make matters worse most of the crew are sick with fever. Unable to move forward or backward and unable to staff the ship, they drift; meanwhile the captain fears he will lose his crew to fever before they ever reach port. Despite their illness, though, the crew try to perform their duties whenever they can so much as roll out of their sick-beds. Community holds them together, even to the extent of Mr. Burns crawling on deck to try to exorcise the spirit of the ship's former captain. In the end, they only just escape death through mutual cooperation. Much of their difficulty is a direct result of their former captain's betrayal of the community. Despite his position as a representative member, he orders his crew to sail into dangerous conditions, and, but for the rebellion of Mr. Burns, he might have succeeded in drowning or starving the crew. Mr. Burns says of him,

> He never meant her [the ship] to see home again. He wouldn't write to his owners, he never wrote to his old wife either – he wasn't going to. He had made up his mind to cut adrift from everything. That's what it was. He didn't care for business, or freights, or for making a passage – or anything. He meant to have gone wandering about the world till he lost her with all hands. (*SL* 61–62)

Even after his death, the captain threatens the crew because he replaced the quinine with a useless substitute and because (from Mr. Burns' perspective) he bars their way past the entrance of the harbor and causes the dead calm. With quinine on board, the delay caused by the calm would not have been nearly so dangerous. In each instance, the former captain's betrayal is real and dangerous; his actions were "a complete act of treason, the betrayal of a tradition which seemed to [the young captain] as imperative as any guide on earth could be" (*SL* 62). The narrator makes it clear that the former captain's actions were not just a physical danger but also a blow against community.

Similarly, in "Heart of Darkness," Marlow presents Kurtz as the culmination of western civilization (*Y* 117, 154). As Miller remarks, "With his plans, his genius, his eloquence, his ideals, he is an example of civilized man at his highest point of development,"[57] and yet he endangers the community. The Russian tells Marlow, "Now, if he [Kurtz] does not say the right thing to them [the Africans] we are all done for" (*Y* 133). The fragility of their position implies Kurtz's betrayal of community. More significant, though, is the attack Kurtz orders on the steamer. In this act, he removes himself from the group and betrays it, as does the former captain in *The Shadow Line*. Besides the physical threat, Kurtz also threatens the group, as had Donkin, through his selfishness. Initially, he goes into the wilderness to propagate his community values (*Y* 91), but after he loses faith in those values, he also loses all feeling for community. He becomes powerful and does not need the mutual affirmation and protection of the group. When he becomes an object of worship among the Africans, his affirmation becomes self-centered rather than mutual. Marlow condemns Kurtz's frame of mind: "'My

Intended, my ivory, my station, my river, my – ' everything belonged to him" (*Y* 116). Because of his attitude, Kurtz raids villages, forces the company to close the Inner Station, and orders the attack on the steamer. Kurtz betrays and jeopardizes every community with which he has contact because his selfishness knows no bounds.

Betrayal in Conrad's works is particularly damning for several other reasons. First, betrayal exposes the community's fragile and ephemeral nature and is unusually devastating when it comes from one with authority; such a betrayal shakes the community's very foundations. Second, the deaths of *The Shadow Line*'s former captain and Kurtz are more than merely poetic justice. Their deaths represent the annihilation of the human when isolated from communion with others. In this way, their deaths are merely a physical manifestation of an already existing condition. The former captain and Kurtz ceased to exist when they cut themselves off from the community. Third, both betrayals occur outside civilization. In each case, the physical danger to the people involved is real, but the isolated surroundings also emphasize a spiritual danger as well. In other words, the betrayal of the leader threatens the group's members with death, and in Conrad's works this means utter annihilation into oblivion: they cease to exist.

In addition to showing betrayal of community, "Heart of Darkness" also affirms the idea of community – but through its absence during most of the story. On Marlow's way to the Outer Station, they land soldiers and custom-house officers, and he remarks: "Some, I heard, got drowned in the surf; but whether they did or not, nobody seemed particularly to care. They were just flung out there, and on we went" (*Y* 60–61). There is a complete want of community here. The crew simply does its job and gets paid. Similarly, at the Outer Station, a group of Africans rests in "the grove of death" waiting to die, and no one even seems to see them (*Y* 66–67). Of the company's chief accountant, Marlow notes, "When a truckle-bed with a sick man (some invalid agent from up-country) was put in there, he exhibited a gentle annoyance. 'The groans of this sick person,' he said, 'distract my attention. And without that it is extremely difficult to guard against clerical errors in this climate'" (*Y* 69). Marlow then sums up the entire scene by saying, "In the steady buzz of flies the homeward-bound agent was lying flushed and insensible; the other, bent over his books, was making correct entries of perfectly correct transactions; and fifty feet below the doorstep I could see the still tree-tops of the grove of death" (*Y* 70). Juxtaposed against human suffering, the company's representative concerns himself with organizing material interests – the company's profits. And so the chief accountant and the others at the Outer Station reject human certainty for organized uncertainty. In this instance and others, "Heart of Darkness" chronicles the dissolution of community and the ethical anarchy that follows.[58]

Victory perhaps most graphically demonstrates the role of community in Conrad's works – both in the moral anarchy that occurs on the island and in the relationship between Heyst and Lena. Essentially alone on the island with the three villains, Heyst and Lena experience the moral anarchy that is possible where community is absent. Without external restraints and a communal contract, the characters experience the effects of a collection of individuals out for themselves. At the close of the novel, all five of the characters are dead. Even more significant is Lena and Heyst's relationship. For Heyst, who was "the most detached of creatures in this earthly captivity, the veriest tramp on this earth, an indifferent stroller going through the world's bustle" (*V* 198–99), and for Lena, who had no one in the world who cared about her (*V* 78), life is wholly unfulfilling. Once they form a relationship, though, all of that changes, and they experience a meaningful existence (until the villains arrive). Unfortunately, Heyst learns this lesson too late and laments to Davidson, "[W]oe to the man whose heart has not learned while young to hope, to love – and to put its trust in life!" (*V* 410).

Lord Jim, however, provides perhaps the clearest example of the effects of community on its members as it shows both the significance and fragility of community. Marlow's constant refrain that Jim is "one of us" emphasizes the existence of community and that the actions of individuals affect the group. Marlow clearly perceives Jim to be a member of the group and is angry because Jim breaches community and because Marlow wants to believe something more than simply consensus forms the group's foundation (or at least he wants to be sheltered from that truth) (*LJ* 40). Appearance and community are the two important issues for Marlow, and the two are intertwined. Marlow asserts that he would have trusted the deck of his ship to Jim based solely on appearance (*LJ* 45), but that is a superficial judgment, and appearance is different from actuality. Jim represents his society, but it is only a surface truth. Once the veneer is stripped away, something else entirely is visible. Jim's appearance of soundness becomes representative of the appearance of the community of the "craft." Jim only appears sound, just as community is only an appearance; beneath its surface, there is nothing to justify its appearance. Jim's appearance juxtaposed against the breach of community reveals the frailty of the group, and because Marlow wishes to repress this knowledge, he wants Jim to suffer.

Brierly is equally angry at Jim. He too recognizes the danger Jim represents to the community and says, "This infernal publicity is too shocking: there he sits while all these confounded natives, serangs, lascars, quartermasters, are giving evidence that's enough to burn a man to ashes with shame. This is abominable. Why, Marlow, don't you think, don't you feel, that this is abominable; don't you now – come – as a seaman?" (*LJ* 67). Brierly's concern is not so much directed toward Jim as a fellow seaman; his concern is with the group as a whole. As one of its members, Jim's actions affect its other members. Brierly recognizes this consequence and wants it to stop. The *Patna* incident itself is bad enough, but Jim's hearing is worse yet because it further publicizes the event. Brierly goes on to say, "This is a disgrace... [W]e must preserve professional decency or we become no better than so many tinkers going about loose. We are trusted. Do you understand? – trusted!... We aren't an organised body of men, and the only thing that holds us together is just the name for that kind of decency. Such an affair destroys one's confidence" (*LJ* 67–68). Brierly's statement gets to the heart of the issue. The "honour of the craft" (*LJ* 46), as Marlow refers to it, is simply a social contract between those of the craft and those who rely on the craft. Nothing else lies at its foundation to guarantee that trust. Only consensus holds it together. Some external restraints exist in the form of hearings and judgments – but no absolutes. In Conrad's works, this phenomenon is true of any voyage on the sea; when human beings are removed from civilization's external restraints, only the trust between crew and passengers, only this social contract, keeps at bay an indifferent universe that holds no absolute judgments over humanity's actions. Once the mutual trust decays, the entire craft becomes untenable. This is why Brierly wants Jim to clear out. The publicity exposes the fragility of the trust and of community itself. If it could happen aboard the *Patna*, then it could happen on other ships as well. Brierly wants this possibility suppressed because it could utterly destroy the community. If the truth of its fragility is not repressed, the whole enterprise may crumble.

Even those not connected with the hearing or the *Patna* react strongly to its crew; when the topic of the *Patna* comes up at one of Jim's many water clerk jobs, Captain O'Brien roars out, "Skunks!... It's a disgrace to human natur' – that's what it is. I would despise being seen in the same room with one of those men" (*LJ* 193–94). O'Brien had no direct contact with the *Patna*'s crew but still responds with extreme anger – to the point of questioning their very humanity. They have injured O'Brien by striking a blow at a part of him. In their breach of community, they injure all members of the group.

The *Patna* incident threatens the trust in the community of seamen and evokes anger on the part of Marlow, O'Brien, Brierly, and others. As a result, they cancel the certificates of those involved. In other words, they cancel their membership in the group so that the *Patna*'s crew can no longer threaten the group. In a sense, the officers cease to exist for the community. Of the five who abandon ship, all disappear in one way or another. George dies on deck (apparently of a heart attack) while trying to abandon ship; the chief engineer goes insane with the d.t.'s; the captain simply disappears;[59] Jim wanders from place to place seeking anonymity; and the second engineer (the only one besides Jim who appears again) also removes himself from the incident by physical distance and by anonymity, and after his one reappearance he too disappears again. Only Jim remains and tries to avoid the fate of the others. He cannot avoid the cancellation of his certificate, but he tries to avoid exclusion from the community.[60] To do so, he first tries to distance himself from the other officers. Several times, he portrays the others as different from himself. Marlow tells us, "He wanted me to know he had kept his distance; that there was nothing in common between him and these men" (*LJ* 103). Later, Jim emphasizes this difference when he says, "Not one of them would face it... They!" And Marlow notes that Jim "moved his hand slightly to imply disdain" (*LJ* 154; ellipsis is Conrad's; see also 24). Even Jim's placement in the lifeboat emphasizes his difference from the others; he tells Marlow, "They sat in the stern shoulder to shoulder, with the skipper in the middle, like three dirty owls, and stared at me" (*LJ* 123). Jim tries to portray the others not only as different sailors from himself but also as wholly different creatures, referring to them as "dirty owls" and comparing the captain's speech to that of a crow (*LJ* 124). By transforming the crew into something different from himself, he strips them of ties to the group, and as discussed earlier, they become others-unlike-self. Jim goes so far as to quit his first job as a water clerk because the second engineer shows up and tries to insinuate a communion between them based upon their mutual guilt, but to acknowledge such a relationship would be to relinquish his community with the men of the sea. In his own mind, he still holds with that community because he feels mitigating circumstances caused his failure. As long as Jim can remain outside the community of the *Patna*'s other officers, he feels he can remain inside the community of seamen. In the end, of course, he is at best only partly successful. He finds he must go to Patusan to hold on to his membership, but by removing himself to Patusan he removes himself physically from the community of seamen.

Even though only consensus holds community together, this fact is not necessarily a negative consequence in Conrad's works. This knowledge must be accepted, but that is all. In fact, just as mutual consensus helps to establish a kind of possible certainty concerning our epistemological experience and avoids solipsism, so also does consensus help to establish a kind of certainty concerning ethics. And the impressionist blurring of boundaries between subject and object find yet another manifestation in communal consensus concerning epistemological experience and ethical actions. The common consent of community members establishes an ethical and epistemological framework and predictability, as it creates a meaning for human existence – not one that is absolute but nevertheless one that can function through cooperation. Throughout his works, Conrad presents an irrational and indifferent universe but still one in which human beings must exist. Knowledge is both subjective and relative because phenomena are contextualized and filtered through human consciousness. At the same time, though, human subjectivity is the one common denominator in Conrad's universe. Consequently, he locates meaning and value in its existence; he affirms those things that affirm human existence and rejects those that reject it. Thus through affirmation of humanity and through social consensus in affirming it, Conrad's works construct a universe that creates meaning for human existence, a universe that, as Stein says, shows us "how to be" (*LJ* 214).

Epilogue

Suspicious of absolutes, Conrad consistently demonstrated the difficulty of universalizing human experience, whether it be objects of consciousness or ethical laws. Nevertheless, he could not accept nihilism, and in humanity and their activities, he finds a means to exist in an indifferent universe. In this way, he was influenced by his times. Born into the perceived certainty of the world of science and the tradition of western civilization, he witnessed the gradual erosion of this certainty into a world of skepticism and relativity in which most long-held assumptions about the nature of human existence came into question. He saw that neither the received truths of society nor the seeming certainty of science could stand up to the buffetings of the modern world. And yet Conrad would not let go of the moorings of an earlier time's seemingly more certain existence – not because those moorings were true nor even because they provided definitive meaning for human existence, but because their alternative was a nothingness that "would have been too dark – too dark altogether" (*Y* 162).

If Conrad's works are tragic, their tragedy lies in their recognition of the failure of an absolute world while still clinging to the conventions of that world. The richness of Conrad's works lies in his own vacillation between a desire for certainty and a recognition that such certainty is illusory. In the end, he was born too early to accept fully and unequivocally a relative universe and too late to believe in the absolutes of his progenitors.

Throughout his literary career, Joseph Conrad sought answers to the problems of human existence and the relationship between human beings and the world around them. Despite shifts in style (from an early convoluted style to a later more direct style), shifts in subject matter (from sea fiction to other topics), and shifts in quality (from greater works to lesser ones),[1] his philosophical presuppositions and impressionism remained constant – as did his views on western civilization, the nature of the universe, and the meaning of human existence. Conrad rejected the absolute world of realism and the scientific century that spawned it and insisted instead upon the relative world of impressionism with individual experience and human subjectivity at its core.

Notes

1 Christopher GoGwilt, *The Invention of the West* (Stanford, CA: Stanford University Press, 1995). See especially 15–42.
2 Diego Martelli, "A Lecture on the Impressionists" (1879), in *Impressionism and Post-Impressionism 1874–1904: Sources and Documents*, ed. Linda Nochlin (Englewood Cliffs, NJ: Prentice-Hall, 1966), 25.

I SUBJECT/OBJECT: SCIENCE AND THE EPISTEMOLOGICAL ORIGINS
OF LITERARY IMPRESSIONISM

1 See, for example, Charles Lyell's *Elements of Geology* (1838) and *The Geological Evidences of the Antiquity of Man* (1863); Charles Darwin's *On the Origin of Species by Means of Natural Selection* (1859) and *The Descent of Man, and Selection in Relation to Sex* (1871).
2 A number of works have investigated the revolutionary changes that occurred across disciplines during the late nineteenth and early twentieth centuries. See, for example, Debora L. Silverman, *Art Nouveau in Fin-de-Siècle France: Politics, Psychology, and Style* (Berkeley: University of California Press, 1989); Stephen Kern, *The Culture of Time and Space: 1880–1918* (Cambridge, MA: Harvard University Press, 1983); Carl E. Schorske, *Fin-de-Siècle Vienna: Politics and Culture* (New York: Vintage, 1981); H. Stuart Hughes, *Consciousness and Society: The Reorientation of European Social Thought 1890–1930*, rev. edn (New York: Vintage, 1977); Samuel Hynes, *The Edwardian Turn of Mind: First World War and English Culture*, new edn (London: Pimlico, 1992); and Roger Shattuck, *The Banquet Years: The Origins of the Avant-Garde in France 1885 to World War I*, rev. edn (New York: Vintage, 1968).
3 See, for example, Auguste Comte's, *Cours de philosophie positive (Course in Positivist Philosophy)* (1830–42) and *Système de politique positive (System of Positivist Polity)* (1851–54); John Stuart Mill's *A System of Logic* (1843) and *Utilitarianism* (1863); Herbert Spencer's *First Principles* (1862); Cesare Lombroso's *L'uomo delinquente (Criminal Man)* (1876); Hippolyte Taine's *De l'intelligence (Intelligence)* (1870); Ernest Renan's *L'avenir de la science (The Future of Science)* (1890); G. H. Lewes' *Problems of Life and Mind* (1874–79); Emile Durkheim's *De la division du*

travail social (The Division of Labor) (1893); and Leslie Stephen's *The Science of Ethics* (1882).

4 For a more extensive discussion of science and literature in the nineteenth century, see Gillian Beer, *Open Fields: Science in Cultural Encounter* (Oxford: Clarendon Press, 1996); Jonathan Smith, *Fact and Feeling: Baconian Science and the Nineteenth-Century Literary Imagination* (Madison: University of Wisconsin Press, 1994); George Levine, ed., *Realism and Representation: Essays on the Problem of Realism in Relation to Science, Literature, and Culture* (Madison: University of Wisconsin Press, 1993); John Christie and Sally Shuttleworth, eds., *Nature Transfigured: Science and Literature, 1700–1900* (Manchester: Manchester University Press, 1989); J. A. V. Chapple, *Science and Literature in the Nineteenth Century* (London: Macmillan, 1986); James Paradis and Thomas Postlewait, eds., *Victorian Science and Victorian Values: Literary Perspectives* (New Brunswick, NJ: Rutgers University Press, 1985); Peter Morton, *The Vital Science: Biology and the Literary Imagination, 1860–1900* (London: Allen & Unwin, 1984); Sally Shuttleworth, *George Eliot and Nineteenth-Century Science: The Make-Believe of a Beginning* (Cambridge: Cambridge University Press, 1984); Diana Postlethwaite, *Making it Whole: A Victorian Circle and the Shape of Their World* (Columbus: Ohio State University Press, 1984); Gillian Beer, *Darwin's Plots* (London: Routledge & Kegan Paul, 1983); Tess Cosslett, *The "Scientific Movement" and Victorian Literature* (New York: St. Martin's Press, 1982); Trevor H. Levere, *Poetry Realised in Nature: Samuel Taylor Coleridge and Early Nineteenth-Century Science* (Cambridge: Cambridge University Press, 1981); G. S. Rousseau, "Literature and Science: The State of the Field," *Isis* 69 (1978): 583–91; M. Millhauser, *Fire and Ice: The Influence of Science on Tennyson's Poetry* (Lincoln: Tennyson Society, 1971); Herbert L. Sussman, *Victorians and the Machine: The Literary Response to Technology* (Cambridge, MA: Harvard University Press, 1968); Aldous Huxley, *Science and Literature* (London: Chatto & Windus, 1963); Leo J. Henkin, *Darwinism in the English Novel 1860–1910: The Impact of Evolution on Victorian Fiction* (New York: Corporate Press, 1940); and Edward Douden, *Studies in Literature 1789–1877* (London: Kegan Paul, 1906), 85–121.

5 Emile Zola, *The Experimental Novel and Other Essays*, trans. Belle M. Sherman (New York: Cassell, 1893), 1.

6 Ibid., 2. In a sense, this is a variation of the nature–nurture argument with Zola clearly coming down on the nurture side.

7 Peter Allan Dale, *In Pursuit of a Scientific Culture: Science, Art, and Society in the Victorian Age* (Madison: University of Wisconsin Press, 1989), 14.

8 Ibid., 7. Compare also Eloise Knapp Hay's comment that "[s]cience is universally worshipped" in Conrad's *The Secret Agent* (*The Political Novels of Joseph Conrad* [Chicago: University of Chicago Press, 1981], 244).

9 Charles Dickens, *Hard Times*, ed. Paul Schlicke (Oxford: Oxford University Press, 1989), 1–2. Hereafter, quotations from *Hard Times* will be taken from this edition and will be followed by their page numbers in parenthesis.

10 Dale, *In Pursuit of a Scientific Culture*, 27.

11 For a more complete discussion of the role of science in the nineteenth century, see Barbara T. Gates and Ann B. Shteir, eds., *Natural Eloquence: Women Reinscribe Science* (Madison: University of Wisconsin Press, 1997); Richard Yeo, *Defining Science: William Whewell, Natural Knowledge, and Public Debate in Early Victorian Britain* (Cambridge: Cambridge University Press, 1993); Tom Sorell, *Scientism: Philosophy and the Infatuation with Science* (London: Routledge, 1991); Patrick Brantlinger, ed., *Energy and Entropy: Science and Culture in Victorian Britain* (Bloomington: Indiana University Press, 1989); George Levine, *Darwin Among the Novelists: Patterns of Science in Victorian Fiction* (Cambridge, MA: Harvard University Press, 1988); R. M. Young, *Darwin's Metaphor: Nature's Place in Victorian Culture* (Cambridge: Cambridge University Press, 1985); Colin A. Russell, *Science and Social Change in Britain and Europe 1700–1900* (New York: St. Martin's Press, 1983); M. T. Green, *Geology in the Nineteenth Century: Changing Views of a Changing World* (Ithaca, NY: Cornell University Press, 1982); David Oldroyd, *Darwinian Impacts: An Introduction to the Darwinian Revolution* (Atlantic Highlands, NJ: Humanities Press, 1980); Greta Jones, *Social Darwinism and English Thought* (Brighton: Harvester, 1980); Susan Faye Cannon, *Science in Culture: The Early Victorian Period* (New York: Dawson and Science History Publications, 1978); Frank Miller Turner, *Between Science and Religion: The Reaction to Scientific Naturalism in Late Victorian England* (New Haven, CT: Yale University Press, 1974); Mikuláš Teich and Robert Young, eds., *Changing Perspectives in the History of Science* (London: Heinemann, 1973); Robert E. Schofield, *Mechanism and Materialism* (Princeton, NJ: Princeton University Press, 1970); Gertrude Himmelfarb, *Darwin and the Darwinian Revolution* (New York: Norton, 1968); John W. Burrow, *Evolution and Society: A Study in Victorian Social Theory* (Cambridge: Cambridge University Press, 1966); Walter F. Cannon, "The Normative Role of Science in Early Victorian Thought," *Journal of the History of Ideas* 30.4 (October–December 1964): 487–502; William Irvine, *Apes, Angels, and Victorians* (Cleveland: Meridian Books, 1959); Alfred North Whitehead, *Science and the Modern World* (London: Macmillan, 1925); and Hugh Elliot, *Modern Science and Materialism* (London: Longmans, Green, 1919).

12 Hay, *Political Novels of Joseph Conrad*, 243.

13 Ian Watt, *Conrad in the Nineteenth Century* (Berkeley: University of California Press, 1979), 152.

14 Mark A. Wollaeger, *Joseph Conrad and the Fictions of Skepticism* (Stanford, CA: Stanford University Press, 1990), 10–11.

15 Frederick R. Karl and Laurence Davies, eds., *The Collected Letters of Joseph Conrad* (Cambridge: Cambridge University Press, 1983–), I: 382. Unless otherwise specified, quotations from Conrad's letters will be taken from this edition.

16 See Hughes, *Consciousness and Society*, 29–31, 38–39.

17 See, for example, Søren Kierkegaard, *Afsluttende Uvidenskabelig Efterskrift* (*Concluding Unscientific Postscript*) (1846); Henri Bergson, *Essai sur les données immédiates de la conscience* (*Time and Free Will: An Essay on the Immediate Data of*

Consciousness) (1889); Wilhelm Dilthey, *Einleitung in die Geisteswissenschaften* (*Introduction to the Human Sciences*) (1883); Friedrich Nietzsche, "Über Wahrheit und Lüge im Ausser-Moralischen Sinne" ("On Truth and Lie in an Extra Moral Sense") (1873); Wilhelm Windelband, *Präludien: Aufsätze und Reden zur Einführung in die Philosophie* (*Preludes: Essays and Lectures Toward Investigations in Philosophy*) (1884); Heinrich Rickert, *Der Gegenstand der Erkenntnis* (*The Object of Knowledge*) (1892).

18 Sanford Schwartz, *The Matrix of Modernism: Pound, Eliot, and Early Twentieth-Century Thought* (Princeton, NJ: Princeton University Press, 1985), 23–24. The proselyte of materialism that Schwartz refers to is Pierre-Jean Georges Cabanis. See his *Rapports du physique et du moral de l'homme et lettre sur les causes premières*, 8th edn (Paris, 1844), 137–38. Compare also Karl Vogt's *Physiologische Briefe für Gebildete aller Stände* (Stuttgart, 1845–47), 206.

19 Wollaeger, *Joseph Conrad and the Fictions of Skepticism*, 8.

20 As suggested in this passage and earlier in the novel (*SA* 41), Ossipon believes in the theories of Cesare Lombroso regarding the relationship between physical appearance and psychological predispositions. Robert G. Jacobs ("Comrade Ossipon's Favorite Saint: Lombroso and Conrad," *Nineteenth-Century Fiction* 23.1 [June 1968]: 74–84) and John E. Saveson ("Conrad, *Blackwood's*, and Lombroso," *Conradiana* 6.1 [January 1974]: 57–62) have discussed Conrad's relationship to Lombroso. Both suggest that Lombroso influenced Conrad (although Saveson qualifies his assertion more than Jacobs does). Clearly, Conrad often portrayed morally unsavory characters as physically unsavory as well (i.e., *LJ* 21, 23–24, 285); however, making the jump from this aspect of Conrad's writing to suggesting that he agreed with Lombroso may be going too far. Lombroso was not the first to suggest physicality and morality are linked, and in *The Secret Agent*, Conrad consistently presents Lombroso unsympathetically. Early in the novel, Karl Yundt says, "Lombroso is an ass" (*SA* 41). Certainly, Yundt himself is not a sympathetic character and could hardly be seen as a mouthpiece for Conrad, but Conrad makes his views of Lombroso particularly clear when he suggests that Ossipon invokes Lombroso as "an Italian peasant" invokes a saint. Given Conrad's background and attitudes, such a comment can only be extremely critical of Ossipon's beliefs.

21 For other discussions of Conrad's relationship with science, see my "Stein's Collections: Order and Chaos in *Lord Jim*," *Conradiana* 28.1 (winter 1996): 48–53; Brian Spittles, *Joseph Conrad: Text and Context* (New York: St. Martin's Press, 1992), 139–59; Donald R. Benson, "Constructing and Ethereal Cosmos: Late Classical Physics and *Lord Jim*," *Conradiana* 23.2 (summer 1991): 133–49; George Levine, "The Novel as Scientific Discourse: The Example of Conrad," in *Why the Novel Matters: A Postmodern Perplex*, ed. Mark Spilka and Caroline McCracken-Flesher (Bloomington: Indiana University Press, 1990): 238–45; Donald R. Benson, "The Crisis of Space: Ether, Atmosphere, and the Solidarity of Men and Nature in *Heart of Darkness*," in *Beyond the Two Cultures: Essays on Science, Technology, and Literature*, ed. Joseph W. Slade

and Judith Yaross Lee (Ames: Iowa State University Press, 1990): 161–75; Patrick A. McCarthy, "*Heart of Darkness* and the Early Novels of H. G. Wells: Evolution, Anarchy, and Entropy," *Journal of Modern Literature* 13.1 (March 1986): 37–60; J. A. V. Chapple, "Conrad's Brooding Over Scientific Opinion," *The Conradian* 10.1 (May 1985): 59–67; Redmond O'Hanlon, *Joseph Conrad and Charles Darwin: The Influence of Scientific Thought on Conrad's Fiction* (Edinburgh: Salamander Press, 1984); Allan Hunter, *Joseph Conrad and the Ethics of Darwinism* (London: Croom Helm, 1983); C. T. Watts, *A Preface to Conrad* (London: Longmans, 1982), 88–91; Stanley Renner, "The Garden of Civilization: Conrad, Huxley, and the Ethics of Evolution," *Conradiana* 7.2 (May 1975): 109–20; C. T. Watts, "*Heart of Darkness*: The Covert Murder Plot and the Darwinian Theme," *Conradiana* 7.2 (May 1975): 137–43; and Marion B. Brady, "The Collector-Motif in *Lord Jim*," *Bucknell Review* 16.2 (May 1968): 66–85.

22 To date, the most comprehensive work on literary impressionism includes Todd K. Bender, *Literary Impressionism in Jean Rhys, Ford Madox Ford, Joseph Conrad, and Charlotte Brontë* (New York: Garland, 1997); Julia van Gunsteren, *Katherine Mansfield and Literary Impressionism* (Amsterdam: Rodopi, 1990); James J. Kirschke, *Henry James and Impressionism* (Troy, NY: Whitston, 1981); James Nagel's *Stephen Crane and Literary Impressionism* (University Park: Pennsylvania State University Press, 1980); H. Peter Stowell's *Literary Impressionism: Chekhov and James* (Athens: University of Georgia Press, 1980); and Maria Elisabeth Kronegger's *Literary Impressionism* (New Haven, CT: College & University Press, 1973). Despite being important contributions to the study of literary impressionism, each has its shortcomings. Although Kronegger helps clarify the relationship between subject and object in impressionist literature, her book draws too close a link between impressionist painting and literature. Similarly, Nagel's book yokes impressionist painting and literature and presents a definition of literary impressionism that incorporates too wide a group of authors. Kirschke's book draws far too close a connection between impressionist painting and literature. It also seems to present contradictory evidence, arguing on the one hand that the impressionist painters directly influenced James and on the other hand that impressionist techniques existed in James' works that appeared before impressionist painting came about. Bender correctly identifies the importance and far-reaching influence of literary impressionism, but his book focuses almost exclusively on visual perception (as is true of the others as well) and sometimes draws too close a tie between impressionist literature and painting. Furthermore, he sometimes seems to fold impressionism into post-impressionism, expressionism, and even cubism. Van Gunsteren avoids some of the traps of linking impressionist literature and painting, but still draws a closer tie between them than I believe exists. Also, her emphasis is almost solely on visual perception. I believe the best work to date is Stowell's opening chapter. He represents well the relationship between subject and object in impressionism; he also shows that the techniques of

impressionist painting and literature are different, but his definition of impressionism is heavily weighted toward visual perception. In addition, on occasion, he also seems to link impressionist painting and literature more closely than I believe is justified.

23 See, for example, Bender, *Literary Impressionism in Rhys, Ford, Conrad, and Brontë*; Jesse Matz, "Walter Pater's Literary Impression," *Modern Language Quarterly* 56.4 (December 1995): 433–56; Stephen Hu, "Hemingway and the Impressionists," *Connecticut Review* 10.2 (spring 1988): 51–59; Todd K. Bender, "Jean Rhys and the Genius of Impressionism," in *British Novelists Since 1900*, ed. Jack I. Biles (New York: AMS Press, 1987), 93–104; George Klawitter, "Impressionist Characterization in *Women in Love*," *University of Dayton Review* 17.3 (winter 1985/86): 49–55; Edward J. Piacentino, "A Study in Contrasts: Impressionistic Perspectives of Antonia and Lena Lingard in Cather's *My Antonia*," *Studies in the Humanities* 12.1 (June 1985): 39–44; Victor Carrabino, "The French *Nouveau Roman*: The Ultimate Expressionism of Impressionism," *Analecta Husserliana* 18 (1984): 261–70; H. Peter Stowell, "Impressionism in James's Late Stories," *Revue de Littérature Comparée* 58.1 (January–March 1984): 27–36; Mary C. Rawlinson, "Proust's Impressionism," *L'esprit Créateur* 24.2 (summer 1984): 80–91; Paul B. Armstrong, "The Hermeneutics of Literary Impressionism: Interpretation and Reality in James, Conrad, and Ford," *Centennial Review* 27.4 (fall 1983): 244–69; Jack F. Stewart, "Impressionism in the Early Novels of Virginia Woolf," *Journal of Modern Literature* 9.2 (May 1982): 237–66; Randall Craig, "Choses Vues: Arnold Bennett and Impressionism," *English Literature in Transition* 24.4 (1981): 196–205; Maurice Beebe, "The *Portrait* as Portrait: Joyce and Impressionism," *Irish Renaissance Annual* 1 (1980): 13–31; Eloise Knapp Hay, "Joseph Conrad and Impressionism," *Journal of Aesthetics and Art Criticism* 34.1 (fall 1975): 137–44; W. V. O'Connor, "Wallace Stevens: Impressionism in America," *Revue des Langues Vivantes* 32.1 (1966): 66–77; and so on.

24 Nagel, *Stephen Crane and Literary Impressionism*, 22.

25 Roger Fry, *Characteristics of French Art* (New York: Brentano's, 1933), 125–49. See also Edmond Duranty, "The New Painting: Concerning the Group of Artists Exhibiting at the Durand-Ruel Galleries" (1876), in *Impressionism and Post-Impressionism 1874–1904*, ed. Nochlin, 5–6.

26 For example, Phoebe Pool argues that Eugène Chevereul's theory of optical mixture led the impressionists "to juxtapose colours on the canvas for the eye to fuse at a distance, thus producing colours more intense than could be achieved by mixing on the palette." (*Impressionism* [New York: Thames & Hudson, 1985], 15). Similarly, Arnold Hauser suggests, "The emphasis on colour and the desire to turn the whole picture into a harmony of colour and light effects is the aim" of impressionism (*The Social History of Art*, trans. Stanley Godman, 2 vols. [New York: Knopf, 1952], II: 875).

27 Martelli writes that impressionism "is a new theory that depends on a different way of perceiving the sensations of light" ("Lecture on the Impressionists," 25). See also Duranty, "The New Painting," 5.

28 See van Gunsteren, *Katherine Mansfield and Literary Impressionism*, 33 and 35.

29 For instance, Erik Ingvar Thurin refers to Whitman's attempt in "Song of Myself" to achieve the "'arrested moment' often sought by Impressionist painters" (*Whitman Between Impressionism and Expressionism: Language of the Body, Language of the Soul* [Lewisburg, PA: Bucknell University Press, 1995], 85–86). See also van Gunsteren, *Katherine Mansfield and Literary Impressionism*, 32.

30 Kirschke, *Henry James and Impressionism*, 82.

31 Beverly Jean Gibbs, "Impressionism as a Literary Movement," *Modern Language Journal* 36.4 (April 1952): 180.

32 Ferdinand Brunetière, "*Impressionnisme dans le roman*," as quoted by Pauline Carrington Bouve, "Impressionism in the Novel," *Gunton's Magazine* 26 (March 1904), 240. Compare also his comment on the novels of Daudet: "If they are not well written, they are magnificently painted" (238).

33 Kronegger, *Literary Impressionism*, 83.

34 Watt, for instance, argues of literary impressionism, "In narration the main equivalents to atmospheric interference in painting are the various factors which normally distort human perception" (*Conrad in the Nineteenth Century*, 178).

35 Calvin S. Brown, "Symposium on Literary Impressionism," *Yearbook of Comparative and General Literature*, 17 (1968): 58. See also van Gunsteren, *Katherine Mansfield and Literary Impressionism*, 51. Similarly, Nagel argues that Stephen Crane's *Red Badge of Courage* is episodic, that it moves from one impression to another (*Stephen Crane and Literary Impressionism*, 124–25).

36 Stowell, *Literary Impressionism: Chekhov and James*, 15. (See also van Gunsteren, *Katherine Mansfield and Literary Impressionism*, 13.) Furthermore, the problem of the fragment may go even deeper than differing media. Lionello Venturi rejects the fragment as uniquely impressionist and argues:

> Another charge made against Impressionists was that they painted only fragments. This is rather amusing. When has a painter existed who represented all of nature? Naturally every artist represents fragments. True painters concentrate in a fragment, the feeling of entire nature, which is nature itself. So did the Impressionists. ("The Aesthetic Idea of Impressionism," *Journal of Aesthetics and Art Criticism* 1.1 [spring 1941]: 42.)

Venturi may overstate the point, since impressionist painting *is* more clearly linked to a specific point in space and time than traditional painting; still, the distinction may be merely one of degree, and if Venturi is right that fragments are not a defining characteristic of impressionist painting, they could not be a defining characteristic of impressionist writing either.

37 See van Gunsteren, *Katherine Mansfield and Literary Impressionism*, 65.

38 Hereafter, when I refer to objects, I mean objects of consciousness as opposed to simply physical objects alone.

39 Stephen Crane, "The Open Boat," in *Tales of Adventure, The Works of Stephen Crane*, ed. Fredson Bowers (Charlottesville: University Press of Virginia, 1970), v: 79–80. Compare a similar incident from *The Mirror of the Sea*:

One wintry, blustering, dark night in July, as I stood sleepily out of the rain under the break of the poop something resembling an ostrich dashed up the gangway. I say ostrich because the creature, though it ran on two legs, appeared to help its progress by working a pair of short wings; it was a man, however, only his coat, ripped up the back and flapping in two halves above his shoulders, gave him that weird and fowl-like appearance. At least, I suppose it was his coat, for it was impossible to make him out distinctly. (*MS* 123–24)

40 Jules Laforgue, "Impressionism: The Eye and the Poet" (1883), trans. William Jay Smith, *Art News* 55.3 (May 1956): 43. Similarly, Théodore Duret writes that the impressionist "only reproduces what he sees" ("The Impressionist Painters" [1878], in *Impressionism and Post-Impressionism 1874–1904*, ed. Nochlin, 9–10). See also Cecilia Waern's comment on impressionists: "They aim at being the reproduction of one impression on the artist's eye, and through his eye on his mind" and that they try "to reproduce, as nearly as possible, the same kind of physical impression on the spectator's eye that was produced on the eye of the artist by the object seen in nature" ("Some Notes on French Impressionism," *Atlantic Monthly* 69 [April 1892]: 536, 537). Compare also C. F. Keary's comment that impressionism is "[w]hat the artist sees *as* he sees it" ("The Philosophy of Impressionism, *Blackwood's Magazine* 163 [May 1898]: 630; emphasis is Keary's).

41 Laforgue, "Impressionism: The Eye and the Poet," 43.

42 [W. S. Sichel], "Fathers of Literary Impressionism in England," *Quarterly Review* 185 (January 1897): 173.

43 Ibid., 175.

44 Ibid., 194.

45 Similarly, William Flint Thrall and Addison Hibbard defined literary impressionism as a "highly personal manner of writing in which the author presents characters or scenes or moods as they appear to his individual temperament rather than as they are in actuality" (*A Handbook to Literature* [New York: Odyssey, 1936], 209).

46 In this analysis, I am partly indebted to two sources. First is Edmund Husserl's assertion that "every conscious process is, in itself, consciousness *of* such and such" (*Cartesian Meditations: An Introduction to Phenomenology*, trans. Dorion Cairns [The Hague: Martinus Nijhoff, 1960], 33; emphasis is Husserl's). In this statement, I believe Husserl implies the necessary existence of the object of consciousness. However, I also infer from this assertion the necessary existence of the source of that consciousness – the subject itself. Second is Maurice Merleau-Ponty's suggestion that empiricism attempted to access the object devoid of subjective factors and that intellectualism attempted to locate the object solely within the perceiving consciousness (*Phenomenology of Perception*, trans. Colin Smith [London: Routledge, 1989], 26–51). I infer from this idea that not just physical objects but all objects of consciousness run a middle course between subject and object. Although these two ideas were catalysts for my own views on literary impressionism, it would be misleading for me to claim

that my analysis carefully follows either of these thinkers' philosophical systems.

47 The terms *positivism* and *idealism* have often been loosely applied to various intellectual movements. By positivism I mean disciplines of thought that looked to the scientific method, with its emphasis on logic and empirical evidence, as the best source for certainty and thus sought to deal with phenomena as free from subjectivity as possible. By idealism I mean those schools of thought that saw reality existing either entirely or primarily within human consciousness and thus sought to deal with phenomena as free from objectivity as possible.

48 Watt suggests something similar when he remarks: "Literary impressionism implies a field of vision which is not merely limited to the individual observer, but is also controlled by whatever conditions – internal and external – prevail at the moment of observation" (*Conrad in the Nineteenth Century*, 178). The "internal and external" conditions, however, include not just the atmospheric conditions and time of day or the observer's personal psychology but also the physical context of the object of consciousness as well as the subject's cultural background. Furthermore, context does not just affect visual perception but all objects of consciousness.

49 Some authors' works also overlap realism and impressionism, either because the authors employ both techniques in their writings or perhaps more often because their realism is really impressionism. Stephen Crane and Henry James exemplify this overlapping of realism and impressionism. Some of Crane's works seem realistic; others seem impressionistic; while still others seem naturalistic. Similarly, James' early works are more realistic while his later works are more impressionistic. I would also argue that James' psychological realism is really a form of impressionism because he emphasizes the relationship between subject and object rather than simply the object itself, as a realist writer would.

50 Letter dated March 10, 1902, *Letters*, II: 390.

51 Ford Madox Hueffer [Ford], "On Impressionism," *Poetry and Drama* 2.6 (June 1914): 173.

52 Watt, *Conrad in the Nineteenth Century*, 170.

53 E. H. Gombrich, *The Story of Art*, 16th edn, revised and enlarged (Oxford: Phaidon, 1995), 513; emphasis is Gombrich's.

54 Ford, "On Impressionism," 174. "Corrected chronicle" is not the best term for this process. The first did not need correction at all, but rather "corrected" is what the culture perceives to be "correct." A better term might be "organized chronicle."

55 Ford Madox Ford, *Joseph Conrad: A Personal Remembrance* (Boston: Little, Brown, 1924), 136–37.

56 Ibid., 194.

57 Ibid., 207.

58 See, for example, ibid., 194–95, 199, 200–1, 205. Also, F. R. Leavis remarks of "Heart of Darkness," "The details and circumstances of the voyage to

and up the Congo are present to us as if we were making the journey ourselves" (*The Great Tradition: George Eliot, Henry James, Joseph Conrad* [New York: New York University Press, 1963], 174).

59 Ford Madox Ford, *The Good Soldier*, ed. Thomas C. Moser (Oxford: Oxford University Press, 1990), 213.

60 H. M. Daleski, *Joseph Conrad: The Way of Dispossession* (London: Faber & Faber, 1977), 116.

61 Albert J. Guerard, *Conrad the Novelist* (Cambridge, MA: Harvard University Press, 1958), 152.

62 Ford, *Joseph Conrad: A Personal Remembrance*, 194–95.

63 Stephen Crane, as quoted by Ford Madox Ford, "Techniques," *Southern Review* 1.1 (July 1935): 31.

64 Henry James, "The Tree of Knowledge," in *The Author of Beltraffio, The Middle Years, Greville Fane, and Other Tales, The Novels and Tales of Henry James*, New York edn (New York: Scribner's, 1909), XVI: 185.

65 Ford, *The Good Soldier*, 103.

66 Watt, *Conrad in the Nineteenth Century*, 272.

67 Ibid., 210.

68 Wollaeger, *Joseph Conrad and the Fictions of Skepticism*, xvi.

69 Letter dated December 9, 1897, *Letters*, I: 420–21.

70 Letter dated September 24, 1919, Edward Garnett, ed., *Letters from Joseph Conrad, 1895–1924* (Indianapolis: Bobbs-Merrill, 1928), 265; emphasis is Conrad's.

71 Letter dated July 20, 1905, *Letters*, III: 276.

72 Watt, *Conrad in the Nineteenth Century*, 147.

73 Robert Penn Warren, "Introduction," *Nostromo* by Joseph Conrad (New York: Modern Library, 1951), xxxviii.

74 Watt, *Conrad in the Nineteenth Century*, 42.

75 Letter dated March 15, 1895, *Letters*, I: 205.

76 Letter dated May 4, 1918, G. Jean-Aubry, *Joseph Conrad: Life and Letters* (Garden City, NY: Doubleday, Page, 1927), II: 204.

77 Hay, *Political Novels of Joseph Conrad*, vii.

78 Watt, *Conrad in the Nineteenth Century*, 173, 179.

79 Letter dated December 5, 1897, *Letters*, I: 416; emphasis is Conrad's. This comment stands in sharp contrast to Conrad's more public assessments of Crane's work that appeared in his essays "Stephen Crane: A Note without Dates" (*NLL* 49–52), "Stephen Crane" (*Last Essays* 93–118), and "His War Book" (*Last Essays* 119–24). For example, in "His War Book," Conrad remarks, "Here we had an artist, a man not of experience but a man inspired, a seer with a gift for rendering the significant on the surface of things and with an incomparable insight into primitive emotions, who, in order to give us the image of war, had looked profoundly into his own breast" (119–20).

80 Hay argues elsewhere, however, that Conrad's view changed to one of gradual acceptance of impressionist methodology. See her "Joseph Conrad and Impressionism," 137–44.

81 For instance, Watt remarks that "Conrad apparently disliked being tarred with the decadent brush" (*Conrad in the Nineteenth Century*, 184). See also Lawrence Graver, *Conrad's Short Fiction* (Berkeley: University of California Press, 1969), 18.

82 Ford, "On Impressionism," 172.

83 Ford, *Joseph Conrad: A Personal Remembrance*, 194; see also vi, 34, 205. Ford's memory is notoriously suspect in this book (at least according to Jesse Conrad and Edward Garnett), but in this instance Ford's assessment seems accurate given the evidence in Conrad's works themselves and the general agreement among commentators on Conrad.

84 Bruce McCullough, *Representative English Novelists: Defoe to Conrad* (New York: Harper, 1946), 336–48. William C. Frierson, *The English Novel in Transition: 1885–1940* (Norman: University of Oklahoma Press, 1942), 214–23. Edward Crankshaw, *Joseph Conrad: Some Aspects of the Art of the Novel* (London: John Lane, 1936), 9. Joseph Warren Beach, *The Twentieth Century Novel: Studies in Technique* (New York: Appleton-Century-Crofts, 1932), 337–65. Ramon Fernandez, *Messages*, trans. Montgomery Belgion (New York: Harcourt, Brace, 1927), 139–51.

85 Extended discussions of Conrad's impressionism include: Bender, *Literary Impressionism in Rhys, Ford, Conrad, and Brontë*; Michael Fried, "Almayer's Face: on 'Impressionism' in Conrad, Crane and Norris," in *So Rich a Tapestry: The Sister Acts and Cultural Studies*, (Lewisburg, PA: Bucknell University Press, 1995), 239–82; Adriaan M. de Lange, "Conrad and Impressionism: Problems and (Possible) Solutions," in *Conrad's Literary Career*, ed. Keith Carabine, Owen Knowles, Wiesław Krajka (Boulder, CO: East European Monographs, 1992), 21–40; Paul B. Armstrong, *The Challenge of Bewilderment: Understanding and Representation in James, Conrad, and Ford* (Ithaca, NY: Cornell University Press, 1987), 109–85; Elena Paruolo, "Reality and Consciousness: Impressionism in Conrad," *L'Epoque Conradienne* 12 (1986): 75–84; Bruce Johnson, "Conrad's Impressionism and Watt's 'Delayed Decoding,'" in *Conrad Revisited: Essays for the Eighties*, ed. Ross C. Murfin (University: University of Alabama Press, 1985), 51–70; Armstrong, "Hermeneutics of Literary Impressionism," 244–69; Todd K. Bender and Sue M. Briggum, "Quantitative Stylistic Analysis of Impressionist Style in Joseph Conrad and Ford Madox Ford," in *Computing in the Humanities*, ed. Richard W. Bailey (Amsterdam: North-Holland Publishing, 1982), 59–64; Fredric Jameson, *The Political Unconscious: Narrative as a Socially Symbolic Act* (Ithaca, NY: Cornell University Press, 1981), 210–42; Watt, *Conrad in the Nineteenth Century*, 169–80, 286–304; Todd K. Bender, "Conrad and Literary Impressionism," *Conradiana* 10.3 (1978): 211–24; Ian Watt, "Impressionism and Symbolism in *Heart of Darkness*," *Southern Review* 13.1 (January 1977): 96–113; Eloise Knapp Hay, "Impressionism Limited," in *Joseph Conrad: A Commemoration*, ed. Norman Sherry (London: Macmillan, 1976), 54–64; Ian Watt, "Pink Toads and Yellow Curs: An Impressionist Narrative Device in *Lord Jim*," in *Joseph Conrad Colloquy in Poland*, ed. R. Jabłkowska (Warsaw: Polish Academy of Sciences, 1975): 11–31; Hay, "Joseph Conrad and Impressionism," 137–44; and

Harold E. Davis, "Conrad's Revisions of *The Secret Agent*: A Study in Literary Impressionism," *Modern Language Quarterly* 19.3 (September 1958): 244–54.

86 Bender, *Literary Impressionism in Rhys, Ford, Conrad, and Brontë*, 102.

87 Donald R. Benson, "Impressionist Painting and the Problem of Conrad's Atmosphere," *Mosaic* 22.1 (winter 1989): 39.

88 Ibid., 34; see also 39.

89 Watt, *Conrad in the Nineteenth Century*, 169; see also 178.

90 Bender, *Literary Impressionism in Rhys, Ford, Conrad, and Brontë*, 50.

91 Adam Gillon, "Conrad as Painter," *Conradiana* 10.3 (autumn 1978): 257. Although Gillon does not argue that Conrad consciously tried to imitate specifically impressionist painting techniques, he does argue for similarities between Conrad's narrative technique and painting techniques in general, among which impressionism would be included. Compare also Daniel Schwarz, who argues of Conrad's narrative technique: "[N]ote how the Post-Impressionist perspective – with its stress on light and shadow – of Marlow's response to the natives mixes foreground and background and focuses on sharply drawn physical shapes... Like Gauguin's paintings, these passages reveal as much as they conceal and depend on the perceiver's gaze to recompose them into significance" (*Reconfiguring Modernism: Explorations in the Relationship Between Modern Art and Modern Literature* [New York: St. Martin's Press, 1997], 97; see also 96). Like Gillon, Schwarz does not argue that Conrad imitates impressionist painting techniques, but he does see post-impressionist painting techniques in Conrad's works, and so the effect is similar – that Conrad's narrative techniques are similar to those of the visual arts.

92 Herbert Howarth, "Symposium on Literary Impressionism," *Yearbook of Comparative and General Literature*, 17 (1968): 45.

93 Eloise Knapp Hay, "Proust, James, Conrad, and Impressionism," *Style* 22.3 (fall 1988): 378; emphasis is Hays'.

94 Wiesław Krajka, "*Lord Jim*: An Impressionistic Novel?" *Folia Societatis Scientiarum Lublinensis* 26 (1984): 61.

95 Guerard, *Conrad the Novelist*, 179, 232; see also 252.

96 Ibid., 226, 218; see also 229.

97 Ibid., 267.

98 Ibid., 258–59.

99 [Walter Pater], "Coleridge's Writings," *Westminster Review* n.s. 29 (January 1866), 107.

2 OBJECTS AND EVENTS IN THE "PRIMITIVE EYE": THE
EPISTEMOLOGY OF OBJECTIVITY

1 Watt, *Conrad in the Nineteenth Century*, 83.

2 Letter dated September 6, 1897, *Letters*, 1: 381.

3 A similar incident occurs in *The Secret Agent*: "Another door opened noiselessly, and Mr. Verloc immobilising his glance in that direction saw at first

only black clothes, the bald top of a head, and a drooping dark grey whisker on each side of a pair of wrinkled hands. The person who had entered was holding a batch of papers before his eyes" (*SA* 18). Because of Verloc's location in space and because the man is holding up papers, Verloc cannot see the man's face. Conrad requires the reader to experience phenomena from a specific physical point of view such that the scene unfolds from Verloc's line of sight rather than from a panoramic view that would take in all of the details of the scene.

4 I am appropriating Laforgue's term here (to somewhat different ends however); see Laforgue, "Impressionism: The Eye and the Poet," 43.

5 Watt, *Conrad in the Nineteenth Century*, 175–79. For responses to Watt, see Johnson, "Conrad's Impressionism and Watt's 'Delayed Decoding,'" 51–70; and Robert S. Baker, "Joseph Conrad," *Contemporary Literature* 22.1 (winter 1981): 116–26.

6 Watt, *Conrad in the Nineteenth Century*, 175.

7 Ibid. Compare Ramon Fernandez's comments about Conrad's narrative technique:

> [H]e applies himself to seizing things at their birth, in their formation, and, so to speak, on the hither side of their definition... An image of the event is communicated to us possessing the qualities of recollection, of a personal, affective recollection, since rememoration's unique medium is the shades of the impression *before* the latter's elucidation by comparison and reasoning. (*Messages*, 144; emphasis is Fernandez's)

8 Johnson, "Conrad's Impressionism and Watt's 'Delayed Decoding,'" 53. Johnson sees the primary importance of these incidents being their bringing out of other possible aspects of the events. For example, he feels that the helmsman's "gripping the spear like something precious" (*Y* 112) represents the very private nature of one's death and the desire to keep that experience to one's self (57–58). But it seems to me that what is most important about these incidents is Conrad's view of the perceptual process itself, its relationship to knowledge and certainty, and its relationship to cultural influence on perceived phenomena.

9 Ibid.

10 Ibid., 52.

11 "The Secret Sharer" includes a similar two-part instance of primitive perception: the young captain sees "something elongated and pale floating very close to the ladder"; then he sees a "headless corpse"; and finally he sees a man (*TLS* 97–98).

12 Some other examples of primitive perception include "The Idiots" (*TU* 84), *Lord Jim* (*LJ* 296–97), "Freya of the Seven Isles" (*TLS* 196), *Nostromo* (*N* 249), *The Secret Agent* (*SA* 198–99), and "Typhoon" (*T* 56).

13 Edward W. Said, *Joseph Conrad and the Fiction of Autobiography* (Cambridge, MA: Harvard University Press, 1966), 187–88.

14 Joseph Conrad, "The Sisters," in *Congo Diary and Other Uncollected Pieces*, ed. Zdzisław Najder (Garden City, NY: Doubleday, 1978), 57.

15 This incident is also an example of the overlapping between limited point of view and blurred boundaries in that the darkness is not just part of the context; it is also the physical factor that limits Byrne's point of view, so that he cannot see the inn clearly. It could also be argued that this incident is a variation on primitive perception.

16 J. Hillis Miller, *Poets of Reality: Six Twentieth-Century Writers* (New York: Atheneum, 1974), 47.

17 Watt, *Conrad in the Nineteenth Century*, 169.

18 Said, *Joseph Conrad and the Fiction of Autobiography*, 142.

19 In the *Patna*'s lifeboat, Jim has a similar experience: "You couldn't distinguish the sea from the sky; there was nothing to see and nothing to hear. Not a glimmer, not a shape, not a sound. You could have believed that every bit of dry land had gone to the bottom; that every man on earth but I and these beggars in the boat had got drowned" (*LJ* 114). In this incident, Jim experiences a complete dissolution of context such that everything beyond the immediate boat disappears and seems as if it no longer exists.

20 Conrad uses fog similarly elsewhere in "Heart of Darkness" (*Y* 45), "An Outpost of Progress" (*TU* 116–17), and *Lord Jim* (*LJ* 398–402).

21 "An Outpost of Progress" refers to a "penetrating, enveloping, and silent" fog that "clings" (*TU* 115).

22 Watt, *Conrad in the Nineteenth Century*, 174.

23 Conrad describes the wilderness in "An Outpost of Progress" similarly: "The river, the forest, all the great land throbbing with life, were like a great emptiness. Even the brilliant sunshine disclosed nothing intelligible. Things appeared and disappeared before their eyes in an unconnected and aimless kind of way" (*TU* 92).

24 Conrad, "The Sisters," 56.

25 Bender, "Conrad and Literary Impressionism," 219.

26 Watt, *Conrad in the Nineteenth Century*, 233.

27 Marlow also notes other examples of absurdity associated with the European traders:

> I avoided a vast artificial hole somebody had been digging on the slope, the purpose of which I found it impossible to divine. It wasn't a quarry or a sandpit, anyhow. It was just a hole... Then I nearly fell into a very narrow ravine, almost no more than a scar in the hillside. I discovered that a lot of imported drainage-pipes for the settlement had been tumbled in there. There wasn't one that was not broken. It was a wanton smash-up. (*Y* 65–66)

> The attempt to douse the fire at the Central Station emphasizes this same kind of absurdity. Marlow notes that the station's inhabitants were

> all cutting capers in the light, with their arms lifted high, when the stout man with moustaches came tearing down to the river, a tin pail in his hand, assured me that everybody was "behaving splendidly, splendidly," dipped about a quart of water and tore back again. I noticed there was a hole in the bottom of his pail. (*Y* 76)

28 Joseph Conrad, "Geography and Some Explorers," in *Last Essays* (New York: Doubleday, Page, 1926), 17.

29 Wollaeger, *Joseph Conrad and the Fictions of Skepticism*, 51.

3   OTHER-LIKE-SELF AND OTHER-UNLIKE-SELF: THE EPISTEMOLOGY OF SUBJECTIVITY

1 Eric Trethewey, "Language, Experience, and Selfhood in Conrad's *Heart of Darkness*," *Southern Humanities Review* 22.2 (spring 1988): 106. See also Deirdre David, "Selfhood and Language in 'The Return' and 'Falk,'" *Conradiana* 8.2 (summer 1976): 137–47.

2 For example, influenced somewhat by Jungian psychology, Guerard saw the search for self as essentially an introspective endeavor, a night journey. One looks within to uncover the self (*Conrad the Novelist*, 1–59). Nancy McNeal takes a similar approach in "Joseph Conrad's Voice in *Heart of Darkness*: A Jungian Approach," *Journal of Evolutionary Psychology* 1 (1979): 1–12. For Otto Bohlmann, discovery of the self is existential. Human beings create their selves, in a sense *ex nihilo*, by accepting their ultimate freedom and responsibility for their choices (*Conrad's Existentialism* [New York: St. Martin's Press, 1991], 46–103). See also Tony E. Jackson, "Turning into Modernism: *Lord Jim* and the Alteration of the Narrative Subject," *Literature and Psychology* 39.4 (1993): 65–85; Suresh Raval, *The Art of Failure: Conrad's Fiction* (Boston: Allen & Unwin, 1986), 45–72; James Clifford, "On Ethnographic Self-Fashioning: Conrad and Malinowski," in *Reconstructing Individualism: Autonomy, Individuality, and the Self in Western Thought*, ed. Thomas C. Heller, Morton Sosna, and David E. Wellbery (Stanford, CA: Stanford University Press, 1986), 140–62; H. M. Daleski, "*Victory* and Patterns of Self-Division," in *Conrad Revisited: Essays for the Eighties*, ed. Murfin, 107–23; Ivo Vidan, "Conrad's Legacy: The Concern with Authenticity in Modern Fiction," in *Joseph Conrad: Theory and World Fiction*, ed. Wolodymyr T. Zyla and Wendell M. Aycock (Lubbock: Interdepartmental Committee on Comparative Literature, Texas Tech University, 1974), 167–86; Ramchander Singh, "Nostromo: The Betrayed Self," *Literary Criterion* 10.4 (summer 1973): 61–66; and Alvin Greenberg, "The Death of the Psyche: A Way to the Self in the Contemporary Novel," *Criticism* 8.1 (winter 1966): 1–18.

3 For example, Chinua Achebe, in his well-known article "An Image of Africa" (*Massachusetts Review* 18.4 [winter 1977]: 782–94), takes Conrad to task for what he feels are inaccurate representations of Africans. Similarly, in his *Conrad's Colonialism* ([The Hague: Mouton, 1969], 35–39), Robert F. Lee discusses the issue of "one of us," focusing only on the nature of westerners themselves, without considering the context of their relationship to non-westerners.

4 The exception to this separation of self and other appears in commentary on the double. However, these commentaries see the double primarily as a manifestation of the self's darker possibilities. Hence, such discussions still look to the self for knowledge of the self. For example, Thomas Moser remarks, "'The Secret Sharer' belongs to Conrad's early period where the

dark powers lurk within us all" (*Joseph Conrad: Achievement and Decline* [Cambridge, MA: Harvard University Press, 1957], 140). See also Herbert L. Carson, "The Second Self in 'The Secret Sharer,'" *Cresset* 34.1 (November 1970): 11–13; Donald C. Yelton, *Mimesis and Metaphor: An Inquiry into the Genesis and Scope of Conrad's Symbolic Imagery* (The Hague: Mouton, 1967), 272–98; Daniel Curley, "Legate of the Ideal," in *Conrad's* Secret Sharer *and the Critics*, ed. Bruce Harkness (Belmont, CA: Wadsworth, 1962), 75–82; Guerard, *Conrad the Novelist*, 14–33; and Robert W. Stallman, "Conrad and 'The Secret Sharer,'" *Accent* 9.3 (spring 1949): 131–43. Guerard argues that Marlow "is loyal to Jim as one must be to another or potential self, to the criminally weak self that may still exist" (147). Steve Ressler also sees the double appearing in "Heart of Darkness" and refers to Marlow as Kurtz's "younger double" (*Joseph Conrad: Consciousness and Integrity* [New York: New York University Press, 1988], 23). See also Ivo Vidan, "The Split Self in Conrad's Fiction," in *Die Modernisierung Des Ich*, ed. Manfred Pfister (Passau, GDR: Richard Rothe, 1989), 275–85. Certainly, the double can represent the self's darker possibilities, but what makes the double a double is not its differences from the self, but rather its similarities, and these similarities are at least as important as the differences.

5 Jackson, "Turning into Modernism," 72–73.

6 Lee argues that this phenomenon continued well into the twentieth century (*Conrad's Colonialism*, 18–34).

7 I am not suggesting that Marlow (or even Conrad for that matter) held unusually enlightened views of non-westerners, but they consistently rejected any *inherent* superiority of western civilization.

8 Guerard argues that "we cannot quite believe the response of Marlow's heart to the beating of the tom-toms. This is, I think, the story's minor but central flaw, and the source of an unfruitful ambiguity: that it slightly overdoes the kinship with the 'passionate uproar,' slightly undervalues the temptation of inertia" (*Conrad the Novelist*, 37). I disagree, however, with Guerard on this point, because it is precisely the similarities between African and European that Conrad wishes to uncover and in so doing to uncover a shifting foundation for western civilization as well.

9 For some recent discussions of other aspects of Conrad and colonialism, see for example Rebecca Carpenter, "From Naïveté to Knowledge: Emilia Gould and the 'Kinder, Gentler' Imperialism," *Conradiana* 29.2 (summer 1997): 83–100; Hugh Mercer Curtler, "Achebe on Conrad: Racism and Greatness in *Heart of Darkness*," *Conradiana* 29.1 (spring 1997): 30–40; Andrea White, "Conrad and Imperialism," in *The Cambridge Companion to Joseph Conrad*, ed. J. H. Stape (Cambridge: Cambridge University Press, 1996), 179–202; Christopher GoGwilt, *The Invention of the West*; John A. McClure, *Late Imperial Romance* (London: Verso, 1994), 8–29; Edward W. Said, *Culture and Imperialism* (New York: Knopf, 1993), 19–31; Mark Conroy, "Colonial Self-Fashioning in Conrad: Writing and Remembrance in *Lord Jim*,"

L'Epoque Conradienne 19 (1993): 25–36; Padmini Mongia, "Empire, Narrative, and the Feminine in *Lord Jim* and *Heart of Darkness*," in *Contexts for Conrad*, ed. Keith Carabine, Owen Knowles, Wiesław Krajka (Boulder, CO: East European Monographs, 1993), 135–50; Gail Fraser, "Empire of the Senses: Miscegenation in *An Outcast of the Islands*, in *Contexts for Conrad*, ed. Carabine, Knowles, Krajka, 121–33; Phil Joffe, "Africa and Joseph Conrad's *Heart of Darkness*: The 'Bloody Racist' (?) as Demystifier of Imperialism," in *Conrad's Literary Career*, ed. Carabine, Knowles, Krajka, 75–90; Chris Bongie, "Exotic Nostalgia: Conrad and the New Imperialism," in *Macropolitics of Nineteenth-Century Literature: Nationalism, Exoticism, Imperialism*, ed. Jonathan Arac and Harriet Ritvo (Philadelphia: University of Pennsylvania Press, 1991), 264–85; Robert Hamner, ed., *Joseph Conrad: Third World Perspectives* (Washington, DC: Three Continents, 1990); and so on. Other important works on Conrad and colonialism include: Benita Parry, *Conrad and Imperialism: Ideological Boundaries and Visionary Frontiers* (London: Macmillan, 1983); John A. McClure, *Kipling and Conrad* (Cambridge, MA: Harvard University Press, 1981); Hunt Hawkins, "Conrad's Critique of Imperialism in *Heart of Darkness*," *PMLA* 94.2 (March 1979): 286–99; and Achebe, "An Image of Africa."

10 Wollaeger, *Joseph Conrad and the Fictions of Skepticism*, 103. Emphasis is Wollaeger's.

11 Ibid., 81.

12 There is a good deal of debate concerning Leggatt. For example, Daniel Curley argues, "Leggatt cannot be considered a 'murderous ruffian' but must on the contrary be held to be what the story itself clearly suggests him to be: the ideal conception of himself that the captain has set up for himself secretly" ("Legate of the Ideal," 81). On the other hand, Guerard remarks, "It is entirely wrong to suppose, as some readers do, that Conrad unequivocally *approves* the captain's decision to harbor Leggatt" (*Conrad the Novelist*, 24; emphasis is Guerard's). I think Lawrence Graver's assessment most accurate: "[J]ust as there is adequate evidence to deny Leggatt's villainy, so there is proof to smudge his status as an ideal figure... One thing can be said with certainty about Leggatt: he is neither higher nor lower, only different" (*Conrad's Short Fiction*, 151).

13 Daleski, *Joseph Conrad: The Way of Dispossession*, 182.

14 Said, *Joseph Conrad and the Fiction of Autobiography*, 157.

15 Jackson, "Turning into Modernism," 72.

16 Armstrong, *Challenge of Bewilderment*, 10.

17 Daleski, *Joseph Conrad: The Way to Dispossession*, 88.

18 Similarly, in *Victory*, Heyst loses himself to his father's ideas for much of his life. Only when he meets Lena does he partially break out of that mold.

19 Raval, *Art of Failure*, 66.

20 Daleski, *Joseph Conrad: The Way of Dispossession*, 67.

21 Ressler, *Joseph Conrad: Consciousness and Integrity*, 23.

22　Daleski, "*Victory* and Patterns of Self-Division," 113.

23　Compare also the narrator's comment in *The Rover* that "people that were out of her [Arlette's] sight were out of her mind also" (*Ro* 161). And in *Under Western Eyes*, the narrator remarks, "There was no longer any Natalia Haldin, because she had completely ceased to think of herself. It was a great victory, a characteristically Russian exploit in self-suppression" (*UWE* 375).

24　Royal Roussel, *The Metaphysics of Darkness: A Study in the Unity and Development of Conrad's Fiction* (Baltimore, MD: Johns Hopkins University Press, 1971), 140.

25　Similarly, in *Under Western Eyes*, Razumov asks himself, "Was it possible that he no longer belonged to himself?" (*UWE* 301).

26　Singh, "Nostromo: The Betrayed Self," 64. See also Wollaeger, *Joseph Conrad and the Fictions of Skepticism*, 166. Daleski makes a similar remark concerning Gould, "When he lets go of everything but the mine, he also loses possession of the self he aspired to establish in undertaking the mining venture" (*Joseph Conrad: The Way of Dispossession*, 127).

27　Warren, "Introduction," xiv.

28　There has been some debate concerning Jim's relationship to Brown. Gustav Morf refers to the "paralyzing influence" of Jim's identifying with Brown (*The Polish Heritage of Joseph Conrad* [New York: Richard R. Smith, (1930)], 157). Guerard notes Jim's "crippling identification with Gentleman Brown" (*Conrad the Novelist*, 145). On the other hand, Daleski argues,

> [I]t seems to me that Brown's insinuation of their "common guilt" [*LJ* 387] and of there being "a bond" [*LJ* 387] between them forces Jim not so much to an identification as to a recognition that the disreputable outlaw is in fact a better man than he morally, for he roundly asserts he would not do what Jim has done: he would not "jump out of trouble" [*LJ* 382] and leave his men in the lurch. (*Joseph Conrad: The Way of Dispossession*, 101)

Watt concurs: "[T]he weight of the evidence is far from supporting the view that Jim acted as he did out of guilt, whether conscious or unconscious, or that any other decision was possible" (*Conrad in the Nineteenth Century*, 342). Wollaeger goes even further, suggesting that "Jim's tragedy begins at the moment he refuses to acknowledge his affinities with Brown, and his refusal ever to awaken to his own denial only adds to its tragic force" (*Joseph Conrad and the Fictions of Skepticism*, 116). I think Morf and Guerard are closer to the mark. When Jim says of Brown and his men, "Men act badly sometimes without being much worse than others" (*LJ* 394), he clearly has himself in mind as well, and therefore it would be difficult to argue that there is no clear identification with Brown or that Jim is not paralyzed by his identification based on the results of his actions.

29　Guerard notes a similar situation in *Victory*: "For Mr. Jones (in an open recasting of the Lord Jim–Gentleman Brown incident) seeks to paralyze Heyst by insisting that they have much in common" (*Conrad the Novelist*, 275). Mr. Jones, however, is not as successful as Brown.

30 Raval, *Art of Failure*, 63–64.
31 Douglas Hewitt, *Conrad: A Reassessment*, 3rd edn (Totowa, NJ: Rowman & Littlefield, 1975), 36.
32 Watt, *Conrad in the Nineteenth Century*, 312.
33 Armstrong, *Challenge of Bewilderment*, 11.
34 Compare also Leggatt's comment: "But you don't see me coming back to explain such things to an old fellow in a wig and twelve respectable tradesmen, do you? What can they know whether I am guilty or not – or of *what* I am guilty, either? That's my affair" (*TLS* 131–32; emphasis is Conrad's).
35 Letter to Charles Chassé dated January 31, 1924 (Jean-Aubry, *Joseph Conrad: Life and Letters*, II: 336).
36 Contrast with Jim's attitude Said's assessment of the young captain in *The Shadow Line*, who "is made to understand the real meaning of 'being oneself,' which is to cross the line of shadowy, unrealized ambitions into a sort of restricted, terrible reality (not particularly friendly or pure) that always falls short of those ambitions" (*Joseph Conrad and the Fiction of Autobiography*, 186).
37 Daleski notes that Jukes in "Typhoon" also contrasts with Jim's untested self-assurance: "At the start of his initiating experience, we recall, the typhoon undermined Jukes's 'faith in himself' [*T* 42]; now his having won through to a 'belief in himself' [*T* 89] is indicative of a newly won knowledge of self. It is in the consciousness of a self that is safely anchored in its own inner firmness that he now feels 'equal to every demand' [*T* 89] and notes the storm 'unmoved' [*T* 89]" (*Joseph Conrad: The Way of Dispossession*, 112).
38 Miller, *Poets of Reality*, 18–19.
39 Guerard, *Conrad the Novelist*, 111.
40 "Letter to Marguerite Poradowska [July 20, 1894]," *Letters of Joseph Conrad to Marguerite Poradowska 1890–1920*, trans. and ed. John A. Gee and Paul J. Sturm (New Haven, CT: Yale University Press, 1940), 72.
41 A somewhat similar idea appears in *An Outcast of the Islands*: "It was not death that frightened him [Willems]: it was the horror of bewildered life where he could understand nothing and nobody round him; where he could guide, control, comprehend nothing and no one – not even himself" (*OI* 149).
42 Raval, *Art of Failure*, 48.

4 "SUDDEN HOLES" IN TIME: THE EPISTEMOLOGY OF TEMPORALITY

1 J. M. Kertzer, "Joseph Conrad and the Metaphysics of Time," *Studies in the Novel* 11.3 (fall 1979): 303.
2 One of the influences for my thinking on impressionist time was Henri Bergson's *Time and Free Will: An Essay on the Immediate Data of Consciousness* (trans. F. L. Pogson [London: George Allen & Unwin, 1910]), in particular

his suggestion that human time contrasts with clock time and that duration is an unsegmented phenomenon. Arnold Hauser also recognized an affinity between impressionism and Bergson's philosophy: "Impressionist thinking finds its purest expression in the philosophy of Bergson, above all in his interpretation of time – the medium which is the vital element of impressionism" (*The Social History of Art*, ii: 925). See also Bender, *Literary Impressionism in Rhys, Ford, Conrad, and Brontë*, 58–59 and Kirschke, *Henry James and Impressionism*, 36. Nevertheless, although Bergson has been an influence, it would be misleading for me to claim my analysis is Bergsonian: his ideas have only been a catalyst for my thinking.

3 De Lange, "Conrad and Impressionism: Problems and (Possible) Solutions," 21.

4 Robert N. Hudspeth argues a somewhat similar point concerning Flora and her father in *Chance*:

> The past is one thing for de Barral, it is something else for Flora. Because she has been a part of the flux and flow of time, her sense of the past is different from his, and this difference is an inescapable barrier between the two. Because they have had different temporal experiences, they cannot possibly understand each other.

In this case, though, the difference in temporal experience is less one of individual subjectivity, as with Verloc and Winnie, than it is the difference of different personal pasts. See "Conrad's Use of Time in *Chance*," *Nineteenth-Century Fiction* 21.3 (December 1966): 288.

5 Robert G. Jacobs, "H. G. Wells, Joseph Conrad, and the Relative Universe," *Conradiana* 1.1 (summer 1968): 52.

6 Ibid. Jacobs also sees Jim's control of time in Patusan represented in the mountain that appears to be frozen in the midst of splitting apart. He argues, "The wonder of it was not that the mountain had split, but that it was in the process of splitting, and that its motion appeared frozen. Like so much of the rest of that world in repose, it appeared static to Marlow; Jim's control over time was complete" (53).

7 Kertzer, "Joseph Conrad and the Metaphysics of Time," 314.

8 In "Heart of Darkness," Kurtz's Intended responds to time somewhat similarly. Kurtz's death stops time for the Intended, but unlike Razumov the Intended finds no way to restart its flow (*Y* 157).

9 William Bysshe Stein, "Conrad's Word-World of Time," in *Aspects of Time*, ed. C. A. Patrides (Manchester: Manchester University Press, 1976), 122.

10 Personal time appears throughout Conrad's works. In addition to the examples cited above, personal time occurs in such instances as *Nostromo* (*N* 466), "Gaspar Ruiz" (*SS* 12), *Chance* (*C* 354), *The Shadow Line* (*SL* 106), *A Personal Record* (*PR* 114), *Lord Jim* (*LJ* 143, 177, 267), "Youth" (*Y* 11–12), and *Under Western Eyes* (*UWE* 69, 112, 160–61, 298).

11 The young captain in "The Secret Sharer" has a similar experience. Near the end of the story, when the captain tries to turn the ship away from the

dangerous shallows, the ocean appears as a homogenous expanse, and without some point of reference he risks running the ship aground: "What I needed was something easily seen . . . All at once my strained, yearning stare distinguished a white object floating within a yard of the ship's side. White on the black water . . . I recognised my own floppy hat" (*TLS* 142). Only when an object of civilization, the hat, appears on the black water can the captain successfully segment space and use the hat to orient the ship and get back on course.

12 In *Under Western Eyes*, Razumov conjures up a similar scene when he says, "The silence of the room resembled now the silence of a deep dungeon, where time does not count" (*UWE* 48). In "a deep dungeon," no contextual demarcations exist to aid the perceiver in telling time.

13 Guerard, *Conrad the Novelist*, 215.

14 Gareth Jenkins, "Conrad's *Nostromo* and History," *Literature & History* 6 (autumn 1977): 149.

15 Ibid., 157. Guerard agrees with Monygham, arguing, "The horizon offered by the book itself seems to me, simply, Dr. Monygham's dark one" (*Conrad the Novelist*, 198). On the other hand, Warren disagrees, "There has been a civil war, but the forces of 'progress' – i.e., the San Tomé mine and the capitalistic order – have won. And we must admit that the society at the end of the book is preferable to that at the beginning" ("Introduction," xxix). I would agree more with Guerard and Jenkins that the differences between the Sulaco revolution and the others are at the very least only temporary and perhaps merely superficial.

16 Hay, *Political Novels of Joseph Conrad*, 163.

17 William Bysshe Stein also argues that there is a difference between eastern and western time. See *"Almayer's Folly*: The Terrors of Time," *Conradiana* 1.1 (summer 1968): 29, and "Conrad's East: Time, History, Action, and *Maya*," *Texas Studies in Literature and Language* 7.3 (fall 1965): 273. However, Stein's argument works from a more linear conception of time, suggesting that Almayer's difficulty is that he lives in and for the future, while the Malays live in the present, without concern for the future. This argument is certainly partly true, but I would argue that the distinction between eastern and western time is more the difference between cyclical time and linear time than a conflict between focusing on past or future.

18 Sue Tyley, "Time and Space in *The Secret Agent*," *The Conradian* 8.2 (summer 1983): 36.

19 Kertzer, "Joseph Conrad and the Metaphysics of Time," 303.

20 See Laforgue, "Impressionism: The Eye and the Poet," 43.

21 After the Greenwich disaster, Verloc reflects: "Fifteen minutes ought to have been enough for the veriest fool to deposit the engine and walk away. And the Professor had guaranteed more than fifteen minutes" (*SA* 174). In other words, he knows Stevie has no notion of linear time intervals, and Verloc obtains a detonator that would allow Stevie time to go to the spot, place the bomb, and return without regard to linear time.

22 Bergson, *Time and Free Will*, 86. Emphasis is Bergson's.
23 Harriet Gilliam, "Time and Conrad's *Under Western Eyes*," *Nineteenth-Century Fiction* 31.4 (March 1977): 421.
24 Daleski, *Joseph Conrad: The Way of Dispossession*, 190.
25 Gilliam, "Time and Conrad's *Under Western Eyes*," 421.
26 Stein, *"Almayer's Folly*: The Terrors of Time," 27, 29, 33.
27 Ibid., 29. See also Stein, "Conrad's East: Time, History, Action, and *Maya*," 273.
28 Guerard, *Conrad the Novelist*, 296. I would argue, however, that this phenomenon is not limited just to characters in Conrad's early works.
29 Hudspeth, "Conrad's Use of Time in *Chance*," 287.
30 Roussel, *Metaphysics of Darkness*, 166.
31 Stein, *"Almayer's Folly*: The Terrors of Time," 29 and 33; see also his "Conrad's East: Time, History, Action, and *Maya*," 273.
32 Kertzer, "Joseph Conrad and the Metaphysics of Time," 308.
33 As noted in Kern's *Culture of Time and Space*, 14.
34 For a more expanded discussion of this phenomenon, see ibid.
35 Stein, "Conrad's Word-World of Time," 122.
36 Bender, *Literary Impressionism in Rhys, Ford, Conrad, and Brontë*, 54.
37 Extended discussions of time and Conrad's narrative technique include: Jakob Lothe, *Conrad's Narrative Method* (Oxford: Clarendon Press, 1989); Werner Senn, *Conrad's Narrative Voice* (Bern, Switzerland: Francke Verlag, 1980); Watt, *Conrad in the Nineteenth Century*, 286–304; Kertzer, "Joseph Conrad and the Metaphysics of Time," 302–17; Gilliam, "Time and Conrad's *Under Western Eyes*," 421–39; Joseph J. Martin, "Edward Garnett and Conrad's Reshaping of Time," *Conradiana* 6.2 (May 1974): 89–105; Stein, *"Almayer's Folly*: The Terrors of Time," 27–34; Clifford Leech, "The Shaping of Time: *Nostromo* and *Under the Volcano*," in *Imagined Worlds*, ed. Maynard Mack and Ian Gregor (London: Methuen, 1968), 323–41; Wendell V. Harris, "Of Time and the Novel," *Bucknell Review* 16.1 (March 1968): 114–29; J. E. Tanner, "The Chronology and the Enigmatic End of *Lord Jim*," *Nineteenth-Century Fiction* 21.4 (March 1967): 369–80; Hudspeth, "Conrad's Use of Time in *Chance*," 283–89; Frederick R. Karl, *A Reader's Guide to Joseph Conrad* (New York: Noonday, 1960), 62–90; R. W. Stallman, "Time and *The Secret Agent*," *Texas Studies in Literature and Language* 1.1 (spring 1959): 101–22; Ben Kimpel and T. C. Duncan Eaves, "The Geography and History in *Nostromo*," *Modern Philology* 56.1 (August 1958): 45–54; Bruce Harkness, "Conrad on Galsworthy: The Time Scheme of *Fraternity*," *Modern Fiction Studies* 1.2 (May 1955): 12–18; Beach, *The Twentieth Century Novel*, 337–65; Donald Davidson, "Joseph Conrad's Directed Indirections," *Sewanee Review* 33.2 (April 1925): 163–77; and Helen Thomas Follett and Wilson Follett, *Some Modern Novelists: Appreciations and Estimates* (New York: Henry Holt, 1918), 332–35.
38 Davidson, "Joseph Conrad's Directed Indirections," 165.
39 Harris, "Of Time and the Novel," 119.

40 Hudspeth, "Conrad's Use of Time in *Chance*," 286.
41 Martin, "Edward Garnett and Conrad's Reshaping of Time," 101.
42 Ford, *Joseph Conrad: A Personal Remembrance*, 136–37.
43 Stein, *"Almayer's Folly*: The Terrors of Time," 27; emphasis is Stein's.
44 Stein, "Conrad's Word-World of Time," 119.
45 Jacobs, "Wells, Conrad, and the Relative Universe," 53.
46 Gilliam, "Time and Conrad's *Under Western Eyes*," 436.
47 Ibid., 437.
48 Ibid., 438.
49 Stallman, "Time and *The Secret Agent*," 113. See also 114.
50 Tyley, "Time and Space in *The Secret Agent*," 35. See also Hay's comment that "The Professor, like the other anarchists, is dreaming of destroying history as well as society; he will use a scientifically clocked bomb to demonstrate his contempt for the accumulated experience of the past" (*Political Novels of Joseph Conrad*, 262).
51 Miller, *Poets of Reality*, 53. Miller later also suggests, "All times are simultaneous in eternity" (59).
52 Kertzer, "Joseph Conrad and the Metaphysics of Time," 306.
53 Hay, *Political Novels of Joseph Conrad*, 219.
54 Kertzer, "Joseph Conrad and the Metaphysics of Time," 314.
55 Daleski, *Joseph Conrad: The Way of Dispossession*, 166.
56 Ibid., 169.
57 Miller, *Poets of Reality*, 41.
58 For a more complete discussion of Conrad's politics see, for example, Hay's *Political Novels of Joseph Conrad*, Avrom Fleishman's *Conrad's Politics: Community and Anarchy in the Fiction of Joseph Conrad* (Baltimore, MD: Johns Hopkins University Press, 1967), and Irving Howe, *Politics and the Novel* (New York: Horizon, 1957), 76–113.
59 Guerard, *Conrad the Novelist*, 194.
60 Hay, *Political Novels of Joseph Conrad*, 213.
61 Daniel R. Schwarz, "Conrad's Quarrel with Politics in *Nostromo*," *College English* 59.5 (September 1997): 552; emphasis is Schwarz's.
62 Ibid., 555–56.
63 Ford, *Joseph Conrad: A Personal Remembrance*, 58; emphasis is Ford's.
64 Guerard, *Conrad the Novelist*, 187.
65 In a letter to John Galsworthy, dated September 12, 1906, Conrad writes of *The Secret Agent*:

> After all you must not take it too seriously. The whole thing is superficial and it is but *a tale*. I had no idea to consider Anarchism politically – or to treat it seriously in its philosophical aspect: as a manifestation of human nature in its discontent and imbecility... As to attacking Anarchism as a form of humanitarian enthusiasm or intellectual despair or social atheism that – if it were worth doing – would be the work for a more vigorous hand and for a mind more robust, and perhaps more honest than mine. (*Letters*, III: 354–55; emphasis is Conrad's)

I believe Conrad is overly modest in his assessment of the novel, which through artistic means arrives at many of the same conclusions as would a more systematic philosophical or political inquiry.

66 Daleski also argues, "It is a further irony that the anarchists may be said to 'lose themselves' not 'in reveries of economical systems derived from what is' [*SA* 61], as the Professor claims, but in a moral nihilism that is so pronounced as to suggest their inner nullity – and so to posit their own ultimate disintegration" (*Joseph Conrad: The Way of Dispossession*, 159).

5 RADICAL RELATIVISM, EPISTEMOLOGICAL CERTAINTY, AND ETHICAL ABSOLUTES: CONRAD'S IMPRESSIONIST RESPONSE TO SOLIPSISM AND ANARCHY

1 Miller, *Poets of Reality*, 5. William W. Bonney also falls into this group of critics (*Thorns & Arabesques: Contexts for Conrad's Fiction* [Baltimore, MD: Johns Hopkins University Press, 1980]); as does Roussel in *Metaphysics of Darkness*.

2 Watt, *Conrad in the Nineteenth Century*, 252.

3 Warren, "Introduction," xxiii.

4 Wollaeger, *Joseph Conrad and the Fictions of Skepticism*, 56.

5 Warren, "Introduction," xx.

6 Wollaeger, *Joseph Conrad and the Fictions of Skepticism*, 13.

7 Ibid., 55–56.

8 Ibid., 78.

9 Guerard, *Conrad the Novelist*, 192.

10 Letter dated November 11, 1901, *Letters*, II: 359.

11 Wollaeger, *Joseph Conrad and the Fictions of Skepticism*, 11–12.

12 Letter dated August 5, 1897, *Letters*, I: 370.

13 Letter dated December 20, 1897, ibid., 425.

14 Other examples of an irrational universe exist in Conrad's works. The narrator of *The Shadow Line* remarks concerning the dead calm, "There was no sense in it. It fitted neither with the season of the year, nor with the secular experience of seamen as recorded in books, nor with the aspect of the sky" (*SL* 87; see also 106). Charles Gould's father feels out of control when forced to accept the San Tomé mine as payment for a "loan" to the government: "[T]he extravagant novelty of this outrage upon his purse distressed his sensibilities" (*N* 56). Later, while alone on the island, Decoud "beheld the universe as a succession of incomprehensible images" (*N* 498; see also 553). The narrator of *The Nigger of the "Narcissus"* refers to their "obscure fate" (*NN* 49). Marlow, in "Heart of Darkness," refers to the uncivilized wilderness as "the incomprehensible" (*Y* 50). In *Lord Jim*, he refers to the world wearing "a vast and dismal aspect of disorder" (*LJ* 313), and Jim complains that the *Patna* incident was both unpredictable (*LJ* 92) and uncontrollable (*LJ* 108).

15 Other examples of an indifferent universe in Conrad's works include the following: The narrator of *The Secret Agent* notes, "The veiled sound filled the small room with its moderate volume, well adapted to the modest nature of

the wish. The waves of air of the proper length, propagated in accordance with correct mathematical formulas, flowed around all the inanimate things in the room, lapped against Mrs. Verloc's head as if it had been a head of stone" (*SA* 195). Even the autobiographical *The Mirror of the Sea* presents this same view of nature: "On that exquisite day of gentle breathing peace and veiled sunshine perished my romantic love to what men's imagination had proclaimed the most august aspect of Nature. The cynical indifference of the sea to the merits of human suffering and courage, laid bare in this ridiculous, panic-tainted performance extorted from the dire extremity of nine good and honourable seamen, revolted me" (*MS* 141–42; see also *MS* 135, 194).

16 Letter to Cunninghame Graham, dated December 14, 1897, *Letters*, I: 423.
17 Letter dated January 31, 1898, *Letters*, II: 30.
18 Warren, "Introduction," xvii.
19 Jean-Aubry, *Joseph Conrad: Life and Letters*, I: 141.
20 Letter to Edward Garnett, dated July [10–15], 1895, *Letters*, I: 234.
21 Miller remarks that "many people are lucky enough to go on with their illusions untouched, in the serene and peaceful state of being deceived" (*Poets of Reality*, 20).
22 Hugh Walpole quotes Conrad as saying to H. G. Wells, "You don't care for humanity but think they are to be improved. I love humanity but know they are not" (Rupert Hart-Davis, *Hugh Walpole* [New York: Harvest, 1952], 162).
23 Letter dated January 31, 1898, *Letters*, II: 30.
24 De Lange, "Conrad and Impressionism: Problems and (Possible) Solutions," 28.
25 Bender, "Conrad and Literary Impressionism," 222.
26 Wollaeger, *Joseph Conrad and the Fictions of Skepticism*, 11. This problem concerned other authors as well. Watt notes that "epistemological solipsism became an important part of the cultural atmosphere of the nineties" (*Conrad in the Nineteenth Century*, 172).
27 Wollaeger suggests, "Skeptic questioning of the reality of other minds ultimately ends in solipsistic self-enclosure and so seals the mind in silence or endless converse with itself" (*Joseph Conrad and the Fictions of Skepticism*, 22).
28 For example, Watt argues, "Marlow's memories of his lonely experiences on the Congo, and his sense of the impossibility of fully communicating their meaning, would in themselves assign *Heart of Darkness* to the literature of modern solipsism" (*Conrad in the Nineteenth Century*, 212).
29 Wollaeger, *Joseph Conrad and the Fictions of Skepticism*, 101.
30 Ibid., 104.
31 Guerard, *Conrad the Novelist*, 141.
32 Ibid., 147.
33 Marlow in fact only partially agrees with Jim's view, but that is beside the point, since Jim believes Marlow concurs completely and is oblivious to Marlow's skepticism.

34 Paul Armstrong sees an uncomfortable side effect of the impressionist method: "The reader of Conrad and Ford may have the experience of living for a time in another's world, but the consequence of this exercise in intersubjectivity is a heightened sense of the solipsism which is always with us even (or especially) when we don't notice it" ("The Hermeneutics of Literary Impressionism," 267). I am not sure, however, that Conrad would wholly agree. Impressionist methodology may remind the reader that all phenomena filters through human consciousness, but its very method of locating the reader at the character's point of experience in space and time attempts to achieve a certain kind of consensus among human subjects that would suggest that there is some overlap of experience. As I argued earlier, the dock workers and the young captain in *The Shadow Line* may look at the ship and see the ship differently, but each still sees a ship.

35 Watt, *Conrad in the Nineteenth Century*, 253; ellipsis is Watt's.

36 Letter dated May 8, 1905, *Letters*, III: 239; emphasis is Conrad's.

37 See Watt, *Conrad in the Nineteenth Century*, 83.

38 Wollaeger, *Joseph Conrad and the Fictions of Skepticism*, 15.

39 Watt, *Conrad in the Nineteenth Century*, 145.

40 Compare also the closing events in "An Outpost of Progress" (*TU* 110–17). Guerard remarks that Kayerts and Carlier "are unequipped for lawless solitude" (*Conrad the Novelist*, 64).

41 In *Lord Jim*, Marlow makes a similar statement: "I mean just that inborn ability to look temptations straight in the face – a readiness unintellectual enough, goodness knows, but without pose – a power of resistance, don't you see, ungracious if you like, but priceless – an unthinking and blessed stiffness before the outward and inward terrors, before the might of nature and the seductive corruption of men – backed by a faith invulnerable to the strength of facts, to the contagion of example, to the solicitation of ideas" (*LJ* 43).

42 Daleski, *Joseph Conrad: The Way of Dispossession*, 65.

43 Letter to Cunninghame Graham, dated August 5, 1897, *Letters*, I: 370.

44 Daleski, *Joseph Conrad: The Way of Dispossession*, 65.

45 Watt argues, "Restraint is tangentially related to the atavism–civilisation duality because it is a quality which is not usually needed in modern society, where all necessary sanctions on conduct are supplied externally" (*Conrad in the Nineteenth Century*, 227).

46 Also compare: "Razumov was one of those men who, living in a period of mental and political unrest, keep an instinctive hold on normal, practical, everyday life" (*UWE* 10).

47 Although no storm occurs in *The Shadow Line*, the dead calm is no less dangerous, especially given the crew's health.

48 Watt, *Conrad in the Nineteenth Century*, 33.

49 Guerard remarks that "betrayal is the ultimate crime" in Conrad's works (*Conrad the Novelist*, 58).

50 See Daleski, *Joseph Conrad: The Way of Dispossession*, 125.

51 Ibid., 134.

52 Stein sees Captain Mitchell as guilty of a similar attitude: "Mitchell exalts wealth above morality and things above humans" ("Conrad's Word-World of Time," 123).

53 Roussel has a more positive interpretation of Hervey's revelation: "Yet despite its pain, Hervey's new awareness is the way to a more positive knowledge. It brings, first, an understanding that the self cannot remain independent of those around it... [T]he only true ground of individual identity lies in the thoughts and heart of another" (*Metaphysics of Darkness*, 35).

54 Daleski, *Joseph Conrad: The Way of Dispossession*, 195; emphasis is Daleski's.

55 Other examples of the importance of communion exist in Conrad's works. For example, *Nostromo*'s Decoud despairs when he loses communion with others – because he was "not fit to grapple with himself single-handed" (*N* 497). The narrator suggests that Decoud "had died striving for his idea by an ever-lamented accident. But the truth was that he died from solitude, the enemy known but to few on this earth, and whom only the simplest of us are fit to withstand. The brilliant Costaguanero of the boulevards had died from solitude and want of faith in himself and others" (*N* 496). By communing with others, Decoud creates a meaning for his existence, and without that communion he finds that "[h]e believed in nothing" (*N* 500). Similarly, in "The Informer," a character must choose between human communion and political ideals. Sevrin poses as a revolutionary but is really a police informer "from conviction" (*SS* 97). He later meets the "Lady Amateur of anarchism" and falls in love with her. Ultimately, he must choose between her and his ideals because "two sentiments of such absorbing magnitude cannot exist simultaneously in one heart" (*SS* 93). Sevrin chooses human communion over an ideal and locates his meaning for existence in humanity, not ideals.

56 Similarly, in "Typhoon," during the storm, the narrator remarks, "Jukes was uncritically glad to have his captain at hand. It relieved him as though that man had, by simply coming on deck, taken most of the gale's weight upon his shoulders" (*T* 39). The companionship the captain provides – the communion between them against the storm – is what matters to Jukes because lack of communion can sap the crew of its will. The narrator notes, "In an instant the men lost touch of each other. This is the disintegrating power of a great wind: it isolates one from one's kind... A furious gale attacks [one] like a personal enemy, tries to grasp his limbs, fastens upon his mind, seeks to rout his very spirit out of him" (*T* 40). The storm isolates crew members and cuts them off from their collective strength. In isolation, they cannot cooperate and protect one another from the dangerous elements, nor can they protect one another from the ethical anarchy of an indifferent universe.

57 Miller, *Poets of Reality*, 30.

58 Marlow encounters this same attitude among the pilgrims of the Eldorado

Exploring Expedition: "They beguiled the time by backbiting and intriguing against each other in a foolish kind of way. There was an air of plotting about that station . . . The only real feeling was a desire to get appointed to a trading-post where ivory was to be had, so that they could earn percentages. They intrigued and slandered and hated each other only on that account" (*Y* 78). The pilgrims are interested only in making money and do not perceive the others as community members but rather as competitors. For them, it is the law of the jungle. Later, at the Inner Station, Marlow remarks, "I pulled the string of the whistle, and I did this because I saw the pilgrims on deck getting out their rifles with an air of anticipating a jolly lark . . . 'Don't! don't you frighten them away,' cried someone on deck disconsolately" (*Y* 146). The pilgrims want to slaughter the Africans – not disperse them. There is a complete want of humanity among the pilgrims.

59   Marlow remarks, "I never saw him again; and, what's more, I don't know of anybody that ever had a glimpse of him after he departed from my knowledge . . . He departed, disappeared, vanished, absconded" (*LJ* 47).

60   Warren notes an interesting contrast between Jim and Monygham, whose "personal story, like the story of Jim, is the attempt to restore himself to the human community and to himself, though he, unlike Jim, survives the attempt" ("Introduction," xi).

EPILOGUE

 1   Among the earliest and most well-known critics of Conrad's later works are Moser (*Joseph Conrad: Achievement and Decline*) and Guerard (*Conrad the Novelist*). (However, most critics of the later works consider *The Shadow Line* to be a notable exception to Conrad's decline.) Dissenting views on Conrad's decline come most notably from Gary Geddes (*Conrad's Later Novels* [Montreal: McGill-Queens University Press, 1980]) and Daniel Schwarz (*Conrad: The Later Fiction* [London: Macmillan, 1982]).

Selected bibliography

Achebe, Chinua. "An Image of Africa." *Massachusetts Review* 18.4 (winter 1977): 782–94.

Armstrong, Nancy. "Character, Closure, and Impressionist Fiction." *Criticism* 19.4 (fall 1977): 317–37.

Armstrong, Paul B. *The Challenge of Bewilderment: Understanding and Representation in James, Conrad, and Ford.* Ithaca, NY: Cornell University Press, 1987.

"The Epistemology of Ford's Impressionism." In *Critical Essays on Ford Madox Ford,* ed. Richard A. Cassell, 135–42. Boston: G. K. Hall, 1987.

"The Epistemology of 'The Good Soldier': A Phenomenological Reconsideration." *Criticism* 22.3 (summer 1980): 230–51.

"The Hermeneutics of Literary Impressionism: Interpretation and Reality in James, Conrad, and Ford." *Centennial Review* 27.4 (fall 1983): 244–69.

Bachelard, Gaston. *The Poetics of Space,* trans. Maria Jolas. Boston: Beacon Press, 1969.

Baker, Robert S. "Joseph Conrad." *Contemporary Literature* 22.1 (winter 1981): 116–26.

Beach, Joseph Warren. *The Twentieth-Century Novel: Studies in Technique.* New York: Appleton-Century-Crofts, 1932.

Beebe, Maurice. "The *Portrait* as Portrait: Joyce and Impressionism." *Irish Renaissance Annual* 1 (1980): 13–31.

Benamou, Michel. "Wallace Stevens: Some Relations Between Poetry and Painting." *Comparative Literature* 2.1 (winter 1959): 47–60.

Bender, Bert. "Hanging Stephen Crane in the Impressionist Museum." *Journal of Aesthetics and Art Criticism* 35.1 (fall 1976): 47–55.

Bender, John and David E. Wellbery, eds. *Chronotypes: The Construction of Time.* Stanford, CA: Stanford University Press, 1991.

Bender, Todd K. *Literary Impressionism in Jean Rhys, Ford Madox Ford, Joseph Conrad, and Charlotte Brontë.* New York: Garland, 1997.

"Conrad and Literary Impressionism." *Conradiana* 10.3 (autumn 1978): 211–24.

"Jean Rhys and the Genius of Impressionism." In *British Novelists Since 1900,* ed. Jack I. Biles, 93–104. New York: AMS Press, 1987.

Bender, Todd K. and Sue M. Briggum. "Quantitative Stylistic Analysis of Impressionist Style in Joseph Conrad and Ford Madox Ford." In *Comput-*

ing in the Humanities, ed. Richard W. Bailey, 59–64. Amsterdam: North-Holland, 1982.

Benson, Donald R. "Constructing and Ethereal Cosmos: Late Classical Physics and *Lord Jim*." *Conradiana* 23.2 (summer 1991): 133–49.

"The Crisis of Space: Ether, Atmosphere, and the Solidarity of Men and Nature in *Heart of Darkness*." In *Beyond the Two Cultures: Essays on Science, Technology, and Literature*, ed. Joseph W. Slade and Judith Yaross Lee, 161–75. Ames: Iowa State University Press, 1990.

"Impressionist Painting and the Problem of Conrad's Atmosphere." *Mosaic* 22.1 (winter 1989): 29–40.

Berg, William J. "L'Oeuvre: Naturalism and Impressionism." *L'Esprit Créateur* 25.4 (winter 1985): 42–50.

Bergson, Henri. *Time and Free Will: An Essay on the Immediate Data of Consciousness*, trans. F. L. Pogson. London: George Allen & Unwin, 1910.

Bevan, Jr., Ernest. "*Nostromo*: The Permanence of the Past." *Conradiana* 10.1 (spring 1978): 63–71.

Bithell, Jethro. *Modern German Literature: 1880–1950*. London: Methuen, 1959.

Bohlmann, Otto. *Conrad's Existentialism*. New York: St. Martin's Press, 1991.

Bongie, Chris. "Exotic Nostalgia: Conrad and the New Imperialism." In *Macropolitics of Nineteenth-Century Literature: Nationalism, Exoticism, Imperialism*, ed. Jonathan Arac and Harriet Ritvo, 268–85. Philadelphia: University of Pennsylvania Press, 1991.

Bonney, William W. *Thorns and Arabesques: Contexts for Conrad's Fiction*. Baltimore, MD: Johns Hopkins University Press, 1980.

Bouve, Pauline Carrington. "Impressionism in the Novel." *Gunton's Magazine* 26.3 (March 1904): 237–42.

Brady, Marion B. "The Collector-Motif in *Lord Jim*." *Bucknell Review* 16.2 (May 1968): 66–85.

Brantlinger, Patrick. "Heart of Darkness: Anti-Imperialism, Racism, or Impressionism?" *Criticism* 27.4 (fall 1985): 363–85.

Bresky, Dushan. "The Style of the Impressionistic Novel: A Study in Poetized Prose." *L'Esprit Créateur* 13.4 (winter 1973): 298–309.

Carabine, Keith, Owen Knowles, and Wiesław Krajka, eds. *Conrad's Literary Career*. Boulder, CO: East European Monographs, 1992.

Contexts for Conrad. Boulder, CO: East European Monographs, 1993.

Carpenter, Rebecca. "From Naïveté to Knowledge: Emilia Gould and the 'Kinder, Gentler' Imperialism." *Conradiana* 29.2 (summer 1997): 83–100.

Carrabino, Victor. "The French *Nouveau Roman*: The Ultimate Expressionism of Impressionism." *Analecta Husserliana* 18 (1984): 261–70.

Carson, Herbert L. "The Second Self in 'The Secret Sharer.'" *Cresset* 34.1 (November 1970): 11–13.

Chapple, J. A. V. "Conrad's Brooding Over Scientific Opinion." *The Conradian* 10.1 (May 1985): 59–67.

Church, Margaret. *Time and Reality: Studies in Contemporary Fiction*. Chapel Hill: University of North Carolina Press, 1963.

Clifford, James. "On Ethnographic Self-Fashioning: Conrad and Malinowski." In *Reconstructing Individualism: Autonomy, Individuality, and the Self in Western Thought*, ed. Thomas C. Heller, Morton Sosna, and David E. Wellbery, 140–62. Stanford, CA: Stanford University Press, 1986.

Conrad, Joseph. *Almayer's Folly*, ed. David Leon Higdon and Floyd Eugene Eddleman. Cambridge: Cambridge University Press, 1994.

The Complete Works of Joseph Conrad. 26 vols. Garden City, NY: Doubleday, Doran, 1928.

Congo Diary and Other Uncollected Pieces, ed. Zdzisław Najder. Garden City, NY: Doubleday, 1978.

The Collected Letters of Joseph Conrad, ed. Frederick R. Karl and Lawrence Davies, 5 vols. Cambridge: Cambridge University Press, 1983–.

Letters of Joseph Conrad to Marguerite Poradowska 1890–1920, trans. and ed. John A. Gee and Paul J. Sturm. New Haven, CT: Yale University Press, 1940.

The Secret Agent, ed. Bruce Harkness and S. W. Reid. Cambridge: Cambridge University Press, 1990.

"Geography and Some Explorers." In *Last Essays*, ed. Richard Curle, 1–21. Garden City, NY: Doubleday, Page, 1926.

Conroy, Mark. "Colonial Self-Fashioning in Conrad: Writing and Remembrance in *Lord Jim*." *L'Epoque Conradienne* 19 (1993): 25–36.

Craig, Randall. "Choses Vues: Arnold Bennett and Impressionism." *English Literature in Transition: 1880–1920* 24.4 (1981): 196–205.

Crane, Stephen. "The Open Boat." In *Tales of Adventure, The Works of Stephen Crane*, ed. Fredson Bowers, v: 79–80. 10 vols. Charlottesville: University Press of Virginia, 1970.

Crankshaw, Edward. *Joseph Conrad: Some Aspects of the Art of the Novel*. London: John Lane, 1936.

Curley, Daniel. "Legate of the Ideal." In *Conrad's* Secret Sharer *and the Critics*, ed. Bruce Harkness, 75–82. Belmont, CA: Wadsworth, 1962.

Curtler, Hugh Mercer. "Achebe on Conrad: Racism and Greatness in *Heart of Darkness*." *Conradiana* 29.1 (spring 1997): 30–40.

Dale, Peter Allan. *In Pursuit of a Scientific Culture: Science, Art, and Society in the Victorian Age*. Madison: University of Wisconsin Press, 1989.

Daleski, H. M. *Joseph Conrad: The Way of Dispossession*. London: Faber & Faber, 1977.

"*Victory* and Patterns of Self-Division." In *Conrad Revisited: Essays for the Eighties*, ed. Ross C. Murfin, 107–23. University: University of Alabama Press, 1985.

David, Deirdre. "Selfhood and Language in 'The Return' and 'Falk.'" *Conradiana* 8.2 (summer 1976): 137–47.

Davidson, Donald. "Joseph Conrad's Directed Indirections." *Sewanee Review* 33.2 (April 1925): 163–77.

Davis, Harold E. "Conrad's Revisions of *The Secret Agent*: A Study in Literary Impressionism." *Modern Language Quarterly* 19.3 (September 1958): 244–54.

Dickens, Charles. *Hard Times*, ed. Paul Schlicke. Oxford: Oxford University Press, 1989.

Epstein, Hugh. "A Pier-Glass in the Cavern: The Construction of London in *The Secret Agent*." In *Conrad's Cities*, ed. Moore, 175–96.

"'Where He Is Not Wanted': Impression and Articulation in 'The Idiots' and 'Amy Foster.'" *Conradiana* 23.3 (autumn 1991): 217–32.

Erdinast-Vulcan, Daphna. "'Sudden Holes in Space and Time': Conrad's Anarchist Aesthetics in *The Secret Agent*." In *Conrad's Cities*, ed. Moore, 207–21.

Ferguson, Suzanne C. "Defining the Short Story: Impressionism and Form." *Modern Fiction Studies* 28.1 (spring 1982): 13–24.

"The Face in the Mirror: Authorial Presence in the Multiple Vision of Third-Person Impressionist Narrative." *Criticism* 21 (1979): 230–50.

Fernandez, Ramon. *Messages*, trans. Montgomery Belgion. New York: Harcourt, Brace, 1927.

Fleishman, Avrom. *Conrad's Politics: Community and Anarchy in the Fiction of Joseph Conrad*. Baltimore, MD: Johns Hopkins University Press, 1967.

Follett, Helen Thomas and Wilson Follett. *Some Modern Novelists: Appreciations and Estimates*. New York: Henry Holt, 1918.

Ford, Ford Madox. *The English Novel*. London: Constable, 1930.

The Good Soldier, ed. Thomas C. Moser. Oxford: Oxford University Press, 1990.

Joseph Conrad: A Personal Remembrance. Boston: Little, Brown, 1924.

The March of Literature: From Confucius to Modern Times. London: George Allen & Unwin, 1939.

Return to Yesterday. New York: Liveright, 1932.

Thus to Revisit: Some Reminiscences. New York: E. P. Dutton, 1921.

"Conrad and the Sea." In *Portraits from Life*, 57–69. Boston: Houghton Mifflin, 1980.

"Techniques." *Southern Review* 1.1 (July 1935): 20–35.

Fraser, Gail. "Empire of the Senses: Miscegenation in *An Outcast of the Islands*." In *Contexts for Conrad*, ed. Carabine, Knowles, and Krajka, 121–33.

Fried, Michael. "Almayer's Face: On 'Impressionism' in Conrad, Crane, and Norris." In *So Rich a Tapestry: The Sister Arts and Cultural Studies*, 239–82. Lewisburg, PA: Bucknell University Press, 1995.

Frierson, William C. *The English Novel in Transition: 1885–1940*. Norman: University of Oklahoma Press, 1942.

Fry, Roger. *Characteristics of French Art*. New York: Brentano's, 1933.

Gardet, Louis, *et al.*, eds. *Cultures and Time*. Paris: Unesco, 1976.

Garland, Hamlin. *Crumbling Idols*, ed. Jane Johnson. Cambridge, MA: Belknap Press, 1960.

"Romantic Biography." *Nation & Athenaeum* 36 (December 6, 1924): 366, 68.

Garnett, Edward. *Friday Nights*. New York: Knopf, 1922.

Garnett, Edward. ed. *Letters from Joseph Conrad, 1895–1924*. Indianapolis: Bobbs-Merrill, 1928.

Geddes, Gary. *Conrad's Later Novels*. Montreal: McGill-Queens University Press, 1980.

Gibbs, Beverly Jean. "Impressionism as a Literary Movement." *Modern Language Journal* 36.4 (April 1952): 175–83.

Gilliam, Harriet. "Time in Conrad's *Under Western Eyes*." *Nineteenth-Century Fiction* 31.4 (March 1977): 421–39.

Gillon, Adam. "Conrad as Painter." *Conradiana* 10.3 (autumn 1978): 253–66.

GoGwilt, Christopher. *The Invention of the West: Joseph Conrad and the Double-Mapping of Europe and Empire*. Stanford: Stanford University Press, 1995.

Gombrich, E. H. *The Story of Art*. 16th edn, revised and enlarged. Oxford: Phaidon, 1995.

Gordon, Jan B. "Walter Pater: Aesthetic Standards or Impressionism?" *Unisa English Studies* 2 (1968): 13–18.

Graver, Lawrence. *Conrad's Short Fiction*. Berkeley: University of California Press, 1969.

Greenberg, Alvin. "The Death of the Psyche: A Way to the Self in the Contemporary Novel." *Criticism* 8.1 (winter 1966): 1–18.

Guerard, Albert J. *Conrad the Novelist*. Cambridge, MA: Harvard University Press, 1958.

Gunsteren, Julia van. *Katherine Mansfield and Literary Impressionism*. Amsterdam: Rodopi, 1990.

Haldar, Indrani. "Perspective and Point of View in Impressionist Painting and Fiction." In *Proceedings of the XIIth Congress of the International Comparative Literature Association*, ed. Roger Bauer and Douwe Fokkema, 562–66. Munich: Iudicium Verlag, 1990.

Hale, Edward E. "The Impressionism of Henry James." *Faculty Papers of Union College* 2.1 (1931): 3–17.

Hamner, Robert, ed. *Joseph Conrad: Third World Perspectives*. Washington, DC: Three Continents, 1990.

Harkness, Bruce. "Conrad on Galsworthy: The Time Scheme of *Fraternity*." *Modern Fiction Studies* 1.2 (May 1955): 12–18.

Harris, Wendell V. "Of Time and the Novel." *Bucknell Review* 16.1 (March 1968): 114–29.

Hauser, Arnold. *The Social History of Art*, trans. Stanley Godman, 2 vols. New York: Knopf, 1952.

Hawkins, Hunt. "Conrad's Critique of Imperialism in *Heart of Darkness*." *PMLA* 94.2 (March 1979): 286–99.

"Conrad and the Psychology of Colonialism." In *Conrad Revisited: Essays for the Eighties*, ed. Ross C. Murfin, 71–87. University: University of Alabama Press, 1985.

Hay, Eloise Knapp. *The Political Novels of Joseph Conrad*. Chicago: University of Chicago Press, 1981.

"Cities Like Whited Sepulchres." In *Conrad's Cities*, ed. Moore, 125–37.

"Impressionism Limited." In *Joseph Conrad: A Commemoration*, ed. Norman Sherry, 54–64. London: Macmillan, 1976.

"Joseph Conrad and Impressionism." *Journal of Aesthetics and Art Criticism* 34.1 (Fall 1975): 137–44.

"Proust, James, Conrad, and Impressionism." *Style* 22.3 (fall 1988): 368–81.

Hemmings, F. W. J. "Zola, Manet, and the Impressionists." *PMLA* 73.4 (September 1958): 407–17.

Henricksen, Bruce. *Nomadic Voices: Conrad and the Subject of Narrative.* Urbana: University of Illinois Press, 1992.

Hewitt, Douglas. *Conrad: A Reassessment.* 3rd edn. Totowa, NJ: Rowman & Littlefield, 1975.

Higdon, David Leon. *Time and English Fiction.* Totowa, NJ: Rowman & Littlefield, 1977.

Hokenson, Jan. "Céline: Impressionist in Language." *L'Esprit Créateur* 13.4 (winter 1973): 329–39.

Howarth, Herbert, *et al.* "Symposium on Literary Impressionism." *Yearbook of Comparative and General Literature,* 17 (1968): 40–68.

Hu, Stephen. "Hemingway and the Impressionists." *Connecticut Review* 10.2 (spring 1988): 51–59.

Hudspeth, Robert N. "Conrad's Use of Time in *Chance,*" *Nineteenth-Century Fiction* 21.3 (December 1966): 283–89.

Hueffer, Ford Madox. "Impressionism – Some Speculations." Parts 1 and 2. *Poetry* 2.5, 6 (August and September 1913): 177–87; 215–25.

"Joseph Conrad." *The English Review* 10.1 (December 1911): 68–83.

"On Impressionism." Parts 1 and 2. *Poetry and Drama* 2.6, 8 (June and December 1914): 167–75; 323–34.

Hughes, H. Stuart. *Consciousness and Society: The Reorientation of European Social Thought 1890–1930.* Revised edn. New York: Vintage, 1977.

Hunter, Allan. *Joseph Conrad and the Ethics of Darwinism: The Challenges of Science.* London: Croom Helm, 1983.

Hynes, Samuel. *The Edwardian Turn of Mind: First World War and English Culture.* New edn. London: Pimlico, 1992.

"The Epistemology of *The Good Soldier.*" *Sewanee Review* 69.2 (April–June 1961): 225–35.

Jackson, Holbrook. *The Eighteen Nineties.* New York: Capricorn, 1966.

Jackson, Tony E. "Turning into Modernism: *Lord Jim* and the Alteration of the Narrative Subject." *Literature and Psychology* 39.4 (1993): 65–85.

Jacobs, Robert G. "Comrade Ossipon's Favorite Saint: Lombroso and Conrad." *Nineteenth-Century Fiction* 23.1 (June 1968): 74–84.

"H. G. Wells, Joseph Conrad, and the Relative Universe." *Conradiana* 1.1 (summer 1968): 51–55.

James, Henry. "The Impressionists." In *The Painter's Eye: Notes and Essays on the Pictorial Arts,* ed. John L. Sweeney, 114–15. Cambridge, MA: Harvard University Press, 1956.

"The Tree of Knowledge." In *The Author of Beltraffio, The Middle Years, Greville Fane, and Other Tales, Novels and Tales of Henry James,* xvi: 165–90. 26 vols. New York: Scribner's, 1909.

Jameson, Fredric. *The Political Unconscious: Narrative as a Socially Symbolic Act.* Ithaca, NY: Cornell University Press, 1981.

Jean-Aubry, G. *Joseph Conrad: Life and Letters.* 2 vols. Garden City, NY: Doubleday, Page, 1927.

Jenkins, Gareth. "Conrad's *Nostromo* and History." *Literature & History*, 6 (autumn 1977): 138–77.

Joffe, Phil. "Africa and Joseph Conrad's *Heart of Darkness*: The 'Bloody Racist' (?) as Demystifier of Imperialism." In *Conrad's Literary Career*, ed. Carabine, Knowles, and Krajka, 75–90.

Johnson, Bruce. "Conrad's Impressionism and Watt's 'Delayed Decoding.'" In *Conrad Revisited: Essays for the Eighties*, ed. Ross C. Murfin, 51–70. University: University of Alabama Press, 1985.

Johnson, J. Theodore, Jr. "Literary Impressionism in France: A Survey of Criticism." *L'Esprit Créateur* 13.4 (winter 1973): 271–97.

Kahl, Russell, ed. *Selected Writings of Hermann von Helmholtz.* Middletown, CT: Wesleyan University Press, 1971.

Karl, Frederick R. *A Reader's Guide to Joseph Conrad.* New York: Noonday, 1960.

Keary, C. F. "The Philosophy of Impressionism." *Blackwood's Magazine* 163 (May 1898): 630–36.

Kern, Stephen. *The Culture of Time and Space: 1880–1918.* Cambridge, MA: Harvard University Press, 1983.

Kertzer, J. M. "Joseph Conrad and the Metaphysics of Time." *Studies in the Novel* 11.3 (fall 1979): 302–17.

Kimpel, Ben and T. C. Duncan Eaves. "The Geography and History in *Nostromo*." *Modern Philology* 56.1 (August 1958): 45–54

Kirschke, James J. *Henry James and Impressionism.* Troy, NY: Whitston, 1981.

"Impressionist Painting and the Reflexive Novel of the Early Twentieth Century." In *Proceedings of the 8th Congress of the International Comparative Literature Association*, ed. Béla Köpeczi and Gyögy M. Vajda, II: 567–73. 2 vols. Stuttgart: Kunst und Wissen, Erich Bieber, 1980.

Klawitter, George. "Impressionist Characterization in *Women in Love*." *University of Dayton Review* 17.3 (winter 1985/86): 49–55.

Krajka, Wiesław. "*Lord Jim*: An Impressionistic Novel?" *Folia Societatis Scientiarum Lublinensis* 26 (1984): 55–62.

Kronegger, Maria Elisabeth. *James Joyce and Associated Image Makers.* New Haven, CT: College and University Press, 1968.

Literary Impressionism. New Haven, CT: College and University Press, 1973.

"Authors and Impressionist Reality." In *Authors and Their Centuries*, ed. Phillip Crant, 155–66. Columbia: University of South Carolina College of Arts and Letters, Department of Foreign Languages and Literatures, 1974.

"From the Impressionist to the Phenomenological Novel." In *The Analysis of Literary Texts: Current Trends in Methodology*, ed. Randolph D. Pope, 129–37. Ypsilanti, MI: Bilingual Press, 1980.

"Impressionistic Literature and Narrative Theory: Stephen Crane." *Review* 4 (1982): 129–34.

"Impressionist Tendencies in Lyrical Prose: 19th and 20th Centuries." *Revue de Littérature Comparée* 43.4 (October–December 1969): 528–44.

Kronegger, Marlies. "Literary Impressionism and Phenomenology: Affinities and Contrasts." *Analecta Husserliana* 18 (1984): 521–33.

Laforgue, Jules. "Impression: The Eye and the Poet," trans. William Jay Smith. *Art News* 55.3 (May 1956): 43–45.

Lange, Adriaan M. de. "Conrad and Impressionism: Problems and (Possible) Solutions." In *Conrad's Literary Career*, ed. Carabine, Knowles, and Krajka, 21–40.

Lee, Robert F. *Conrad's Colonialism*. The Hague: Mouton, 1969.

Leech, Clifford. "The Shaping of Time: *Nostromo* and *Under the Volcano*." In *Imagined Worlds*, ed. Maynard Mack and Ian Gregor, 323–41. London: Methuen, 1968.

Levenson, Michael H. *A Genealogy of Modernism: A Study of English Literary Doctrine 1908–1922*. Cambridge: Cambridge University Press, 1984.

Levine, George. "The Novel as Scientific Discourse: The Example of Conrad." In *Why the Novel Matters: A Postmodern Perplex*, ed. Mark Spilka and Caroline McCracken-Flesher, 238–45. Bloomington: Indiana University Press, 1990.

Lothe, Jakob. *Conrad's Narrative Method*. Oxford: Clarendon Press, 1989.

Martin, Joseph J. "Edward Garnett and Conrad's Reshaping of Time." *Conradiana* 6.2 (May 1974): 89–105.

Matz, Jesse. "Walter Pater's Literary Impression." *Modern Language Quarterly* 56.4 (December 1995): 433–56.

May, Brian. "Ford Madox Ford and the Politics of Impressionism." *Essays in Literature* 21.1 (spring 1994): 82–96.

McCarthy, Patrick A. "*Heart of Darkness* and the Early Novels of H. G. Wells: Evolution, Anarchy, and Entropy." *Journal of Modern Literature* 13.1 (March 1986): 37–60.

McClellan, Edwin. "The Impressionistic Tendency in Some Modern Japanese Writers." *Chicago Review* 17.4 (1965): 48–60.

McClure, John A. *Kipling and Conrad: The Colonial Fiction*. Cambridge, MA: Harvard University Press, 1981.

Late Imperial Romance. London: Verso, 1994.

"Problematic Presence: The Colonial Other in Kipling and Conrad." In *The Black Presence in English Literature*, ed. David Dabydeen, 154–67. Manchester: Manchester University Press, 1985.

McCullough, Bruce. *Representative English Novelists: Defoe to Conrad*. New York: Harper, 1946.

McNeal, Nancy. "Joseph Conrad's Voice in *Heart of Darkness*: A Jungian Approach." *Journal of Evolutionary Psychology* 1 (1979): 1–12.

Meixner, John A. "Ford and Conrad." *Conradiana* 6.3 (September 1974): 157–69.

Meyerhoff, Hans. *Time in Literature*. Berkeley: University of California Press, 1955.

Miller, J. Hillis. *Poets of Reality: Six Twentieth-Century Writers*. New York: Atheneum, 1974.

Minkowski, Eugène. *Lived Time: Phenomenological and Psychopathological Studies*, trans. Nancy Metzel. Evanston, IL: Northwestern University Press, 1970.

Mongia, Padmini. "Empire, Narrative, and the Feminine in *Lord Jim* and *Heart of Darkness*." In *Contexts for Conrad*, ed. Carabine, Knowles, and Krajka, 135–50.

Moore, Gene M., ed. *Conrad's Cities*. Amsterdam: Rodolphi, 1992.

Morf, Gustav. *The Polish Heritage of Joseph Conrad*. New York: Richard R. Smith, [1930].

Moser, Thomas. *Joseph Conrad: Achievement and Decline*. Cambridge, MA: Harvard University Press, 1957.

Muller, Herbert. "Impressionism in Fiction: Prism vs. Mirror." *American Scholar* 7.3 (summer 1938): 355–67.

Nagel, James. *Stephen Crane and Literary Impressionism*. University Park: Pennsylvania State University Press, 1980.

"Impressionism in 'The Open Boat' and 'A Man and Some Others.'" *Research Studies* 43.1 (March 1975): 27–37.

"Literary Impressionism in *In Our Time*." *Hemingway Review* 6.2 (spring 1987): 17–26.

Newton, Joy. "Emile Zola and the French Impressionist Novel." *L'Esprit Créateur* 13.4 (winter 1973): 320–28.

Nochlin, Linda, ed. *Impressionism and Post-Impressionism: 1874–1904*. Englewood Cliffs, NJ: Prentice-Hall, 1966.

O'Connor, W. V. "Wallace Stevens: Impressionism in America." *Revue des Langues Vivantes* 32.1 (1966): 66–77.

O'Hanlon, Redmond. *Joseph Conrad and Charles Darwin: The Influence of Scientific Thought on Conrad's Fiction*. Edinburgh: Salamander Press, 1984.

Øverland, Orm. "The Impressionism of Stephen Crane: A Study in Style and Technique." In *Americana Norvegica*, ed. Sigmund Skard and Henry H. Wasser I: 239–85. Philadelphia: University of Pennsylvania Press, 1966.

Parry, Benita. *Conrad and Imperialism: Ideological Boundaries and Visionary Frontiers*. London: Macmillan, 1983.

Paruolo, Elena. "Reality and Consciousness: Impressionism in Conrad." *L'Epoque Conradienne* 12 (1986): 75–84.

Pater, Walter. *The Renaissance: Studies in Art and Poetry*, ed. Adam Phillips. Oxford: Oxford University Press, 1986.

[Pater, Walter]. "Coleridge's Writings." *Westminster Review* n.s. 29 (January 1866): 106–32.

Perosa, Sergio. "Naturalism and Impressionism in Stephen Crane's Fiction." In *Stephen Crane: A Collection of Critical Essays*, ed. Maurice Bassan, 80–94. Englewood Cliffs, NJ: Prentice-Hall, 1967.

Peters, John G. "Stein's Collections: Order and Chaos in *Lord Jim*." *Conradiana* 28.1 (winter 1996): 48–53.

Peyre, Henri. "Impressionism in Art and Literature: Random Thoughts Around a Centennial." *Centerpoint* 1.3 (1975): 29–40.

Piacentino, Edward J. "Another Angle of Willa Cather's Artistic Prism: Impressionistic Character Portraiture in *My Antonia*." *Midamerica* 9 (1982): 53–64.

"A Study in Contrasts: Impressionistic Perspectives of Antonia and Lena Lingard in Cather's *My Antonia*." *Studies in the Humanities* 12.1 (June 1985): 39–44.

Pool, Phoebe. *Impressionism*. New York: Thames & Hudson, 1985.

Poulet, Georges. *Studies in Human Time*, trans. Elliott Coleman. Baltimore, MD: Johns Hopkins University Press, 1956.

Raval, Suresh. *The Art of Failure: Conrad's Fiction*. Boston: Allen & Unwin, 1986.

Rawlinson, Mary C. "Proust's Impressionism." *L'Esprit Créateur* 24.2 (summer 1984): 80–91.

Ray, Martin. "The Landscape of *The Secret Agent*." In *Conrad's Cities*, ed. Moore, 197–206.

Renner, Stanley. "The Garden of Civilization: Conrad, Huxley, and the Ethics of Evolution." *Conradiana* 7.2 (May 1975): 109–20.

Ressler, Steve. *Joseph Conrad: Consciousness and Integrity*. New York: New York University Press, 1988.

Rewald, John. *The History of Impressionism*. 4th revised edn. New York: Museum of Modern Art, 1973.

Riechel, D. C. "Monet and Keyserling: Toward a Grammar of Literary Impressionism." *Colloquia Germanica* 13.3 (1980): 193–219.

Roberts, Andrew. "*Nostromo* and History: Remarkable Individuality and Historical Inevitability." *The Conradian* 12.1 (May 1987): 4–16.

Rogers, Rodney O. "Stephen Crane and Impressionism." *Nineteenth-Century Fiction* 24.3 (December 1969): 292–304.

Roussel, Royal. *The Metaphysics of Darkness: A Study in the Unity and Development of Conrad's Fiction*. Baltimore, MD: Johns Hopkins University Press, 1971.

Said, Edward W. *Culture and Imperialism*. New York: Knopf, 1993.

Joseph Conrad and the Fiction of Autobiography. Cambridge, MA: Harvard University Press, 1966.

Sarvan, C. P. "Racism and the *Heart of Darkness*." *International Fiction Review* 7.1 (winter 1980): 6–10.

Saveson, John E. "Conrad, *Blackwood's*, and Lombroso." *Conradiana* 6.1 (January 1974): 57–62.

Schorske, Carl E. *Fin-de-Siècle Vienna: Politics and Culture*. New York: Vintage, 1981.

Schwartz, Sanford. *The Matrix of Modernism: Pound, Eliot, and Early Twentieth-Century Thought*. Princeton, NJ: Princeton University Press, 1985.

Schwarz, Daniel R. *Conrad: The Later Fiction*. London: Macmillan, 1982.

Reconfiguring Modernism: Explorations in the Relationship Between Modern Art and Modern Literature. New York: St. Martin's Press, 1997.

"Conrad's Quarrel with Politics in *Nostromo*." *College English* 59.5 (September 1997): 548–68.

Senn, Werner. *Conrad's Narrative Voice*. Bern: Francke Verlag, 1980.

Shattuck, Roger. *The Banquet Years: The Origins of the Avant-Garde in France 1885 to World War I.* Revised edn. New York: Vintage, 1968.

[Sichel, W. S.] "Fathers of Literary Impressionism in England." *Quarterly Review* 185 (January 1897): 173–94.

Silverman, Debora L. *Art Nouveau in Fin-de-Siècle France: Politics, Psychology, and Style.* Berkeley: University of California Press, 1989.

Singh, Ramchander. "Nostromo: The Betrayed Self." *Literary Criterion* 10.4 (summer 1973): 61–66.

Smith, Allan Gardner. "Stephen Crane, Impressionism and William James." *Revue Française d'Etudes Américaines* 8.17 (May 1983): 237–48.

Smith, George E. III. "James, Degas, and the Modern View." *Novel* 21.1 (fall 1987): 56–72.

Spencer, Sharon. *Space, Time and Structure in the Modern Novel.* New York: New York University Press, 1971.

Spittles, Brian. *Joseph Conrad: Text and Context.* New York: St. Martin's Press, 1992.

Stallman, Robert W. "Conrad and 'The Secret Sharer.'" *Accent* 9.3 (spring 1949): 131–43.

"Time and *The Secret Agent.*" *Texas Studies in Literature and Language* 1.1 (spring 1959): 101–22.

Stein, William Bysshe. "*Almayer's Folly*: The Terrors of Time." *Conradiana* 1.1 (Summer 1968): 27–34.

"Conrad's East: Time, History, Action, and Maya." *Texas Studies in Literature and Language* 7.3 (fall 1965): 265–83.

"Conrad's Word-World of Time." In *Aspects of Time*, ed. C. A. Patrides, 114–25. Manchester: Manchester University Press, 1976.

Stewart, Jack F. "Impressionism in the Early Novels of Virginia Woolf." *Journal of Modern Literature* 9.2 (May 1982): 237–66.

Stouck, David. "Willa Cather and the Impressionist Novel." In *Critical Essays on Willa Cather*, ed. John J. Murphy, 48–66. Boston: G. K. Hall, 1984.

Stowell, H. Peter. *Literary Impressionism, James and Chekhov.* Athens: University of Georgia Press, 1980.

"Impressionism in James's Late Stories." *Revue de Littérature Comparée* 58.1 (January–March 1984): 27–36.

Stronks, James B. "A Realist Experiments with Impressionism: Hamlin Garland's 'Chicago Studies.'" *American Literature* 36.1 (March 1964): 38–52.

Symons, Arthur. *Dramatis Personae.* Indianapolis, IN: Bobbs-Merrill, 1923.

Sypher, Wylie. *Rococo to Cubism in Art and Literature* (New York: Vintage Books, 1963).

Tanner, J. E. "The Chronology and the Enigmatic End of *Lord Jim.*" *Nineteenth-Century Fiction* 21.4 (March 1967): 369–80.

Thrall, William Flint and Addison Hibbard. *A Handbook to Literature.* New York: Odyssey, 1936.

Thurin, Erik Ingvar. *Whitman Between Impressionism and Expressionism: Language of the Body, Language of the Soul.* Lewisburg, PA: Bucknell University Press, 1995.

Tobin, Patricia Drechsel. *Time and the Novel: The Genealogical Imperative.* Princeton, NJ: Princeton University Press, 1978.

Tretheway, Eric. "Language, Experience, and Selfhood in Conrad's *Heart of Darkness.*" *Southern Humanities Review* 22.2 (spring 1988): 101–11.

Tyley, Sue. "Time and Space in *The Secret Agent.*" *The Conradian* 8.2 (summer 1983): 32–38.

Venturi, Lionello. "The Aesthetic Idea of Impressionism." *Journal of Aesthetics and Art Criticism* 1.1 (spring 1941): 34–45.

Vidan, Ivo. "Conrad's Legacy: The Concern with Authenticity in Modern Fiction." In *Joseph Conrad: Theory and World Fiction*, ed. Wolodymyr T. Zyla and Wendell M. Aycock, 167–86. Lubbock: Interdepartmental Committee on Comparative Literature, Texas Tech University, 1974.

"Ford's Interpretation of Conrad's Technique." In *Joseph Conrad: A Commemoration*, ed. Norman Sherry, 183–93. London: Macmillan, 1976.

"The Split Self in Conrad's Fiction." In *Die Modernisierung Des Ich*, ed. Manfred Pfister, 275–85. Passau: Richard Rothe, 1989.

Waern, Cecilia. "Some Notes on French Impressionism." *Atlantic Monthly* 69.4 (April 1892): 535–41.

Warren, Robert Penn. "Introduction." *Nostromo* by Joseph Conrad. New York: Modern Library, 1951.

Watt, Ian. *Conrad in the Nineteenth Century.* Berkeley: University of California Press, 1979.

"Impressionism and Symbolism in *Heart of Darkness.*" *Southern Review* 13.1 (January 1977): 96–113.

"Pink Toads and Yellow Curs: An Impressionist Narrative Device in *Lord Jim.*" In *Joseph Conrad Colloquy in Poland, 5–12 September 1972*, ed. R. Jabłkowska, 11–31. Warsaw: Polish Academy of Sciences, 1975.

Watts, Cedric. *A Preface to Conrad.* London: Longmans, 1982.

"*Heart of Darkness*: The Covert Murder Plot and the Darwinian Theme." *Conradiana* 7.2 (May 1975): 137–43.

Weisstein, Ulrich. "A Bibliography of Critical Writings Concerned With Literary Impressionism." *Yearbook of Comparative and General Literature* 17 (1968): 69–72.

"Butterfly Wings without a Framework of Steel?: The Impressionism of Katherine Mansfield's Short Story 'Her First Ball.'" *Primeiro Congresso de Literatura Comparada* (1990): 57–77.

Wertheim, Stanley. "Crane and Garland: The Education of an Impressionist." *North Dakota Quarterly* 33.1 (winter 1965): 23–28.

[Westley, F. C.] "Literary Impressionists." *The Spectator* 59 (June 19, 1886): 810–11.

White, Andrea. "Conrad and Imperialism." In *The Cambridge Companion to Joseph Conrad*, ed. J. H. Stape, 179–202. Cambridge: Cambridge University Press, 1996.

Wollaeger, Mark A. *Joseph Conrad and the Fictions of Skepticism.* Stanford, CA: Stanford University Press, 1990.

Yelton, Donald C. *Mimesis and Metaphor: An Inquiry into the Genesis and Scope of Conrad's Symbolic Imagery.* The Hague: Mouton, 1967.

Zietlow, Paul. "Pater's Impressionism Reconsidered." *ELH* 44.1 (spring 1977): 150–70.

Zola, Emile. *The Experimental Novel and Other Essays*, trans. Belle M. Sherman. New York: Cassell, 1893.

Index